MW00333633

Westchester County

"Westchester County's Enterprises" by Joan G. Ford

Produced in cooperation with
The County Chamber of Commerce, Inc.

Windsor Publications, Inc.
Chatsworth, California

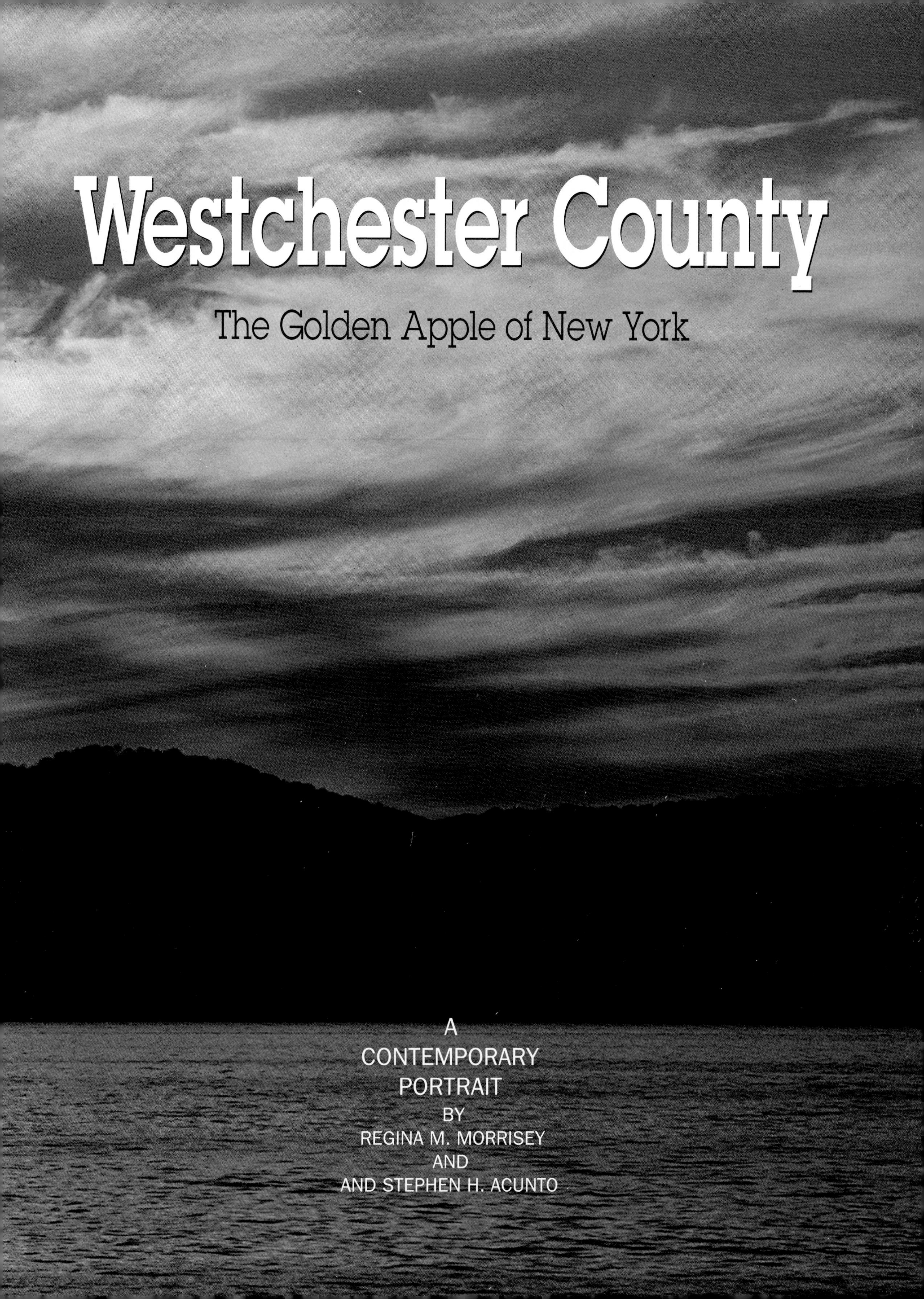

Westchester County

The Golden Apple of New York

A
CONTEMPORARY
PORTRAIT
BY
REGINA M. MORRISEY
AND
AND STEPHEN H. ACUNTO

Windsor Publications, Inc.—Book Division
Managing Editor: Karen Story
Design Director: Alexander D'Anca
Photo Director: Susan L. Wells
Executive Editor: Pamela Schroeder

Staff for *Westchester County: The Golden Apple of New York*
Senior Manuscript Editor: Jerry Mosher
Photo Editor: Lisa Willinger
Senior Editor, Corporate Profiles: Judith L. Hunter
Production Editor, Corporate Profiles: Justin Scupine
Proofreader: Mary Jo Scharf
Customer Service Manager: Phyllis Feldman-Schroeder
Editorial Assistants: Elizabeth Anderson, Dominique Jones, Kim Kievman, Michael Nugwynne, Kathy B. Peyser, Theresa J. Solis
Publisher's Representatives, Corporate Profiles: Hannah Dresser, Tom Hildebrandt
Layout Artist: Bonnie Felt
Layout Artist, Corporate Profiles: Lisa Barrett
Designer: Christina Rosepapa

Caption Writer: Patricia A. Perito, Harrison, N.Y.

Windsor Publications, Inc.
Elliot Martin, Chairman of the Board
James L. Fish III, Chief Operating Officer
Michele Sylvestro, Vice President/Sales-Marketing
Mac Buhler, Vice President/Acquisitions

Published 1990
Printed in the United States of America
First Edition

Library of Congress Cataloging-in-Publication Data
Morrisey, Regina M., 1946-
Westchester County : the golden apple of New York : a contemporary portrait / by Regina M. Morrisey and Stephen H. Acunto ; "Westchester County's enterprises" by Joan G. Ford. — 1st ed.
p. 224 cm. 23 x 31
"Produced in cooperation with The County Chamber of Commerce, Inc."
Includes bibliographic references and index.
ISBN 0-89781-367-7
1. Westchester County (N.Y.)—Civilization. 2. Westchester County (N.Y.)—Description and travel. 3. Westchester County (N.Y.)—Economic conditions. 4. Westchester County (N.Y.)—Industries. I. Acunto, Stephen H., 1949- . II. Ford, Joan Genell. III. Title.
F127. W5M67 1990
974.7'277—dc20 90-37228
CIP

Boats form a graceful trail in the water at Playland in Rye. Photo by Peter Britton

CONTENTS

Arrivals
Ferris
ONLY

PREFACE

ur thanks to the staffs of many local and county offices for providing data and support for this fresh look at Westchester County. Special thanks to the assistance of the The County Chamber of Commerce, Inc., the office of Westchester County Executive Andrew P. O'Rourke, the Westchester County Planning Department, Westchester County Office of Economic Development, the Council for the Arts in Westchester, the Westchester County Department of Parks, Recreation & Conservation, and the Westchester/ Putnam School Board Association.

Thanks also to municipal planners, city managers, and town and village officials who provided assistance in gathering information about new local undertakings. Their interest in serving this effort is appreciated. Part of the appeal of doing business and living in Westchester County was apparent in the courteous and efficient way people answer the phones in such offices and guide visitors around municipal quarters—from the smallest colonial town hall to the modern courthouse and library to the art deco Westchester County Offices. People do make the process of doing business in Westchester pleasant.

Thanks also to the business owners, executives, and residents, and to school and hospital administrators, who were eager to share the details of a way of living and work that few counties can claim. The county's historical societies brim with over 300 years of recollections. A look around reveals there are plenty of reasons for businesses to hum to life serving local residents and clients around the globe. Stylish Westchester County has all of the elements of a good life to suit the present and to underwrite a bright future for living and working in the nation's Golden Apple.

Regina M. Morrisey
Stephen H. Acunto

The Old Croton Trailway offers joggers and hikers miles of scenic paths with views such as this one. Photo by Linda Zila

Pepsico's sculpture gardens, shown here, feature works by Rodin, Calder, and Segal, set amidst grounds designed by landscape architect Russel Page. Located in Purchase, the gardens are visited by strollers, art lovers, students from neighboring SUNY Purchase, and the 1,000 employees who work at Pepsico's offices there. Photo by Rich Zila

PART

1

THE GOLDEN APPLE

1

WELCOME TO THE GOLDEN APPLE

As the twenty-first century beckons, Westchester County, New York, is emerging as a preferred address in the national and international business community. While still maintaining its twentieth-century reputation as the classic bedroom community for Manhattan's movers and shakers, the county has expanded its horizons to welcome the best of business. Westchester has many vibrant corporate boardrooms linked to expanding global business fronts. It has high-caliber educational institutions for all ages, modern, well-equipped hospitals, and an array of extraordinary opportunities for healthful living. It also has a welcome mat out for the discerning entrepreneur of the 1990s who wants to live and work in beautiful Westchester.

Westchesterites hesitate to call their richly endowed county a "suburb" as increasing numbers of workers commute to the county and its nearly 28,000 places of business, creating a powerful business current of its own. In reality, Westchester is not a "sub" anything.

True, Westchester County still has its three bustling commuter train lines serving residents who work in the concrete canyons of New York City. Lines of suited executives wait at train stations throughout the county each weekday morning to commute to Manhattan.

Over the last 40 years, however, Fortune 500 executives living in Westchester County began to embrace the idea of working here. Their enthusiasm for spending

The Tappan Zee Bridge spans three miles over the mighty Hudson, a river that bears its founder's name. In 1609 Henry Hudson explored this significant waterway and wrote of the great promise he saw in the land. The Tappan Zee Bridge stands as testimony that people are still migrating to Westchester to take advantage of its abundant resources. Photo by Rich Zila

RIGHT: All aboard! A Metro North conductor ensures passengers safe boarding and exiting. The Metropolitan Transportation Authority estimated that in mid-1989, 95,000 to 100,000 people boarded their trains each day for an average of 190,000 trips both into and out of Westchester. Photo by Linda Zila

FAR RIGHT: Commuters who are hard pressed for time needn't worry: Metro North serves Westchester with more than 500 trains weekdays and 250 trains on the weekends. Photo by Rich Zila

FACING PAGE: Ten Bank Street, an impressive display of steel and glass in downtown White Plains, is a 12-story office building with 4,000 square feet for retail use. Photo by Rich Zila

more time in a spacious and naturally beautiful environment has sparked corporate growth and has made Westchester County an internationally known corporate locale.

Nearly 900,000 people live in Westchester County, calling one of its six cities, 14 towns, or 23 villages home. Approximately 465,000 people work in the county, some of whom commute from the boroughs of New York City and from other counties to work in Westchester's corporate headquarters.

THE SETTING

Within its 450 square miles, Westchester County offers sites for modern office buildings of glass and steel that each day reflect the county's sumptuous woods, sparkling ribbons of rivers and broad lakes, and tall grass marshland skirting the Long Island Sound. A drive past a corporate office building in any corner of Westchester offers a mirror image of the tranquil environment that draws some of the biggest national and international companies here.

Even the weather cooperates with business in Westchester, where the day sky reflected in those glass structures is a blue sky about 60 percent of the year and the average annual temperature is 52 degrees Fahrenheit. The year-round weather experience proves to be an invigorating one. Temperatures in the depth of January range from 21 degrees to 38 degrees and in July's high summer, the range is from 62 degrees to 85 degrees. The average temperature in January is 30 degrees and in July, 74 degrees.

The county's terrain is dominated by two bands of hilly ranges running parallel with the Hudson River and the border with Connecticut. The southeastern corner of the county lies on the edge of Long Island Sound and is jagged with bays and estuaries. In some places, marshland rims the water on land that was formed in the last ice age.

The Manhattan Hills of the Hudson Highlands are the dominant feature of the county's north-central and northwestern borders. About three-fourths of the county's land is forested, with hardwoods and oaks prevailing in mostly acidic soil. Slate and schist bedrock predominate under the hilly terrain and broad valleys that run north-south in most of the county.

CORPORATE CULTURE

Offering a choice setting and an excellent quality of life to employees made sense to Lila Acheson Wallace and Dewitt Wallace, who founded *Reader's Digest.* They ran their publishing oper-

logos in creating Westchester's corporate parks. Small and medium-sized businesses co-exist in comfortable yet distinctive campus settings. These enclaves for corporate growth and expansion are welcomed by neighbors and government—and are encouraged to be part of home/office communities.

Westchester's corporate parks encourage their own brand of relaxed professionalism; they are subdued settings that quietly defer to their residential neighbors. The design trends favored in the county provide an atmosphere of uncrowded and understated expansion by business that has a favorable visual impact for neighbors and maximum attractiveness for employees.

A quiet bike ride can lead to simple pleasures waiting to be discovered throughout Westchester County. Photo by Peter Britton

ation in several Pleasantville locations in the 1920s. The Wallaces then built a landmark, cupola-topped, red-brick headquarters in 1939 to keep their worldwide base in Westchester. General Foods and International Business Machines followed in the 1950s and after to leave enduring impressions on the corporate landscape.

Pepsico, Texaco, CIBA GEIGY, NYNEX, Nestlé, TWA, and MCI have followed suit in opening major operations in the county. Each has carved its own niche in Westchester communities with gracefully landscaped headquarters and modern architecture to present its corporate identity.

Fortune 500 and 1000 companies have made a graceful imprint beyond their own interests and world-renowned

SMALL BUSINESS SUPPORT

Westchester's status as a preferred corporate address has attracted new, small businesses that support big business—from advertising, printing, and video production companies to architects, engineers, attorneys, and accountants, to office supply and maintenance firms and office plant doctors. Then too, a legion of local businesses serving communities have immigrant histories—from the well-known Italian family on the waterfront in Ossining that operates a restaurant started years ago by their grandparents, to the young Korean green grocer who came from Seoul to Yonkers a few years ago and works a 14-hour day, his ticket to enjoying the Westchester life-style.

There is a lively corps of small business owners from every ethnic and racial background whose stores, offices, and shops line the commercial districts of the cities, towns, and villages throughout the county. There is vital manufacturing in progress throughout the southern sector and a strong work force to support it.

On any given day, retail and consumer businesses open their doors for the family looking for a new home—be it a family from Japan or from a borough of New York City. The shopkeepers and department store clerks serve the single person buying new furniture and the senior citizen in search of easy care appliances. A host of little and not-so-little businesses exist for people of every age who love their suburban home and seek gardening expertise, a swimming pool, new kitchen and bath fixtures, and the insurance agent to arrange coverage that will protect it all.

Nearly 20 major commercial banking institutions with over 250 branches do business in the county. In addition, there are a dozen savings and loan institutions and savings banks. In all, about 50 banking institutions are actively serving Westchester County in approximately 350 branch offices.

These ready financial service resources make doing business in Westchester easy for residential customers and businesses. The county has ranked among the top 10 in New York State in retail sales volume for years.

WHITE PLAINS—COUNTY SEAT

A prime example of the county's transformation from bedroom community to corporate boardroom can be found in White Plains, the county's seat of government. Located in a corridor known for its high-powered business focus, White Plains has been redeveloping through an infusion of corporate interest and municipal renewal. Still a vital residential city of apartment buildings, townhouses, and single-family homes, White Plains is the site of many futuristic office buildings that cluster near its train station and along major streets in its substantial commercial area.

A purposeful renewal of the city that began two decades ago continues to propel White Plains to new heights as an attractive home for business. It is evolving as a modern and well-used transportation center for bus and rail. Retail development has kept up with business through new shops and Fifth Avenue department stores—noticeable imports from Manhattan. Restaurants are plentiful and cosmospolitan. As a cityscape, White Plains is becoming markedly

The elaborately embellished buildings on Ossining's Main Street date primarily from the 1870s, after fires early that decade resulted in a flurry of rebuilding. The Greek Revival building from 1845, center, fortunately survived the fires and remains the only wooden commercial example of that style in the county. Photo by Rich Zila

The gentle tide of the Long Island Sound washes slowly onto the inlets along Westchester's southeastern corner. Passersby are seen here enjoying the view off of Umbrella Point in New Rochelle. Photo by Rich Zila

modern, yet it is given to preserving green space and adhering to a workday pace that snaps to the beat of business with a friendly yet determined face.

TRAIN LINES

The Metropolitan Transportation Authority operates a three-prong, north-south rail system in the western, eastern, and central sections of the county. Whether a commuter travels to and from a Westchester municipality on the Hudson River Line in the west, the Harlem Line in the center of the county, or the New Haven Line in the east, the ride traces a unique business path.

Running parallel to the Hudson River, the Hudson River Line weaves through big and small municipalities from Yonkers to Peekskill where industry and residential life flourish. Mid-county, roughly through Westchester's center, the Harlem Line traces the Bronx River through White Plains. The river pools in tranquil spots in Bronxville and Tuckahoe where willow trees arch overhead. A bicycle and walking path parallels its course as the river narrows under a leafy canopy in Scarsdale, only to peek out again once along a ball field or corporate lawn in White Plains and towns north. More waterways follow the course of the rail north in beautiful communities to the border with Putnam County.

The municipalities along the Long Island Sound served by the New Haven Line trains pass in a kaleidoscopic view of business, industry, and established residential neighborhoods from Mount Vernon and Pelham to Rye, New Rochelle, and Port Chester. From Grand Central Station, the first stop in Mount Vernon is reached in a swift 24 minutes. Residents of Pelham, New

Employees and guests of The Reader's Digest Association enjoy a spectacular corporate art collection adorning the halls and offices of the company's landmark headquarters in Pleasantville, shown here. Photo by Rich Zila

Rochelle, Larchmont, Mamaroneck, and Rye all boast of their swift commutes. Visible from the train are the tree-lined streets and Main Street stores of more than a half-dozen nautical Sound towns strung like jewels along the Old Boston Post Road or U.S. Route 1 all the way to the county's border with Connecticut.

Amtrak runs trains on its northeast and eastern routes to and from major cities, among them Boston and Buffalo, Philadelphia and Washington, D.C., from Yonkers and Croton Harmon on the Hudson line.

The commuter trains of Metro North serve a growing number of people making a reverse commute to any of 47 stops in Westchester cities and towns from Manhattan for their day's work. The Metropolitan Transportation Authority estimated in mid-1989 that 95,000 to 100,000 people boarded their trains each day for an average of 190,000 trips both into and out of Westchester. The giant rail company itself employs more than 1,400 out of its White Plains headquarters.

ROAD NETWORKS

About one-third of Westchester's labor force is an office force; they work in the northern region of Westchester as readily as the south, using a network of interstate, state, county, and local roads to reach all points. There are more than 3,200 miles of local and state roads in the county, making its major cities just 10 to 30 minutes apart. The county spawned the first United States parkway—the Bronx River Parkway—in 1927, and has few peers in its diverse and far-reaching road connections. They fan out for easy access to neighboring business areas in New Jersey, New York City, Rockland County, Putnam County, Connecticut, and Long Island.

There is the New York State Thruway, or Interstate 87, running from New York and New Jersey to the southwestern part of the county and extending westward across the Tappan Zee Bridge over the Hudson River into Rockland County and to Albany and Buffalo.

The Tarrytown Corporate Center, shown here, is a complex of seven buildings located off of the intersection of Interstate 87 and the Cross Westchester Expressway. The center includes the luxurious Westchester Marriott Hotel among its 125 tenants. Photo by Rich Zila

"Station stops: Mount Vernon . . . Fleetwood . . . Bronxville . . ." The distinctive architectural forms of many periods can be seen by passengers from the window of Harlem Line trains. Bronxville's mission-styled Gramatan Arcade, shown here, was enclosed in 1929 for shops like M. Kalish, whose namesake established a dry cleaners, tailor, and furrier business there. Photo by Rich Zila

Interstate 95, on the county's eastern border, links Westchester to the New England states to the north and New York City and Long Island to the south. Interstate 287 is an east-west belt that crosses the county from Tarrytown on the Hudson River to Rye on the Long Island Sound.

Interstate 684 cuts through the county's wooded northeast central suburbs from White Plains for about 30 miles to North Salem and the Putnam County border.

Beginning at the county's southern border, the Bronx River Parkway hugs its bubbling namesake and threads through prime commercial and residential property to White Plains. It connects at the Kensico Reservoir with the Taconic State Parkway. The scenic roadway extends north toward the state capital in Albany between the Hudson River and the Massachusetts border.

The Saw Mill River Parkway cuts across a lush swath from Yonkers in a northeasterly direction and merges with I-684.

Another road which feeds into I-684 is the Hutchison River Parkway, which parallels I-95. The Hutchison River Parkway also connects with the Merritt Parkway into Connecticut.

Across southern Westchester County, the Cross County Parkway links the Henry Hudson Parkway in New York City, the Saw Mill River Parkway, the Deegan Expressway (I-87), and the Bronx River Parkway, and it connects

U.S. Route 1, also known as the Boston Post Road, was one of Westchester's earliest overland routes. Following the Long Island Sound shore, the Boston Post Road made possible the establishment of commercial and residential communities. Photo by Rich Zila

An Amtrak train on the Hudson Line races over the tracks near Bear Mountain bridge. Amtrak provides interstate service and makes stops at Croton-Harmon, New Rochelle, and Rye train stations. Photo by Rich Zila

the Sprain Brook Parkway and the Hutchison River Parkway. The "Hutch" accesses New York's major airports—LaGuardia and John F. Kennedy. This lower Westchester system ties all points in the south together and allows several approaches to central and northern points.

AIRPORT

Centrally located Westchester County Airport has proven to be a major asset to the business traveler who must take shuttle flights to Boston or Washington, D.C., or who needs regularly scheduled flights to Chicago, Detroit, or points south. Airlines operating out of the Westchester County Airport include United, Northwest, Business Express, American Eagle, Allegheny Commuter, and Piedmont.

Located in Harrison, five miles northeast of White Plains, the 750-acre airport has shuttle and commercial airplanes that stand side-by-side with corporate jets. The shuttles of Westchester County are an alternative to those available at New York metropolitan LaGuardia and John F. Kennedy airports, which are within an hour's drive from central Westchester and 25 minutes from southern sections of the county.

The original Westchester airport structure, erected in 1946, served an estimated 368,000 planing and 363,000 de-planing passengers in 1989. It is giving way to more modern facilities that will include restaurants, lounges, and a host of modern travel amenities.

BUS SYSTEM

Businesses based in Westchester County depend on several bus companies to transport their employees. The county's bus system is the fourth-largest transit system in the state. Westchester County oversees the Bee

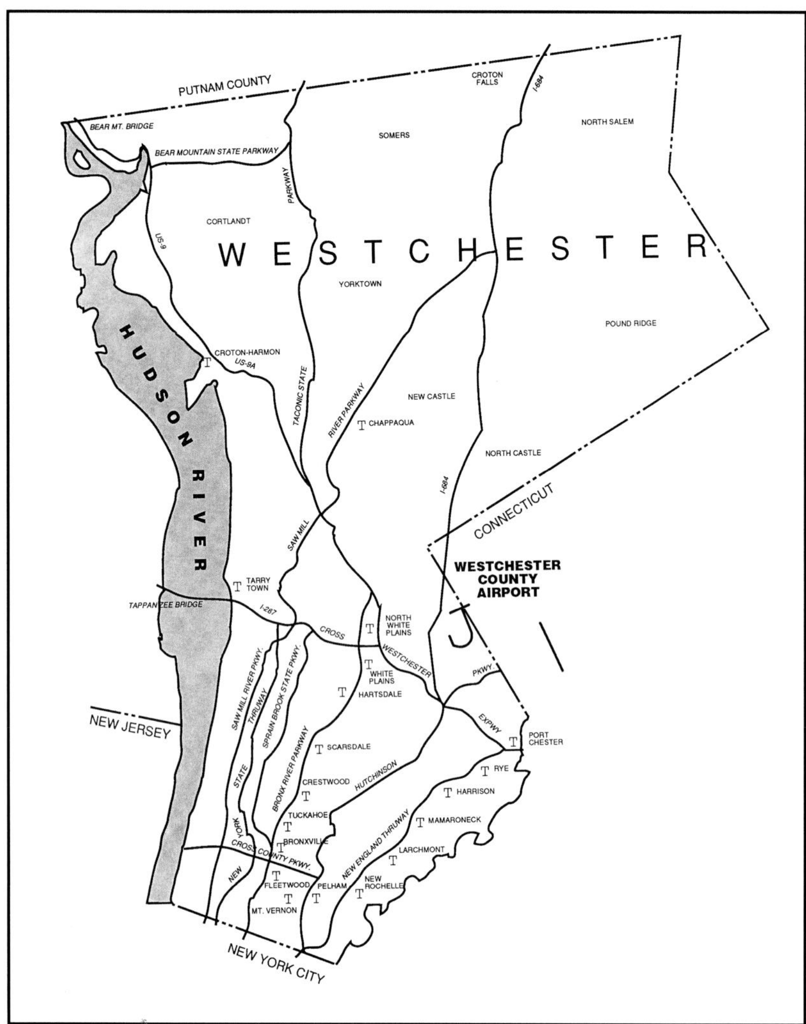

Shown here are Westchester's major road networks. Courtesy, Westchester County Department of Planning

FACING PAGE, TOP: Cars zoom along the Cross Westchester Expressway, a route that links the Sound shore communities on the east with the Hudson River Valley communities on the west. Photo by Rich Zila

FACING PAGE, BOTTOM: The control tower at Westchester County Airport oversees the safety of more than 700,000 passengers annually. The facility provides about 70 daily flights on scheduled carriers by major corporations as well as individual light-plane owners. Photo by Rich Zila

Line system, a public bus system using six private companies to carry 100,000 passengers each day. The 300-bus fleet has over 50 routes. In addition, there are 21 vans in the system for people who cannot use the scheduled route service. The county-operated service has transport counselors to inform business, colleges, libraries, and senior citizens about the growing system and map out bus use for local residents. Bus service between New York City and Westchester is modern and booming.

One of the largest private bus companies, Liberty Lines in Yonkers, employs more than 900 people. In addition, dozens of limousine services operate in the county and there are more than 2,000 registered taxi cabs, most radio controlled. About 40 motor freight carriers are based in Westchester, hauling freight to businesses within and beyond its borders. United Parcel package delivery service employs 750 people who work out of its Elmsford facility and a number of other delivery services make runs in the county.

EDUCATION

More than ever, business seeks a bright, enthusiastic, and educated work force to achieve its goals and grow.

Westchester's population is a markedly well-educated one. The county boasts a score of established public and private institutions of higher education. Forty public school districts and highly rated private schools and parochial schools ready the majority of the county's high school graduates for college.

The county's schools prepare children for the complex life of the twenty-first century with state-required courses that are among the most demanding in American education. New York teachers qualify to teach in the county's systems after rigorous course work in subject matter and teacher training. Westchester County schools rank among the state's best, and regularly achieve state and national recognition for excellence and innovation.

The children of the county enjoy airy, well-maintained, cheery classroom space that is often equipped with computers, video aids, and audio aids to bolster their textbook resources. They also are exposed to a well-rounded day punctuated by physical exercise, music programs, art programs, and trips to the nature and historic preserves that are sprinkled throughout the county.

Students in Westchester schools tend to stay in school. The county has one of the lowest dropout and absentee rates in the state. About 70 percent of the county's students continue their education beyond high school.

The adult population also profits from easy access to the intellectual and cultural offerings in the county and in nearby New York City.

COLLEGES

The Purchase Campus of the State University of New York and Westchester Community College in Valhalla are the two public institutions of higher education in the county. The university at Purchase focuses on liberal, fine arts, and arts degrees in four-year programs. The county's top-ranked community college has a vast array of medical, technical, professional, and liberal arts two-year programs leading to associate degrees.

Among special degree-granting institutions, New York Medical College, also in Valhalla, is one of the country's oldest private medical colleges and the third-largest of its kind. It offers medical, administrative, and public health degree programs and is located at the huge Westchester County Medical Center complex—a key part of the county's substantial health care network.

Iona College in New Rochelle, established in 1940 as a Catholic men's college, recently combined with Elizabeth Seton College of Yonkers, a former two-year Catholic women's college, to form

a major private college for southern Westchester County.

Several colleges founded as women's Catholic colleges continue to serve Westchester higher education in unique ways. The College of New Rochelle, Mercy College in Dobbs Ferry, Manhattanville College in Purchase, and Marymount College in Tarrytown are liberal arts bastions in the county that have expanded programs into the areas of business management and communications.

Pace University in Pleasantville and White Plains grants degrees in the arts and sciences and business, and Polytechnic Institute in Hawthorne grants master's degrees in several technical, business, and engineering fields.

Sarah Lawrence College thrives on its strong liberal arts tradition. Concordia College in Bronxville and The King's College in Briarcliff Manor were established by Protestant founders. The two schools have a Christian emphasis, with secular courses as well as those designed to prepare people for Christian ministry and living.

The Westchester Business Institute in White Plains, the Monroe Business Institute in New Rochelle, and the Berkeley School in White Plains are among the top postsecondary institutions devoted to training people for

RIGHT: Educators across Westchester know physical education is important for fostering a strong body—an essential ingredient for a healthy mind. Softball is just one of the many activities these New Rochelle High School students partake in throughout the school year. Photo by Rich Zila

BELOW: Westchester's caring employees, such as this lifeguard at the Pound Ridge swimming pool, make the county's children feel safe and secure. Photo by Geoffrey Kerrigan

careers in business. Education is seen as a continuing process by all of these institutions. They cultivate courses to serve adults who want to improve their business sense, their computer and technological literacy, and to enhance the quality of life in Westchester. These schools form partnerships with corporations and offer very specific courses for employees. They send interns to corporations for direct training and experience. Businesses sponsor intellectual and cultural programs through area colleges that are open to all in the community.

The sum total of this massive public and private education effort is a highly qualified, working population. Westchester County schools are producing an educated work force equipped to fill all sorts of managerial and professional slots, secretarial and administrative jobs, and positions in complicated technical fields, new industry, and transportation and service industries.

SPORTS AND RECREATION

Westchester County devotes 23,295 acres to parkland that serves as the setting for outdoor fun in villages and cities and in 30 county parks and 27 town parks. The county also has an extensive network of hiking and horse trails and nature preserves. It has games courts in 17 cities and villages, and a variety of picnic and swim areas. The private and public golf courses of Westchester include Saint Andrew's, the oldest in the United States.

Westchester's fabled country clubs center on golf and a swirl of social activities. They dot the county, attracting tennis and swimming enthusiasts as well. In addition, shore clubs sprinkled on acreage along the Long Island Sound and Hudson River add sailing and power boating to the activities list. Adjacent to the shore clubs are marinas and parklands, including Playland in Rye, a county amusement park that is an art deco landmark and an attraction to children of all ages.

There are tennis, racquet, and health clubs to suit the fitness buff. The county's lakes and reservoir system attract fishermen year-round. The Bronx River Parkway has a devoted bicycle ridership that has exclusive use of the road on Sundays for several months of the year. There is no reason to sit still in Westchester when the outdoors offers so many diversions.

With more than 3,500 hotel rooms available in the county, getting away

The 110-foot-tall art deco music tower dominates the amusement mall at Playland in Rye. Built by the Westchester County Parks Commission between 1923 and 1927, the distinctive 279-acre recreation complex was designated a National Historic Landmark in 1987. Photo by Rich Zila

In contrast to the southern part of the county, northern Westchester is a semi-rural area that is home to apple orchards and horse farms such as the Sunnyfield Farm shown here. Photo by Geoffrey Kerrigan

from the routine of life can be accomplished in short trips. The getaways range from bed-and-breakfast establishments on quaint village streets to modern hotels, complete with pools, saunas, and exercise rooms. And the county's museums and historic sites offer points of interest to residents and visitors alike.

HEALTH CARE

The county's population is wide-ranging in age. Self-contained communities for adults offer their residents complete facilities for healthful indoor and outdoor activities. Towns remain devoted to providing services for young families and an increasing number of facilities are opening to serve child care needs. There are impressive health resources in Westchester, with hospitals in every corner of the county and specialized facilities and medical groups in practice in every direction. There is no reason to leave Westchester County for health care needs—from neonatal care to nursing homes. More than 20 hospitals in the county provide 3,500 beds for a vast array of medical services.

HOUSING

The market for residences has been a consistently strong one. In 1984 there were 2,875 housing units authorized to be built in the county for a total construction cost of more than $422 million.

Westchester's housing portrait is complex, and with good cause. A southern industrial city such as Mount Vernon has a population of about 64,000, while North Salem in horse country has fewer than 5,000 residents. With the county traditionally bent on home rule, each municipality makes provisions for its own destiny and is responsible for its own master plan for development. Watersheds and bodies of water are especially protected. In northern towns, planners have shown a preference for multi-acre zoning that bodes well for the successful executive seeking secluded property for building a new home. In southern areas, cooperative

apartments and condominiums have a greater share of planning interest and prove valuable to single people starting their careers. Altogether, Westchester has highly varied, affordable living.

THE GOLDEN APPLE

Westchester's history begins in the colonial days and its housing stock reflects the influences of the Dutch, English, Irish, German, Italian, and Eastern European immigrants who brought a piece of the Old World with them. It also shows itself as the well-maintained "bedroom" community that grew out of the post-World War II boom. The broad streets of contemporary family homes remain the distinctive havens that commuters first chose in the 1950s and 1960s.

The setting may be Victorian or art deco, colonial, modern, or ultra modern. Westchester County's added quality of life and consistent value emerge as it becomes distinguished as both bedroom and boardroom community. Crown it next to the Big Apple as the Golden Apple. It has always had an eye for business.

ABOVE: Well laid-out neighborhoods such as Sleepy Hollow Manor in North Tarrytown, are desired for their stylish houses, large manicured lawns, and tree-lined streets. Photo by Rich Zila

LEFT: Neighborhood corner stores, such as Archie's in Pleasantville, are busy as early as 5:30 a.m. with regulars stopping in for their morning coffee and newspaper. For many residents the groceries mean that it's just a short walk to the store for a last minute item or two. Photo by Barbara Brundage

LIBERTY OR DEATH

2

A WORKING HISTORY

or three-quarters of a century after the summer of 1609 when Henry Hudson, working for the Dutch East India Company, guided the ship *Half Moon* up the river that bears his name, Dutch fur traders profited mightily in Westchester. Indians of various tribes stood willing to exchange mink, beaver, and other pelts for European trinkets. The prized pelts constituted the main cargo of ships returning to Holland in those years.

But by the 1670s, Westchester's fur resources were growing scarce and the place was left to farmers and the like who wanted to settle down.

Hudson had been on the wrong track when he sailed upriver in search of a northwest route to the Orient. But the natural bounty he discovered prompted some Dutchmen to forego the Orient and settle for land from Manhattan northward. A patroonship on the Hudson River was granted in 1646 to Adriaen van der Donck, who later built a gristmill on a waterway that would be known as the Saw Mill River. This land was dubbed "Yonkers" by the English colonists, many of whom had been working their way into the area on the north and east from the Massachusetts Bay and Connecticut settlements. The wanderers were called "Johnnies," a name that became "Yankees" on the Dutch tongue. People from other parts of Europe made their way little by little into the area. As early as 1643, a missionary wrote that his head reeled with the chatter of 18 languages he had heard by the docks of New Amsterdam on the tip of Manhattan Island, downriver from van der Donck's patroonship.

Depicted here is the reading of the Declaration of Independence at the Court House in White Plains, July 8, 1776. Not everyone was for the break with England, and many individuals in the county wrestled with their consciences throughout the ensuing war. Courtesy, Westchester Historical Society

Huguenots found the New World much safer than eighteenth-century France. This painting is G. A. Harker's version of the first encounter between the Native Americans and the Huguenots. With the help of German Jacob Leisler, the refugees founded New Rochelle on Long Island Sound. They named the colony after their former home in France, La Rochelle. Courtesy, Westchester Historical Society

Many of the area's settlers had fled religious persecution. Huguenots left Catholic persecution in La Rochelle, France, and in 1688 some of the refugees founded New Rochelle on Long Island Sound with the help of a German named Jacob Leisler. Though Leisler was hanged in 1691 for promoting himself as governor of New York and staging a rebellion against English rule, he is honored for his friendship to the first 33 families in New Rochelle with a bronze statue that still graces tree-lined North Avenue.

Leisler negotiated the late 1680s purchase of the Huguenots' 6,100 acres from John Pell, Lord of Pell's Manor, whose property spread far to the south of New Rochelle, including part of today's Pelham Manor area. The purchase gave the 10.4-square-mile settlement nine miles of scalloped shoreline, where today regal sail and power boats and deep sea charter vessels plow the waterway.

North on the Sound, English flatboats and barges laden with settlers from Greenwich, Connecticut, rode low on the same body of water in the 1660s. Their crews and passengers sighted giant heaps of clam and mussel shells that Siwanoy Indians discarded on the shore. The shell heaps dwindled as settlers burned them to make lime used to build their homes.

The English of Rye (which was first called Hastings) spread to Port Chester and across to Poningoe (which means the land between two rivers) to claim what is now Harrison and White Plains. Outlawed local Siwanoy and Mohegan Indians steered clear of the settlement, but some settlers routinely risked stiff fines to pass their whiskey around native campfires and place bets on wrestling warriors.

Dutch vessels patrolling the Sound struck fear into the first English residents of Rye. But the Dutch lost political control of the area to the English in 1664 in a takeover engineered by the Duke of York and Albany, brother of Charles II and later himself King James II. There was an order to take power "with humanity and gentleness" and without forcing the English language or religious beliefs on the Dutch. Two centuries later, the Dutch language was still spoken in the Hudson Valley although English, obviously, had won out.

Westchester was made a county in 1683 and named for a city in England. Still, the Dutch policy of granting large estates to individuals continued: Philipsborough Manor was granted to Frederick Philipse in 1693; Cortlandt

The Westchester Indians attacked the homestead of Adriaen van der Donck in the late 1600s. Dutch relations with the Indians in Upstate New York were reasonably good but pressure from New England or New Jersey conflicts caused local flare-ups all along the Hudson Valley. Courtesy, Westchester Historical Society

Manor to Stephanus Van Cortlandt in 1697; and Scarsdale Manor to Caleb Heathcote in 1701. Farmers coming into the area became tenants to these patrician landowners.

Mount Vernon was part of Eastchester in 1733 when John Peter Zenger, publisher of the *New York Weekly Journal,* wrote disparagingly about a rigged election arranged by Royal Governor William Crosby at Saint Paul's Church. Zenger's trial for seditious libel found him not guilty and set a precedent for freedom of the press that the country's founding fathers would make part of the Constitution. Saint Paul's Church still stands, gracing South Columbus Avenue in Mount Vernon and the historic landmark listings of the National Trust.

The English of Connecticut, who had ushered settlers into Rye in 1660, lost it and the northeast and eastern corner of the county to New York. It would take years of court review to determine which state controlled the area. Indians left or succumbed to the potent liquor and sickness carried by the settlers. With smallpox, tuberculosis, measles, and venereal disease carried across the Atlantic Ocean to blunt their numbers, the Indians were rarely seen in Westchester by the middle of the eighteenth century.

Westchester Indians had been part of the Wappinger Confederacy, which was kin to the Algonquians. The agrarian Indians torched grass to smoke out their prey, and their cleared land became the first acreage used for farming and homesteads. Their wigwams, made from bent sapplings or poles covered with bark, stood near Wampus Lake and in areas now called Bedford, Pound Ridge, Cortlandt, Yorktown, and Somers. The Indians were called

Before the Revolution, Lancaster Underhill and his sons, utilizing the water power at Bronxville, carried on a gristmill and sawmill, and a factory for the carding of wool. About 1840, the mill, pictured here in a contemporary engraving, came into the hands of James P. Swain, who used it as a grist mill and a screw and axle factory. Courtesy, Westchester County (NY) Archives

Wappings, Wecquaesgeeks, Kichawans, Tankitekes, Sequins, and other names. Many of these names were linked to the land they settled. All of them knew the Hudson River as "Shatamuc," or "the river that flows both ways." Many of the Indians' place names remain today. Some, like Katonah, are named for the chiefs who sold off land.

Many settlements in Westchester grew around points along rivers and streams where water moved swiftly enough to turn a mill and grind harvests of grain. Given livestock, fowl, wheat, corn, rye, and barley, most settlements hummed with the sounds of the sawmill, gristmill, smithy, cordwainery, cooperage, bakery, and brewery. Philipsburg Manor in North Tarrytown and Muscoot Farm in Somers are among the county's lovingly maintained restorations that in sight, sound, and costume are devoted to the life of the early residents.

The rocky land of Westchester yielded the stones for walls that still stand today. Gracefully following the contour of the land in several communities that protect them as historic treasures, the stone walls divided farms and kept grazing livestock safe in vast common pastures.

Throughout the 1700s, Westchester's bountiful timber was fashioned into cabins and rough-hewn houses that peeked out of the forests near dirt paths and wider wagon routes like the first leg of the Boston Post Road in the east and the Albany Post Road in the west. Clearly marked with mileage posts from New York City, the roads served coach and mail. From shore to shore, in the 1700s stagecoaches pulled up in front of inns such as the Square House in Rye, where traveling gents downed ale or rum and argued the merits of separating from England.

REVOLUTION

The debate grew heated with each trade restriction and tax. Taxation increased when King George needed money to fight a war in 1744 and the French and Indian War from 1755 to 1763. Westchester settlements sent their quota of troops to the battlefield, troops that had to leave fields untended and unprofitable. Quaker settlers, who had crossed Long Island Sound to take up residence in different locations throughout Westchester, refused to fight and paid dearly in extra taxes for their pacifism.

From the earliest days in the colonies, homes were brightened with little more than handmade quilts and candles. Prosperity allowed colonists grander items imported from Europe, accounting for a brisk shipping business. In the 1700s, families scurried to the docks on the Hudson River and Long Island Sound to deposit produce for sloops that arrived with finery from the port of New York. With revolution, Westchester became "Neutral Ground" ripe for raiding by British cowboys, rebel skinners, and brutish apolitical others. Families buried valuables, hid livestock in barren fields, and said goodbye to fighting-age men. Homes and churches were looted and left unrepaired for fear they would be subjected to new assault.

Some colonists had grown cool to the English crown, but in Westchester, divided loyalties separated local families and friends. Many were likely to agree with the Loyalist paper *Westchester Farmer* and feel dubious about the passionate "Crisis Papers" penned by Thomas Paine, who spent the last days of his life in New Rochelle.

As he made camp with George Washington's troops in the darkest days of the war, Paine was said to have used a soldier's drum for a desk to write for the Revolution. Westchester's place in publishing history was assured when Paine's work—120,000 copies of *Common Sense*—was spread throughout the colonies, the equivalent of 10 million copies today.

When Paine retired to a house that is preserved on North Avenue in New Rochelle, local officials denied this devoted revolutionary character the right to vote. His new hometown denied Paine this right on the grounds that he had accepted honorary citizenship from the French after aiding their revolt.

During the Revolution, Westchester residents had spotted handsomely outfitted French soldiers on the march. Mount Kisco was the prized location of a church that served late in the war as headquarters for Washington's army in a rendezvous with the troops of General Comte de Rochambeau. The 5,000 Frenchmen, dressed in white uniforms trimmed in green, blue, or bright yellow, set up tents beside the ragtag American soldiers while the two generals plotted a movement of 10,000 men for the pivotal Battle of Yorktown, Virginia, in 1781.

The graveyard of this same "Church at North Castle Corners," which served as a hospital for soldiers wounded in the 1776 Battle of White Plains, remains under the watchful care of Mount Kisco historians. Similar sacred ground, monuments, and historic sites are protected in dozens of locations in the county.

White Plains had been the site of a convention of New Yorkers who established the new state constitution in July 1776. With the outbreak of war, some White Plains courthouse records were carted to North Salem for safety. Three patriots from North Salem are credited with altering the course of the war by capturing Major John André. At 29, André was a smooth and dashing British operative who was aiding the traitor Benedict Arnold. Arnold, trusted commander of the vital fortifications at West Point, was involved in a

Revolutionary War pamphleteer and author of* Common Sense, *an incendiary tract that urged independence from Britain, Thomas Paine spent much of his life in Westchester. His house on North Avenue in New Rochelle has been preserved and is open to the public. Courtesy, Westchester Historical Society

Riding steamboats became the rage of the early 1800s. Passengers could choose from a number of competing companies and ride in high style on ships such as the* Drew *and the* St. John *of the "People's evening line" between New York and Albany. By 1843 the voyage took just seven hours, 21 minutes. Courtesy, the Alice and Hamilton Fish Library, the Alice Desmond Collection

plan to weaken the fort and complete the grip that the British hoped would cut off New York from New England to defeat the Revolution. Without Arnold's treason, the British dared not attack West Point with fewer than 20,000 men.

Three men from the north woods—John Paulding, Van Wart, and David Williams—walked into the pages of history in September 1780 when they refused to be taken in or bribed by André as he crossed the county with Arnold's papers outlining weakened defenses at West Point for the British. They intercepted André in or near North Salem while searching for cattle thieves. He was hung by orders of General George Washington on October 2.

John Jay, the first chief justice of the United States, figures in the history of Rye and the town of Bedford. Jay's family had homes in both places. The Homestead on Route 22 in the Katonah area of Bedford is maintained as the Jay family's later residence, with furnishings from the eighteenth and nineteenth centuries in rooms that now serve for many musical and history-related events.

GROWTH OF COMMERCE

By war's end, the new Americans of Westchester had seen seven bleak harvests and the destruction left by rampaging outlaws. They were anxious to rebuild their lives, reopen town meetings, and start new businesses. The county's first true housing boom started in the late 1700s. New prosperity filled cargo sloops of a bustling, free nation.

Startled Hudson River residents reported that it sounded "like the devil in a sawmill" when Robert Fulton's steamboat, the *Clermont,* chugged by on its first run to Albany in 1807. A technological wonder, the vessel made the trip in 32 hours.

Fulton had built the new boat for Robert R. Livingston, a New York politico who briefly held a monopoly on

The Mamaroneck dock around 1910 was host to powerful steamers such as the* Rene Elaine Davis *(left) which were an essential part of the early economy. Barges and cargo boats shuttled between New York City and upcounty ports. Courtesy, Mamaroneck Historical Society

steamboating in New York waters. As chancellor of the state, Livingston had administered the oath of office at the new country's inauguration of George Washington in 1789. He also was a man of some taste. Livingston's third steamboat, the *Paragon,* afforded passengers spacious accommodations and "the best in fine wines, all manner of dainties and even ice cream in the hot season," according to one astonished Russian artist who painted this "whole floating town."

Riding steamboats became the rage of the early 1800s, one that was fueled by heady competition from new companies that built faster and faster boat models. Racing steamboats was popular among companies and tended to attract swarms of patrons to come aboard, until an explosion or two dissauded people from choosing only the speediest boat. But by 1843, the run to Albany took just seven hours, 21 minutes. It was a stylish ride in a steamboat that boasted a rococo drawing room where passengers lolled away the time.

Dozens of workaday vessels plowed the waters around Westchester with the glamour boats, some going all the way to the locks of the Erie Canal. Construction of the canal inland to Lake Erie insured the Hudson River's favorable status as a commercial waterway for all manner of businesses in the nineteenth century. Ferries shuttled between Oyster Bay and Rye on the Long Island Sound from the first years of Rye's settlement. In the 1800s, barges and cargo boats followed a hectic schedule as they shuttled between New York City, the "window open to the world," and upcounty ports. Crews heaved crates and barrels of manufactured and imported goods onto county docks and hauled aboard locally produced grain, fruits, and vegetables.

Westchester, an obliging farmer for the great city, would become its water bearer when drawing plans were unfurled for the creation of the Croton Aqueduct in the 1840s. The Roman-modeled system tapped the Croton River, some 40 miles from the city, and

The Croton Aqueduct, shown here in 1852, carried water approximately 40 miles from the Croton River to New York City. Courtesy, Westchester Historical Society

carried its waters over hills and valleys to provide the first adequate water supply to the city. A great engineering achievement of the mid-nineteenth century, the project consumed years and the lives of several workers, many of them the newest immigrants to the county.

The Croton Aqueduct brought water to a booming city population, as crop failure in Ireland and political upheaval on the European continent had driven the century's first sizable waves of immigrants across the Atlantic. They were Irish, English, Scotch, German, Scandinavian, and Italian. The latter group's numbers would swell as the century ended. Work for the laboring newcomer could be found on the water project and in laying the first railroad track in the county.

By 1844, a train from New York City could reach Mount Vernon, Bronxville, Tuckahoe, Scarsdale, and all the way to White Plains. Three years later, crews had worked their way to Croton Falls at the Putnam County border. The smoke from their engines did not blacken the wool of grazing sheep as protesting farmers once feared it would. Instead, there was brisk business to be done supplying the city overland with milk dropped off at Westchester depots.

Around Somers and North Salem, enterprising businessmen lured farmers from their milking pails to gaze at exotic animals from Africa. In Somers,

Hachaliah Bailey imported an elephant, "Old Bet," that thrilled his neighbors in 1808. Following a path of potatoes tossed before her, Old Bet was coaxed down country roads in the dark of night and kept under wraps so that people had to pay to see her. The town has remembered this event by preserving the Elephant Hotel, now housing town offices, and a statue of the elephant on a 15-foot pillar at the same Route 100 location.

North Salem's circus—June, Angevine, Titus and Company— brought the first hippopotamus to America. Circus animals wintered in huge barns in the area and toured far into the Midwest. The 1842 road trip of June, Angevine, Titus and Company covered 2,482 miles and took 184 days, of which 151 were spent traveling. Still, they exhibited their curious livestock in 85 towns and cities. The June mansion still stands in North Salem on June Road.

The new rail era prompted many Westchester farmers to head into the middle of America. They were in the market to sell off land in the county just as prospering captains of industry from New York City began to scoop up acres for their stylish country retreats.

Merchants in Scarsdale, White Plains, Bedford, and Mount Kisco were among those stocking the carriages of wealthy people on new estates in the middle of the county. In Waccabuc, the nine children of wealthy Robert Hoe could romp on the Mead Street estate he outfitted for them in 1838. One of his sons would invent the rotary printing press in 1847 and revolutionize the newspaper industry.

In Tarrytown on the Hudson River, William Paulding and his son built a Gothic revival summer retreat, Lyndhurst, that rail mogul Jay Gould would make even more elaborate years later. Just to the south, writer Washington Irving lived in more modest surroundings at Sunnyside on the Hudson from 1835 to 1859. His 21 volumes still occupy shelf space in the study of his wisteria-draped cottage. The charmed residence attracts legions of visitors who know him for two short stories—"The Legend of Sleepy Hollow" and "Rip Van Winkle."

Simeon Leland, a prominent New York City innkeeper, constructed a castle that still stands in New Rochelle, and John Stapleton, inventor of the trolley, erected his own majestic digs in the same city. In Yonkers, John Bond Trevor, a broker, built a fine home styled on the best architecture exhibited at the Centennial Exhibit of 1876.

These and other mansions survive to

Photographs were often keepsakes and badges of pride. Everyone gets into the act in this photo of Hopper's Grocery at the corner of Railroad and Lexington in White Plains in 1895. Courtesy, Westchester Historical Society

FACING PAGE, BOTTOM: An excavation crew cleared the way for this stretch of the Westchester & Boston Railroad in 1901. Courtesy, Westchester Historical Society

Italian immigrant craftsmen who worked on the Stephenson House in Croton are shown here in 1910. Thousands of Italian immigrants poured into Westchester from the crowded tenements of New York City. Many settled permanently in the area. Courtesy, Westchester Historical Society

the present day and find new life as museums, country clubs, college libraries, classroom buildings, and headquarters of several religious and historical organizations.

IMMIGRATION

Immigrants readily left behind the frightful tenements of New York to be servants for the fine residences of the wealthy in Westchester. Estates spread across acres dotted with housing for the carriage man, groundskeeper, and grape gardener. Such serviceable lodgings were built with nineteenth-century flair and were provided to the hired help. These servants quarters stand today as highly prized and charming country homes.

Many immigrant railroad, dam, and tunnel workers of the mid-nineteenth century settled in plain-faced row houses in enclaves that arose in the county's towns, villages, and cities. Here, people heard only their native tongue spoken. They devotedly built their own churches and centered family lives around them, and they kept to themselves behind cherished lace curtains brought from home. Longtime residents skirted the noisy saloons catering to immigrant workmen. When the Civil War erupted in 1861, many immigrants went off to the battlefields, earning the grudging respect of old-timers who had spurned them. The hardship of war drew Westchesterites together in the end.

The Tigers of the New York Regiment boarded trains to the Deep South armed with a year's supply of Dr. Benjamin Brandreth's "pure vegetable pills," which were manufactured in Ossining (then called Sing Sing). The pills made at the local factory were swallowed from Paris to Peoria and were the subject of wondrous newspaper testimonials.

Westchester military academies practiced war games and graduated cadets who would be officers and gentlemen of the 1800s. Girls' academies flourished in the county as finishing schools producing gentlemen's wives. Rows of cadets at an Ossining academy who were too young to have entered the Civil War were stiff and solemn as they saluted the black-draped train bearing the body of President Abraham Lincoln on the tracks of the Hudson River line in 1865.

When New York City called for more water from its Westchester source in the 1880s, fresh immigrant labor was again available. Work on the Croton Dam and its 30 miles of tunnels drew thousands of Italian immigrants to Westchester. When the new immigrant Italians spilled onto the teeming streets of New York, many of the newcomers were shepherded north by padroni hired to line up able-bodied crews for the newest backbreaking project.

One padrone who brought workers to Mount Kisco was known to extract $12 of the $14 of a laborer's weekly wages for food and lodgings at the rooming house he ran. It would be a long time before immigrant families were treated fairly. There was nothing for the families to do but console themselves in village gathering spots.

Many of Westchester's young men who survived the Civil War attended this reunion of the Cromwell Post of the Grand Army of the Republic in 1907. Courtesy, Westchester Historical Society

Laborers were said to have nodded grimly when they heard that a keg of dynamite hurled into one padrone's parlor had ended his role in their lives.

Despite having one such villain exit the picture, the laborers had tough going in Westchester. Slighted by English-speaking neighbors, they created their own neighborhoods, planted gardens, penned chickens and assorted livestock, and filled the air with arias and arguments in the language of Italy. In Ossining the hobnail boots of the workmen tapped uphill each morning out of an insular valley settlement called The Hollow. In Mount Kisco, the mandolin was strummed into the night air on Sutter's Row. Years later Sutter's Row would be level land selected for a shopping area called Bazaar Mall. Ossining would remember The Hollow with a charming sketch copied on souvenir T-shirts and sold by the local historical society.

In Tuckahoe, Italian and Irish immigrants worked in the marble quarries but coolly stayed to themselves when the whistle called a halt to a day's work. Proud men like Michael Dalton of the Benedict Quarry, who cut the stone for the lions gracing the steps of the 42nd Street New York Public Library, dressed in a somber suit and carried his black tool bag to the quarry much like a surgeon entering the operating room. Such accomplished workers accepted as their own the proud reputation of Tuckahoe for homes, hotels, and chuches built from fine marble. In Mount Pleasant, quarry workers could claim praise for the Dolomite marble that was used to build St. Patrick's Cathedral in Manhattan.

Both Italian and Irish groups were filled with skilled artisans who apprenticed for nearly a decade in their trade and eventually started their own businesses in Westchester. They became wealthy carving gravestones and statuary and building some of the county's exquisite stone mansions. Others established road construction companies and other contracting firms that built the county's arching bridges and graceful walls.

In the 1880s and 1890s, nine million people came to America. Another nine million came in the first decade of the

1900s. Immigrants from Eastern Europe and Russia fled the sting of persecution, particularly persecution against Jews. Leaving Ellis Island, some refused to be shunted into the cramped tenements on Manhattan Island and flocked to booming southern Westchester cities such as Yonkers, where factories such as Alexander Smith and Sons, then the world's largest carpet maker, had been operating at full speed since the 1860s. Other Jewish families chose New Rochelle, White Plains, Mount Kisco, and Peekskill, where tradesmen and skilled craftsmen could make a living. In each community, this newest insular group built temples and networks for philanthropic and social programs that are apparent to the present day.

In Mount Kisco, businesses were begun with clanging backpacks of goods carried from house to house on the valley floor. Peddlers who stuck to the grind eventually graduated to the horse and buggy trade, then swept the entrances of their own fine establishments on Main Street.

Jewish immigration in the 1920s brought a group of professionals and workers who formed a cooperative in Goldens Bridge called The Colony. Life at the 150-acre summer place centered around a refurbished barn where social, intellectual, and political activism was nurtured. Considered avant-garde in its thinking, the group roughed it in tents during the first years of the cooperative. Men, women, and children built the Colony roads, and dammed a brook and created their "swimming hole."

Speaking Polish, Russian, German, and heavily accented English and dressed in clothing uncommon to northern Westchester, The Colony's residents then braced themselves for anti-Semitic encounters with local people. But their tents became summer homes which today stand as year-round residences vital to the life of Goldens Bridge, a hamlet of the town of Lewisboro.

Goldens Bridge, Katonah, and Purdys were moved in the late 1800s to accommodate the waters of the Croton Reservoir system and road beds that would precede I-684. Purdys' houses

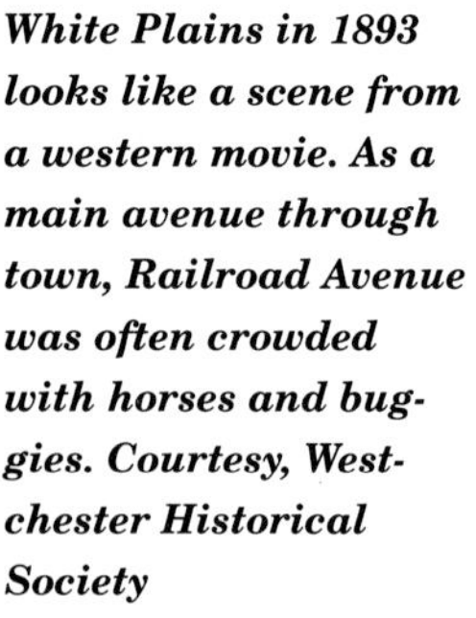

White Plains in 1893 looks like a scene from a western movie. As a main avenue through town, Railroad Avenue was often crowded with horses and buggies. Courtesy, Westchester Historical Society

and businesses were moved to the top of a hill and the old hamlet was flooded, transforming the area into the seven-million-gallon Lake Titicus that glistens today. Similar circumstances led Katonah residents to plan a new village it would inhabit in 1897. Its park-like main boulevard is one of the avenues where the Katonah Village Improvement Society planted many of the first 200 trees it purchased. The village retains the beautiful touches furnished by the society and individual Victorian-era homebuilders.

After 1825, Ossining merchants and manufacturers were irked by the village's unwanted association with Sing Sing, the infamous prison of gangster movie fame. One hundred convicts were put to work constructing the stone prison on the Hudson River that year in the village of Sing Sing. The name stems from the Sint Sinck tribe that first inhabited the place—the Indian name means "stone upon stone."

The 1,000-member prison population, ordered to be silent under the eyes of guards, worked in the prison factory turning out goods "made in Sing Sing" that were often confused with village ware. Village businessmen took pains to maintain a separate identity for their goods and were relieved when the hamlet's name was changed.

Even far back in the history of its little villages, Westchester had factories that produced hats, boots, tools, and spectacles. The first condensed milk operation in the United States churned in the county. The late nineteenth century industrial age meant new business to southern Westchester. In the 1880s, Westchester's foundry and machine shop products earned their owners $2.3 million. Southern blacks moving north during and after the Civil War began to carve niches in area cities, attracted by jobs in the factories and service industry. Westchester remained desirable to workers and the trolley would connect Westchester cities and towns and speed the workers' route.

A day's labor in Westchester was extremely varied. Work on board fishing boats heading out to sea and work aboard yachting vessels attracted new people to Westchester waters. Country hotels and horse and carriage firms lured patrons who wanted shade trees, cool breezes, and the chance to glimpse through the wrought iron gates and over the stone walls of the estates. The

White Plains' finest sit proudly for a group portrait in 1907. Courtesy, Westchester Historical Society

In the early 1900s, sponsored by local schools and organizations such as the American Legion, Little League, and others, amateur baseball teams organized all across America. This co-ed team, pictured at an unidentified Westchester event in 1918, was probably unusual in its day. Courtesy, Westchester County (NY) Archives

naturally beautiful and glamorous Westchester reputation was established early on.

INDUSTRIAL INROADS

In the 1860s, Yonkers was home to the Otis Elevator Company, while Peekskill had the Fleischmann Company, then known as Standard Brands. Plenty of businessmen rode to New York City, where they would climb aboard elevators that Otis workers made. Horace Greeley, one of the best-known commuters of the 1800s, wrote articles in the *New York Tribune* about the quality of service provided by railroad workers in the 1860s.

By 1899 the Mobile Company of America produced a steam-driven automobile in Tarrytown. Chevrolet and Fisher Body plants turned out car products in Tarrytown throughout the early 1900s. Ward Motor Vehicle Company was building electric trucks in Mount Vernon in 1905.

New York Telephone Company kept linemen on the road as they connected the homes of Westchester to the new communication system. Gas light companies preceded electric light companies in hiring local workers. P.R. Malloy and Company, Inc., of Port Chester produced the filament that gave off the first feeble light of the electric bulb in the early 1900s. Westchester Lighting Company was operating a gas plant in Pelham by then, and the Yonkers Electric Lighting and Power Company had been operating since 1885 under the first franchise for such a business in the county. Ward Leonard Electric was open for business in Bronxville in 1897.

The motion picture industry found New Rochelle an attractive location for producing silent films, and cartoonists set up their drafting tables in the same city. In 1903 the Sanitas Fabric Wall Covering Company of Buchanan brought a new decorating tool to homemakers nationwide.

Early twentieth-century legends in Westchester business include Mint Products of Port Chester, later known as the Life Savers Corporation. With new packaging and a new independent sales force operating from 1914 to 1916, the company boosted sales of mint candy from 940,000 rolls to 22 million rolls. It opened its Port Chester plant in 1920 and would supply the armed forces of World War II with a rationed pack of mints a day for every soldier. At war's end, the count was 250 million rolls.

Westchester bought bonds and sent soldiers to World War I and World War II. Its industries captured awards from the Army and Navy for production efforts that blew the roof off existing records. Barges and tugs built at U.S. Shipbuilding in Yonkers were part of the Normandy invasion and General Douglas MacArthur's command in the Pacific campaigns of World War II. Burroughs Wellcome and Company, an international pharmaceutical firm that opened a Tuckahoe plant in 1925, would supply first aid kits for soldiers and contribute medicine through United Nations programs to recovering countries after the war. The Fifth Avenue Rex Company that had produced lady's compacts and cigarette cases before the war made Purple Hearts that were awarded to wounded soldiers. Filling one order filed by the U.S. government, the New Rochelle Company made 15 million uniform buttons for Russian soldiers.

Factory employment would increase in Westchester by 68 percent from 1939 to 1947. Suburbanization accounted for Tudor- and Mediterranean-style homes of southern Westchester and art deco shopping areas in the early 1900s "downtown." This would stagger during the Depression, but from 1947, it would again soar and the business of Westchester County cities would take on new dimensions.

Increasingly rare, the old swimming hole was once a treasured part of growing up in America. Shown here on a summer day in 1917 are children enjoying the cool water of the Bronx River, north of Tibbets Avenue. Courtesy, Westchester County (NY) Archives

3

WESTCHESTER'S CITIES

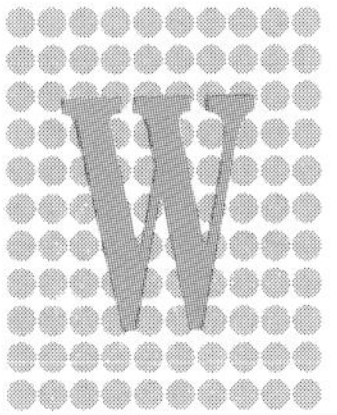

Westchester County's story from World War II to the present mirrors modern history's demographic shifts of people around the globe, finding new Americans from Asia, the Middle East, the Caribbean, and Latin America clustering in urban centers. The new groups are making their mark as surely as groups from the British Isles and Europe threaded the fabric of life in nineteenth-century Westchester.

At the same time, some cities that faltered with age in the 1950s have been bolstered and transformed by an array of renewal and restoration programs that have allowed them to catch up economically with the brand-new suburban neighborhoods that sprouted by villages and towns.

Westchester's six cities have been changed and revitalized in different ways. They profit from the public funds spent to restore and beautify their oldest neighborhoods. The cities have lively business interests, educational and health resources, diverse residential stock, and a sense of community identity.

The cities share one of the most prized benefits of peaceful communities—a consistently low crime rate. In an era of national concern about crime, Westchester County has been found to have fewer incidents to worry about. A 1988 Federal Bureau of Investigation study of national crime statistics released reports that Westchester County experienced well below half the rate of crime of neighboring New York City.

A close look at each city, from Yonkers (the largest) to White Plains (the center of government and commerce), reveals a wealth of living resources and the diverse

The enterprising cities of Westchester County are the address chosen by many small and large businesses. The Westchester Financial Center, shown here, is one of the dynamic new office sites built in downtown White Plains in recent years. Photo by Rich Zila

Yonkers rises from the east bank of the Hudson River and allows for beautiful vistas of the Palisades on the tributary's west bank. The Palisades, great walls of rock, span almost 50 miles to the north. Photo by Rich Zila

commercial, corporate, and industrial businesses that propel the county's thriving economy.

YONKERS

By night, the City of Yonkers—the fourth-largest city in the state—is a hilly land mass by the Hudson River that appears nearly Mediterranean in a panorama of terraced, twinkling lights. About 195,000 people live in the 18-square-mile city, turning on the lamps that light its hills and valleys.

The city has seven hills that rise more than 300 feet above sea level, dotted with houses—about 76,000 units were recorded in the 1980 census. Across the Hudson River is the ageless stone curtain palisades of New Jersey. To the north is Hastings and to the south is posh Riverdale, a residential section of the Bronx that is favored by international dignitaries and diplomats.

Just about every ethnic group to enter America has had a foothold in the sprawling city of Yonkers, especially since it burst on the industrial scene of the 1800s. It was then that the Otis Elevator Company engraved its name and the words "Yonkers, N.Y." on the contraptions that lifted people and wares to new heights. Carpets and hats turned out in other riverside factories boosted the economy and renown of the city. Tall smokestacks and factory yards teeming with immigrant workers altered the waterfront that had served as a sloop and stagecoach stop for a small farm community in the 1700s.

Wealthy New York businessmen of the 1800s built a sprinkling of ornate houses with a river view in Yonkers. They added to a mix of Georgian, federal, and Greek revival houses that served the wealthy of the post-Revolutionary era. With the 1830s came interest in the early Gothic revival style; with the 1850s, Italianate revival. The 1860s and 1870s ushered in French Second Empire, and in the 1870s and 1880s high Victorian Gothic was the fashion. The Queen Anne style held court in the 1890s before architects came full circle to find new ways to interpret the early colonial dwellings in the shingle style and colonial revival. Yonkers played host to them all.

New residential areas east of the river began to be developed in the late 1800s that reflected several of these architectural styles. Called Park Hill, Ludlow Park, and Shonnard Park, the gracious neighborhoods fanned up and away from the point where industry, commerce, and tenement housing vied for dominance by the river. Commercial Gettys Square lured its customers from these new neighborhoods.

The construction of railroads, and later parkways, would account for the slices of development in the city. Yonkers' five glacial ridges provide the ripple of valleys and hills that naturally divide these neighborhoods north to south.

Close to the Hudson, one industrial sector currently flourishes, poised for continued new development. Ornate municipal buildings stand where officials grapple with the issues of renewal, a changing society, and growth. Nearby are artfully designed nineteenth-century houses, some in disrepair and others in stages of revival. Many houses share neatly swept and tree-shaded sidewalks with apartment buildings on the terraced streets form the shoreline uphill to Broadway. Yonkers blends into prominently residential Hastings to the north on Route

Yonker's grand Victorian homes stand proudly on the hills overlooking the Hudson River. Photo by Rich Zila

The entrance rotunda of the Yonkers City Hall, built circa 1907, is topped by a richly ornamented, shallow, gilded dome which rests on marble columns. Photo by Rich Zila

FACING PAGE, TOP: Lyndhurst, the first of noted architect Alexander Jackson Davis' large country houses in the Greek revival style, was largely influential in establishing the romantic movement in architecture and landscape design. The elegant estate, built in 1838, is now a museum open to the public. Photo by Rich Zila

FACING PAGE, INSET: The youthful grace of sisters Dorothy and Helen Gould is immortalized in stone at Lyndhurst. Their grandfather, the railroad magnate and financier, Jay Gould, purchased the property in 1880. Photo by Rich Zila

9, which begins in Manhattan as the famed Broadway and continues north through Albany.

The Hudson River Museum and Andrus Planetarium overlook the river from a high point of Untermeyer Park on Broadway and are part of the nineteenth-century mansion, Glenview, owned by financier John B. Trevor. Trevor and a business partner once stymied wealthy Jay Gould of Lyndhurst Castle in Tarrytown in his bid to corner the gold market. It was a sweet victory Trevor may have savored while strolling the expansive riverside estate that is now, like Lyndhurst to the north, open to the public.

But Yonkers has more claim to fame than old world capitalist glory. Leapfrog across the hills past the well-established industry and business of the Saw Mill River Road and Nepperhan Avenue areas toward the city's eastern border and one will find what locals consider to be the birthplace of the American shopping center—the Cross County Shopping Center. In the 1950s, Yonkers was among the first to deliver the goods in this unique plaza, bowing to the automobile's role in modern life and providing parking lots that few city streets could offer. The resulting boom in shopping made the center a magnet for consumers for miles around.

The city that invented the place to "shop 'til you drop" never really let go of its key role. The shopping center houses scores of stores, including John Wanamakers and Sterns department stores. Central Avenue courses due north from the shopping center to White Plains and brims with more stores. A large stock of middle income and upper income housing flanks the hills hugging Central Avenue, from apartment complexes to townhouses to single-family homes that continue into Scarsdale and Hartsdale, making the area a bustling market for an upscale audience.

The New York State Thruway, which passes the Cross County Shopping Center, carves the eastern section from the rest of Yonkers. The eastern area shows its relative newness in its wide streets and stock of post-World War II houses. Nationally known Sarah Lawrence College is in this leafy corner of the city near Bronxville. Much of the eastern edge of Yonkers overlooks the tree-lined Bronx River and parallel parkway with a phalanx of turreted and terraced apartment buildings. The area extends from the residential Woodlawn section of the Bronx in the south past Bronxville in the north to Crestwood, another section brimming with large, well-kept, single-family homes.

Today, about 10 percent of Yonkers' land is used for commerce or industry. Precision Valve employs 550 in the city. Refined Sugars, employing 500, has its headquarters in the city.

Tom Carvel housed his ice cream business in Yonkers and Dellwood milk trucks roll from the city. Industry and massive warehouses have lined Nepperhan Avenue for years and include small concerns like the Acme Brief Case Company, Inc., which employs 100 workers. Kawasaki & Nissho Iwai, international manufacturer of railroad cars, and the multi-national Schott Corporation, which sells glassware for laboratories and homes, have headquarters conveniently located near the Hudson Line and the river. The 22-acre New York City Port Authority

Industrial Park at Yonkers is a river site for diverse businesses.

Retail, office, and high-tech space is available on several thoroughfares, among them Tuckahoe Road, Yonkers Avenue, McLean Avenue, and Broadway. There is modern office space on Executive Boulevard by the Saw Mill River Parkway.

Three hospitals operate in the city: Saint John's Riverside Hospital, Saint Joseph's Medical Center, and Yonkers General. Laboratories and medical supply companies are engaged here and serve a wide populace. Bus Associates, with 900 on staff, and Liberty Lines, a company employing more than 800, are headquartered in Yonkers.

Yonkers is the site of a major county sewage treatment facility where 70 million gallons of sewage are treated each day. It serves areas to Briarcliff Manor, Mount Kisco, White Plains, and Mount Vernon.

Given Route 9, the Saw Mill River Parkway, the New York State Thruway, the Sprain Brook Parkway, the Bronx River Parkway, and city thoroughfares, Yonkers serves the county with about 40 percent of its land devoted to roads. Access points abound in the city for the rest of Westchester and the metropolitan area.

The city's recreational stock includes centralized Tibbetts Brook Park and Pool, site of family picnics, ethnic fairs, and colorful heritage day events. Dunwoodie Golf Course and nationally famous Yonkers Racetrack are also centralized attractions. Numerous restaurants and cinema centers are scattered in the city.

Ethnic diversity remains a hallmark of Yonkers. From Germany, Russia, and Eastern European countries, immigrants in search of factory jobs flocked to Yonkers after English, Irish, Scotch, and Italian immigrants. Blacks from the South competed for factory jobs and started their own businesses in the city. All of these groups graced the landscape with distinctive houses of worship whose domes and spires still command attention.

Today's newest groups include Cubans, Central Americans, and Caribbean and South American immigrants who live in the city with Greek, Portuguese, Middle Eastern, and Oriental immigrants, many of whom began settling in Yonkers in the 1950s. In addition, families of Japanese businessmen in the United States for a three-to-five-year hitch are discovering that Yonkers' wealth of residential choices is abundant.

Yonkers' substantial housing market comes as a surprise to those who have not known about the offerings of this big hometown. Its price range for housing is equally attractive among Westchester cities. Being big, it has taken on its share of the nation's struggles and burdens. But many solid neighborhoods support Yonkers in its transition to the next century, the newest immigrant wave, and the newest riverside industries to stamp "Yonkers, New York" on their wares.

NEW ROCHELLE

The waterfront mansions here sell for millions and their fortunate occupants, like everyone else in New Rochelle, need just 30 minutes to reach Grand Central from the city's train station—all the more time to spend in New Rochelle, where the good life has been lived on the Long

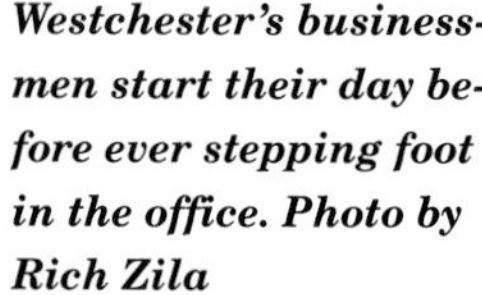

Westchester's businessmen start their day before ever stepping foot in the office. Photo by Rich Zila

Children grow up with pride in the racially integrated community of New Rochelle. Photo by Rich Zila

Island Sound for 300 years.

Defying the ill effects of age, the city continues to attract attention for its development potential. There is a $300-million revival proposed by a private sector group that calls for building a luxury condominium tower next to the city's train station and adding other modern space in the central downtown corridor for commercial and retail use. It is the latest proposed infusion of funds for the heart of the city in decades of applied effort.

New Rochelle is home to approximately 70,000 people and is the site of two gracefully designed college campuses—30-acre Iona College and the 50-acre College of New Rochelle—that boost its population by about 16,000. It has an attractive range of housing for citizens from all walks of life. More units are proposed within the city, including innovative ways to transform unused space above retail storefronts for new apartments.

Residential bounty aside, the city of 10.67 square miles has been successful in modernizing its downtown district for business and in maintaining its nine miles of shoreline and over 1,200 acres of recreational land. Bound to beat the odds in the urban gamble for continued business and real estate development, it has renewed blocks of handsome stores and offices.

One hundred storefronts in about 50 buildings boast restored facades that retain the best of their late-nineteenth-century Gothic and early-twentieth-century art deco origins. The buildings are within a 10-block area by the city's Main Street. Nine sites in the central business district have been selected for renewal projects that are under environmental review. The sites include locations on Division Street, Huguenot Street, and Memorial Highway.

Expansion and change are overtaking an enclosed mall in the center of the city, where moviegoers will have their choice of a dozen theaters, and new stores and restaurants will be added to the 100 establishments already in operation there, including Macy's and Bally of Switzerland. Travelers to this section of Westchester can stay in the city's modern hotel rooms and enjoy quick access to major New York airports and to Amtrak trains bound for a number of cities in the northeast.

Doctors have offices in the city to be close to the massive New Rochelle Hospital. Several nursing homes operate here. Law firms, banks, and realtors are among the 800 businesses that open each work day. Among small- to medium-sized businesses are over 100 in the categories of light and heavy industry. Longine Wittnauer, Inc., a jewelry firm, employs 300 people. They can

ABOVE: Westchester County's boating enthusiasts enjoy more than a dozen municipal marinas and private yacht and boat clubs that dot the waterfront on both the Long Island Sound and the Hudson River. The gilt cupola of the New Rochelle Yacht Club, shown here, helps sailors navigate the waters of the Long Island Sound. Photo by Rich Zila

rely on a public transportation system that provides bus service to the area, as well as the trains of the Metro North New Haven Line.

Interstate 95 makes New York, Connecticut, and Long Island accessible to New Rochelle's businesses and residents. The Hutchinson River Parkway also serves the city's industrial southern section and predominantly residential western and northern sections.

In the late 1960s and early 1970s, three major department stores and a string of other businesses pulled out of New Rochelle in an exodus that would test its resolve for decades. It has been tackling the universal concerns associated with inner city blight and social stresses in economically depressed neighborhoods. New Rochelle also has remained home to a strong middle-class black population. There are plenty of white collar neighborhoods for all races in New Rochelle and continued effort to maintain working class neighborhoods throughout the city.

Depressed streets continue to disappear in older sections as New Rochelle tries to house a greater diversity of people in its downtown sector while opening it up to fresh retail business opportunities. Some would like to build up the area for throngs to stroll and shop under the stars and bright city lights.

Apartment dwellers in tall, brick buildings by the Long Island Sound enjoy a day at choice spots on the fishing pier and twin beaches of the city's nearby Hudson Park, and they have congregated near the band shell in the park on concert nights for years. Five Island Park, the largest waterfront park to be opened on the sound in over 30 years, has beckoned residents to cross over by causeway or boat since 1981. On Davenport Neck, tennis has

RIGHT: New Rochelle's small sailing vessels can be seen in silhouette against the glittering Long Island Sound. Photo by Rich Zila

long vied with water sports for popularity at shore clubs that share the peninsula's space with single-family homes.

Residents from all over the city find their sea legs in the armada of recreational boats that leave the slips of a dozen New Rochelle yacht clubs and a municipal marina for weekend adventure. Glen Island, a 105-acre county-operated recreation area, attracts the land lover from New Rochelle and nearby towns.

Inland and moving northward, distinctive, beautiful, and massive houses on and around North Avenue, Webster Avenue, Pinebrook Boulevard, and Quaker Road live up to the American dream that artist Norman Rockwell brushed to life in this city. Like Rockwell's paintings, the look of any number of New Rochelle streets is comfortable, inviting, and serene.

In addition to the mall and downtown stores, there are large shopping areas in the northern section of the city to accommodate an increasing number of residential shoppers. Wykagyl Country Club, in the northern section of town, adds to the area's upscale appeal.

Off the Sound's shore, 60-acre Davids Island, formerly the Fort Slocum military post, awaits a billion-dollar development for the luxury housing market. New Rochelle serves about 25,000 residential units now, including the latest designs in townhouses, well-kept cooperative apartment buildings, and single-family homes.

Founded in 1688 by French Huguenots, New Rochelle remains the proud and strong-willed Queen City of the Sound. So far, the cast of the city's resident admirers has been a stellar one. It includes renowned performing artists such as Robert Merrill, Jan Peerce, and Renata Scotto, producer and playwright Ossie Davis, actress Ruby Dee, and author E.L. Doctorow. Its Foy Park is named for the Broadway family.

New Rochelle's fate has been tied to the business and family concerns of generations of upwardly mobile people. It will continue to depend on residents, business owners, and city officials who grasp the American dream and refuse to let go of it.

MOUNT VERNON

Mount Vernon has a place in colonial

New Rochelle City Hall, shown here, is a wonderful example of adaptive re-use. Formerly a high school, the building, which might otherwise have been torn down, was spared through the efforts of preservationists. Photo by Rich Zila

history as part of the original Town of Eastchester. The city truly came into its own in the 1850s as a planned community for working people near a new train station in southernmost Westchester. The four-square-mile industrial center that is today a city of 65,000 people was until then pastoral exurbia. In 1851 a visionary clothing store owner from New York City named John Stevens followed through on a dream of creating a city of homes. Mount Vernon was born. It's motto: "City of Beautiful Homes."

Stevens gathered others around him who saw the possibilities of building a thousand simple, frame houses where people of modest means could find a better life than that offered in crowded New York City. Within a year of buying the land and organizing a home association, there were 300 houses under construction. The Stevens family history records a whirlwind summer of 1851, when families in groups of 50 came by train to picnic, peer at lot maps, and choose the sites of their dream houses.

Mount Vernon became a place for industry in 1853 when a concerned citizens' group backed growth. The group reportedly had no trouble collaring sleepy-eyed morning commuters at the train station to buy shares of stock for a new local factory where scores of resident machinists could work.

Because of a peculiar train schedule, the commute in 1853 was a long haul. Local businessmen worried that the machinists who commuted to the city would soon tire of the trip. One speech maker at a factory rally represented the cause of weary machinists and all of those who wanted to see the planned community of Mount Vernon prosper. "Many who commuted for the purpose of going to New York and who were therefore obliged to leave their little home—which in fact was no home at all to them—leaving at early dawn or before and returning late at night—would be benefitted by the building of such a machine shop."

From the beginning Mount Vernon had a modest view of itself and its workaday houses. There were and still are very fine, large houses in Mount Vernon akin to those in neighboring

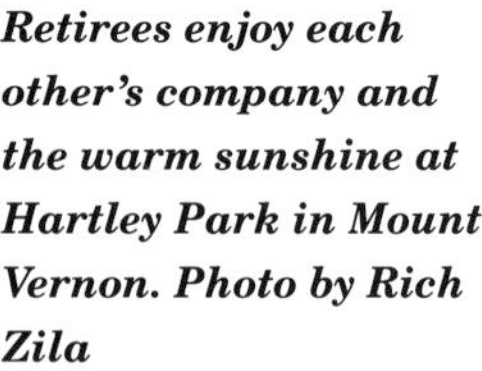

Retirees enjoy each other's company and the warm sunshine at Hartley Park in Mount Vernon. Photo by Rich Zila

Westchester Gardens in Mount Vernon provides gracious living for apartment dwellers. Photo by Rich Zila

Bronxville, Eastchester, Pelham, and New Rochelle. But when Mount Vernon was coming into its own in that rail rush, locals said industry should be cultivated. It would put Mount Vernon on the map.

One pro-industry city father in 1853 pointed out that Mount Vernon lacked the hilltop vistas of the Hudson River that nearby Yonkers was proud to offer and it missed the alluring nine miles of shoreline of which New Rochelle boasts. From the start, Mount Vernon was cast among the three industrious southern cities as the sturdy one between Yonkers, the "Queen City of the Hudson," and New Rochelle, the "Queen City of the Sound."

In that tradition, Mount Vernon offers a wide range of opportunities for work and for housing. There is much middle-income, affordable, multi-unit housing in the city, as well as a wide range of beautiful upscale family homes. There are well-built apartment complexes, some dating back to the 1930s in several areas. Elmsmere, Hunts Woods, and Pasadena Park abound in fine housing. Chester Heights and Chester Hill are quiet neighborhoods that serve the first-time homeowner and large families.

Many apartments are sold as cooperative or condominium units in the city. They retain value due in large measure to Mount Vernon's location, which is prized by commuters who reach Grand Central by rail nonstop in 24 minutes. Mount Vernon has a substantial neighborhood of apartment buildings called Fleetwood in the northwest corner of the city that has its own train station and shopping district as well as access to several major highways.

Fourth Avenue in southern central Mount Vernon is a shopping hub. The city's government buildings and Mount Vernon Hospital are in this area. Nearby Gramatan Avenue houses offices for banks, law firms, and other businesses. The city is served by Gannett Westchester Rockland Newspapers and local weeklies.

A bustling Fourth Avenue was photographed in an 1870s newspaper, full of gents in straw hats and ladies carrying parasols, all of them craning their necks to watch a circus performer cross overhead on a tightrope. At that time, shops, hotels, and department stores flourished in Mount Vernon, including one establishment that lured shoppers to its furniture department for afternoon tea served by kimono-dressed Japanese ladies.

The city grew quickly through the early twentieth century. German immigrants left a mark in the northwest section of the city, bringing with them classical music that provided all of the recreation many early residents seemed to need. Soon there was an opera house in Mount Vernon, and then motion picture theaters to draw crowds to Fourth Avenue in the 1920s. The crowds came from different sections of the city; Italian families congregated together, Eastern Europeans and southern blacks

Members of a wedding relish the revitalization of Peekskill. Riverfront Green, a park on the water's edge, is the setting for special events and elegant passenger boats. Photo by Linda Zila

had their own sections. By the hard-pressed 1930s, there were more than two dozen houses of worship in which residents could gather to pray for an end to the Great Depression.

Various stretches of Mount Vernon serve as roadbed and train track bed and frame different neighborhoods. Trains stop on the New Haven and Harlem lines in the city's three stations. Greenbelts lie to the west by the Bronx River Parkway and to the east by the Hutchinson River Parkway. In the north is the Cross County Parkway, linking a network that puts Mount Vernon business in close proximity to New York City, New Jersey, Long Island, and Connecticut.

Mount Vernon is one of the most convenient; central locations in the tristate area. Industrial property hugs the southernmost section of the city and there is a mix of industrial and commercial property along the southeast corridor that is paralleled by Route 22 and the Hutchinson River Parkway. The southern area borders Pelham Bay and the Bronx and there is easy access for a large pool of employees via a complex bus system and New York City subways that run to Mount Vernon's southern border.

Manufacturers of every type run their operations in Mount Vernon. Tool and dye firms, semiconductor firms, metal stamping, plumbing, and heating companies, and graphics and printing outfits operate here. A nationally known mail order company was started in the city by Lillian Vernon, and Consumer Union's renowned publishing and product testing operations for *Consumer Reports* magazines and books operate here.

Litton Industries, Rockwell International, Sirco International Corporation, and Wachtel Kuklauer are firms that employ from 200 to 400 people. Top 500 companies in New York listed by Crain's Business Edition in 1989 operate in Mount Vernon. Big, small, and middle-size industrial firms have always received a welcome.

It is apparent that many sections of Mount Vernon, quick to accept the worker and provide housing, are now dedicated to keeping in shape. Projects to revitalize the areas near the city's oldest retail center continue to shake the dust of time from facades.

As a full-grown city approaching the year 2000, this urban place is subject to the wrenching tests of its mettle that many cities face today. Mount Vernon continually renews its energy with newcomers who value the wide price range of its housing, its central location, stable tax base, and business-oriented reputation.

PEEKSKILL

Peekskill overlooks the Hudson River as it curves sharply to the northwest beneath the city's commanding hillside perch. The city's history dates back to a 1600s Dutch fur trader named Jan Peek, and the area was on George Washington's mind during the Revolutionary War when the British attacked a weakly defended American barrack and warehouse as river ice melted in March 1777.

Peekskill was long ago a major stop for cargo and passenger boats on the Hudson, from sloops to steamers. By the mid-1840s it was a major center in the county for iron works. Peekskill's gritty workers turned out stoves and plows for America's homes and farms for decades. The Civil War disrupted, then decimated, the plow trade in the South, but iron works continued operating in Peekskill into the 1930s.

Three major companies produced stoves there at the turn of the century. One prominent employer of the trade until 1931, the Naylor Brothers Iron and Brass Foundry and Machine Shops, also put food on the tables of a diversified immigrant and southern black population. In hard times, the workers fished in the river for sturgeon, or "Albany Beef," to survive.

Other Peekskill residents found steady work preparing yeast for sale by Fleischmann Company, later Standard Brands, a company which boasted that it had 1,000 employees laboring in the largest yeast factory in the world in the later 1940s. Clothing manufacturers provided jobs in the city for a similarly long time.

The 1980s turned out to be a boom decade for Peekskill. The transition was marked by the addition of 330,000 square feet of industrial space and approval of more than 2,300 new housing units. Between 1985 and 1988, 1,100

Situated on approximately 250 acres in Buchanan, Indian Point Nuclear Generating Station, IP2, owned and operated by Con Edison, provides 915 megawatts of electricity to more than one million people and services. According to the company, IP2 is Con Edison's most economical source of electricity. Photo by Rich Zila

Birds of all kinds can be observed close-up at the Edith C. Read Park and Wildlife Sanctuary in Rye. The 170-acre natural preserve includes a quarter-mile of shoreline along the Long Island Sound, and a saltwater lake with seven wooded islands. Photo by Rich Zila

units were built, adding to the housing stock in the older core city of Peekskill and its numerous residential neighborhoods. Today, apartment complexes and closely set single- and multi-family homes stand within city limits, and modern homes built after World War II spread to its edges and beyond in the town of Cortlandt.

The wide ribbon of Route 9 speeds traffic alongside the city of about 20,000 people as it responds to a fourth decade of urban renewal. The 4.5-square-mile city has made headway in restoring decaying neighborhoods in a block-by-block assault on blight. Buildings beyond hope were leveled and new ones erected. Hundreds of apartments were rehabilitated through years of programs that devoted attention to acres and acres of city streets.

City parkland and parking space was created. New municipal buildings, including a central police station, court, library, and community center have been added to the center city, as well as senior citizen housing. Here building facades were also freshened by entrepreneurs who sided with city officials in reclaiming very serviceable work space. In this area, Peekskill houses the oldest bank in Westchester, Lincoln First Bank on North Division and Main Street. The bank opened as Westchester County National Bank in 1833 with Pierre Van Cortlandt as its president. New restaurants sprout on Division Street thanks to local and federal economic development loans.

Nearby is the Peekskill Paramount Center for the Performing Arts, a restored theater where thousands hear a variety of music every year. It is one of the biggest beneficiaries of the 450-space parking building the city erected in the heart of the business district. Two such structures were erected as part of the city's renewal. The major office developments were initiated late in the last decade, enhancing the central business district's potential. Structural renewal and social services continue to be the focus of the city's mayor, common council, and city manager.

Peekskill's residents are lured to stores on Route 6, a busy east-west central thoroughfare that extends into Putnam County and then Connecticut. Route 35 and Route 202, which runs south past Peekskill Community Hospital into Yorktown Heights, offer more shopping choices. In Peekskill's business center, space is taken by neighborhood stores and is also scooped up for offices by engineers, architects, accountants, and other non-retail businesses.

Fresh attention is apparent beyond the city's core. Central Avenue, the gateway to the city's waterfront, was the focal point in the late 1980s for development of a new artist's colony and dining spot to be centered around a restored gristmill. At the river's edge is Riverfront Green, a park that has been the setting for culinary feats accomplished by volunteers raising funds for local health projects. Over the years they have broken records assembling the largest omelet, sandwich, popcorn ball, and lasagna for crowds contribut-

Re-enactors, such as this guard at the John Jay Homestead in Katonah, provide a glimpse into Westchester's role and activities during the beginning of the American Revolution. Photo by Geoffrey Kerrigan

ing to the Peekskill Area Health Center.

Three hundred acres of land formerly owned by nonprofit institutions became part of the open market during the 1980s and are developed or in review for development. Housing in Peekskill proves to be among the steadiest sellers in the area. The city had 8,518 housing units in a wide price range in 1989, drawing new people of every age to this corner of the county.

In the city's industrial section, the 90-acre Charles Point Industrial Park is a huge, modern complex where a large portion of the county's garbage is processed in a garbage-to-energy plant.

81 Main Street shines in the afternoon sunlight. This building offers businesses 120,000 square feet of office space on five stories in downtown White Plains. Photo by Rich Zila

More space for industry lies within this area and an $11-million road modernization project was set in motion in the late 1980s to provide swift passage between the industrial park and Route 9. Tracks of the Metropolitan Transportation Authority's Hudson Line lie between the river and Route 9, serving rail passengers of the Metro North and Amtrak. To the north lies Camp Smith, a New York National Guard post on a large reservation, and to the south is Indian Point, a mega power source for the metropolitan region.

In 1956, Con Edison was the first electric company in the United States permitted to develop a commercial nuclear plant. Since then, three Con Edison plants have sprung up on the riverbank in nearby Buchanan; one of them is now operated by the Power Authority of the State of New York. Nearly 800 workers are employed at Indian Point.

River watch groups and industry have negotiated the issues of river purity and industrial operations since the 1970s and the river's overall health shows in the fish now spawning and living in it. Peekskill residents with a river view in this corner of the county are among those to profit from the fresh attention given to the area.

RYE

Rye City has stood alone since 1944, claiming independence from the town of Rye that was settled in the 1660s by English families who came from neighboring Greenwich. Over its lifetime, the six-square-mile city has proven to be dedicated to providing a high quality of life for its 15,000 residents.

Rye's two miles along Long Island Sound consist of high-priced land for its people and marshy tall grass for about 200 types of birds that frequent its county-run conservancy. Inland, houses dot large properties along winding, quiet, wooded streets and stand side-by-side on avenues westward to Interstate 95.

A parcel of Rye's shorefront is set aside for the county's Playland, complete with a direct access road from the interstate for visitors. The peninsula of Milton Point juts out quietly into the water, its contour known to those who take shelter in the 350-slip city marina in Milton Harbor.

Rye has shown itself to be content with a premier residential reputation. In 1989, there were about 5,500 resi-

The White Plains civic center serves local and county residents. The Court House, left, distinguishes White Plains as Westchester's county seat and the library provides a wealth of information services. Photo by Rich Zila

Redevelopment in White Plains hasn't stopped shoppers from frequenting Mamaroneck Avenue businesses. Shown here are pedestrians browsing among the offerings of Aspasia, a long-established jewelry store. Photo by Linda Zila

dential properties, the overwhelming number of them owner-occupied, single-family homes. Apartments in old and new buildings tend to be cooperative or condominium units, and ultra modern townhouses also can be found.

A municipal park, country club, and golf course are open to residents, as are the trails and museum of Rye Nature Center. The city has excellent schools, a large library, a center for the arts, and a center for the performing arts. It can rely on United Hospital in nearby Port Chester for health emergencies and care.

Rye has corporations operating facilities within its borders, as well as some commercial properties to be developed. Avon Products, Inc., New York Life Insurance Company, Mutual of Omaha, and Companion Life Insurance Company have facilities in Rye. Banks, law firms, and professional offices occupy quaint buildings surrounding Purchase Street, a smartly outfitted avenue of shops near the train station. Purchase Street stands to the side of Route 1 (the Boston Post Road), a thoroughfare connecting Westchester shore towns with New York City and points in Connecticut and Massachusetts.

I-95 serves Rye travelers with the same destinations and I-287 is equally accessible for Westchester and Rockland County travel. Metro North trains make runs on the New Haven Line to Grand Central Station in 38 minutes. All of these routes provide access for the captains and lieutenants of indus-

ABOVE AND FACING PAGE: The multi-block Galleria changed the pulse of downtown White Plains. Anchored by leading department stores J.C. Penney and Abraham and Strauss, the enclosed shopping mall provides indoor parking, and houses about 150 specialty stores including an assortment of eateries located amidst sunlit interior landscaping. Photos by Rich Zila

try who staked out residential parcels from large estates that made up the area before the twentieth century.

The Rye Historical Society preserves the records of the gentlemen farmers to gentlemen yachtsmen who make up Rye's past. The society restored the Square House, a circa 1670s tavern that was a stagecoach stop for colonial travelers, and transformed it into a museum. An area of neutral ground on the outskirts of battle during the American Revolution, Rye served as one of the homes of John Jay, the first chief justice of the U.S. Supreme Court.

Rye City has maintained a tranquil atmosphere for its modern homeowners and the retail businesses that serve them. That atmosphere also suits the workings of legal, commercial, and professional firms that have chosen it as an accessible county home base.

WHITE PLAINS

Distinguished as county seat, birthplace of the State of New York, and keeper of Westchester's records since pre-Revolutionary days, White Plains is an upbeat, 10-square-mile mecca for business, communications, commerce, living, and the law.

White Plains has been recharged in the last half of the twentieth century with sparkling new urban vistas that hold promise for the next century of business. Each workday morning, the city now welcomes about 300,000 people to its high-rise office buildings, courts, government offices, hotels, health facilities, classrooms, shops, boutiques, and topshelf department stores. At night, it tucks about 47,000 residents into homes that range from stucco mansions to singles studios in a wide range of quiet neighborhoods that encircle downtown.

Downtown, attorneys from all over the county duly make appearances before judges in a modern, 20-story courthouse. Federal, state, county, and city government officials convene in nearby buildings, and local newspapers and radio and cable stations run on deadline. The *New York Times* and Associated Press maintain satellite offices in the center of the city while Prodigy, the national computer information service, has a staff of 450 at its Hamilton Avenue headquarters. Corporate neighbor AT&T on the same block employs 1,000.

County shoppers spend in shops on Mamaroneck Avenue, Post Road, Bloomingdale Road, Main Street, and the enclosed Galleria Shopping Mall. The upscale Fifth Avenue and homespun American department stores of White Plains are plentiful and varied. They include Bloomingdale's, Neiman Marcus, Saks Fifth Avenue, Macy's, Abraham & Strauss, J.C. Penney, and Sears Roebuck & Company. The Fashion Mall and Westchester Pavilion are two new multimillion-dollar shopping meccas being proposed.

At noon, executives and office workers from Fortune 500 companies stroll the city's streets to a host of restaurants. In summer, they stop to hear music played by the fountains of North Broadway and Main Street in programs sponsored by the county. Modern sculpture catches the eye in front of new glass, steel, and brick buildings. They rise along the city's wide boulevards, giving White Plains a roomy, open for business air. A new train station and central bus terminal is adorned with an eye-catching clock tower.

The Trans Center serves commuters from the city and workers who spill out of the new office buildings and industries at day's end. The city has numerous companies within its borders that supply goods and services: along short Water Street near Main Street, C.P. International, Inc., a computer programming firm, employs 400 people at its computer terminals; at Ocean Packing, another 400 employees move perishable goods to market. Metro

North employees clear the tracks at centralized yards of the Harlem Line for the wide-ranging crowd.

Hotels in the heart of the city cater to the general public with banquet facilities and to the corporate traveler's meeting and rest agenda. The city entered 1990 with phase three of upgrading five parking structures serving the driving public that stops at hotels such as midtown La Reserve, Holiday Inn, Crowne Plaza, and White Plains Hotel.

Business rules the Platinum Mile, a stretch of highly developed real estate

Texaco Inc., a worldwide organization, is located in Harrison on Westchester's famous Platinum Mile. The building spans the length of more than three football fields and incorporates an underground parking garage for 1,400 cars. Photo by Rich Zila

FACING PAGE: Friends relax in Kensico Park in Valhalla. This tree-lined park at the base of Kensico Dam hosts a wide range of county-run entertainment programs. Photo by Linda Zila

that borders the I-287 extending eastward to the City of Rye and I-95, the New York to New England interstate. The I-287 crosses west into Rockland County and is central Westchester's vital belt parkway. International and national business concerns are lined up for review along this corridor of prized real estate. Texaco's headquarters for 1,300 employees is located here on Westchester Avenue. Gannett Westchester Rockland Newspapers houses the news gathering and printing and distribution operation for its dozen daily newspapers and for national *USA Today.* NYNEX offices are on nearby Red Oak Lane, as is Stouffer's Westchester Hotel.

Nearby North Street serves business interests, including General Foods Corporation and its 3,600 employees. Bloomingdale Road houses major medical concerns, including New York Hospital Cornell Medical Center. White Plains Hospital, Saint Agnes Hospital, and Burke Rehabilitation Center are also in the city. Health Maintenance Organizations and doctors in private practice draw many clients to White Plains.

Pace University has a city campus on spacious North Broadway, a boulevard with a lush green center divide full of flowers, statues, and park benches. The flowery view pleases the eye of students, residents, and office workers along this thoroughfare. Access to I-287 and to the Bronx River Parkway serve the population and that of nearby North White Plains.

Neighborhoods called Gedney and Ridgeway fill corners of the city with beautifully maintained houses of every design. More homes sit on Battle Hill and in Rosedale. Residents enjoy the public golf course of Maple Moor, which skirts the Hutchinson River Parkway. Private clubs also serve up manicured courses here. White Plains is a golfer's mecca. Westchester Hills, Ridgeway, Century, and Fenway are key private clubs. Residents congregate indoors at the Westchester County Center, a much-frequented and recently renovated art deco building used for everything from concerts and antique and collectible shows to circuses.

To the north, Kensico Park, at the base of the Kensico Dam, is an outdoor gathering place where the county operates a wide range of summer entertainment programs.

Major corporations have been transforming partners in White Plain's twentieth-century history, but realtors, banks, and city officials also look to a future of closer relations with the latest maverick entrepreneurs. The space and support are in White Plains for a wide-ranging interconnection of businesses that will come about with the dawn of the twenty-first century.

4

A HAVEN FOR MIND AND BODY

ore than 11,000 babies were born in Westchester hospitals in 1988 and are now under care in one of the most modern health care systems in the world. Parents can rush newborns to one of the county's 14 general care hospitals if accidental poisoning, an inexplicable fever, or a fall prompts a trip to the emergency room.

Encouraged by caring professionals, some children must learn to be brave for treatment of the serious diseases or disabilities that make hospital visits a routine part of their lives. But most of the county's children, treated to excellent neonatal, natal, and pediatric care, will not see the inside of a hospital until they volunteer to be candy stripers as teenagers or watch their babies delivered in ultramodern facilities.

Westchester's citizens over 55 are likely to make use of the county's health care facilities to stay fit for an active life-style. Whether they need to confer with a specialist in sports medicine for tennis elbow or deal with life-threatening illness, patients benefit from a wide range of modern, million-dollar diagnostic equipment that area nonprofit hospitals have worked hardto secure.

Medical advances in equipment and treatment are routinely embraced in the county's hospitals. Westchester residents are accustomed to getting the best that medicine has to offer. This expectation of excellence is the standard setting under which the county's hospitals must continually operate. It is directly tied to the quality of life in Westchester and is seen in the adoption of current national trends in

Westchester's hospitals maintain standards of excellence by constantly refining and improving their treatment. At Four Winds, a private psychiatric hospital, innovative, individualized therapy in traditional surroundings nourishes each patient's ability to build a healthy foundation for the future. Shown here is the art therapist at an exhibit of patients' art work. Courtesy, Four Winds Hospital

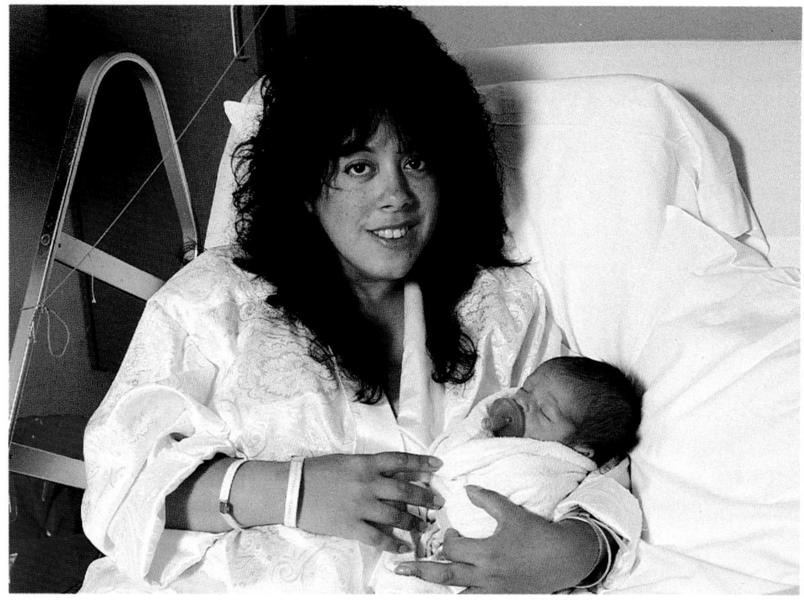

Mother and newborn at White Plains Hospital Medical Center receive a complete range of family-centered care. The Obstetrical and Gynecological Units provide nursing care to pre- and postpartum obstetrical and gynecological patients. A nursery is staffed by medical personnel especially trained in the care of newborns. Photo by Rich Zila

treatment and equipment by local hospitals.

The $1.2-million Digital Subtraction Angiography allows highly sophisticated imaging of the vascular system of stricken heart patients. The CAT scan offers a speedy method of sharply defining small structures in the body to insure proper and immediate treatment of illness. The Magnetic Resonance Array is another innovative method of seeing hard-to-examine internal systems of the body, including the brain. The sensitive new Candela Miniscope is used with the laser lithotripter, a non-surgical therapy that fragments calcium stones blocking kidney function. The new treatment allows a shorter hospital stay and convalescence than former types of treatment.

Add nuclear medicine, the latest equipment for mammography, and electrocardiograms and electroencephlograms readily available to Westchester residents in local hospitals, and one sees how well the community hospitals keep pace with world-renowned health facilities.

Like New York City hospitals, Westchester County hospitals also adhere to stringent codes and regulations administered by the New York State Health Department. Certification for medical professionals in New York follows rigorous training and demands high educational standards.

Westchester hospitals attract doctors with high standards who want to work in an attractive environment and in equally attractive office and living space nearby. Nurses and other health professionals are attracted to the system for the working environment offered in the county. United Hospital in Port Chester was among local hospitals in the 1980s that made a major drive to attract professionals in nursing and other specialties with salaries and ben-

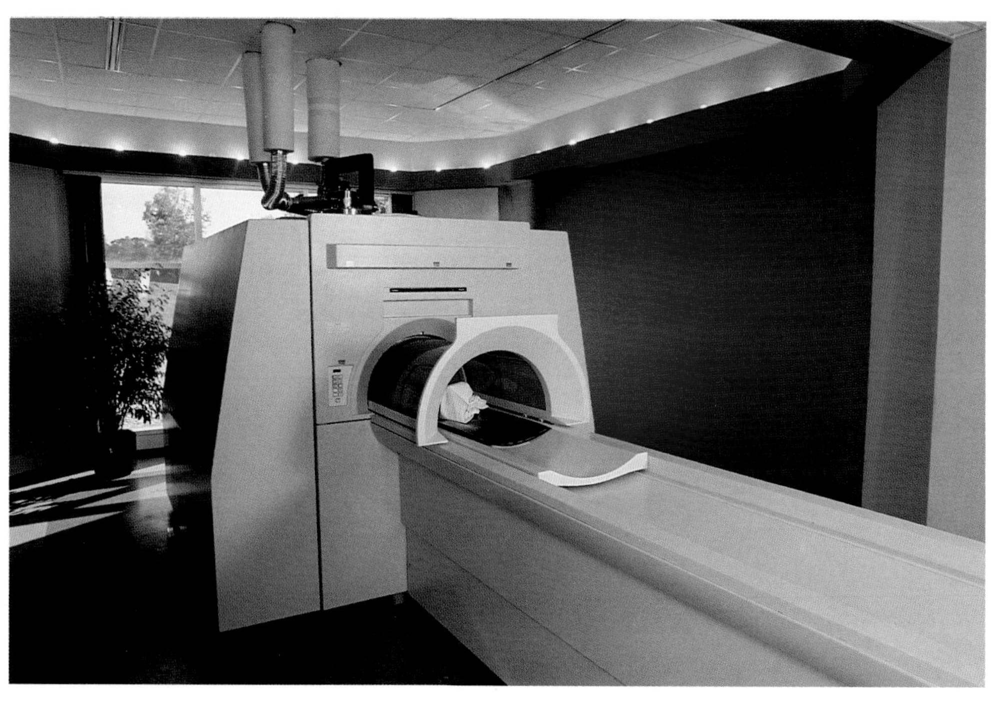

Westchester's hospitals have the latest equipment available. The Magnetic Resonance Imager takes pictures without exposing patients to radiation. Photo by Robert Frerck/TSW Click/Chicago Ltd.

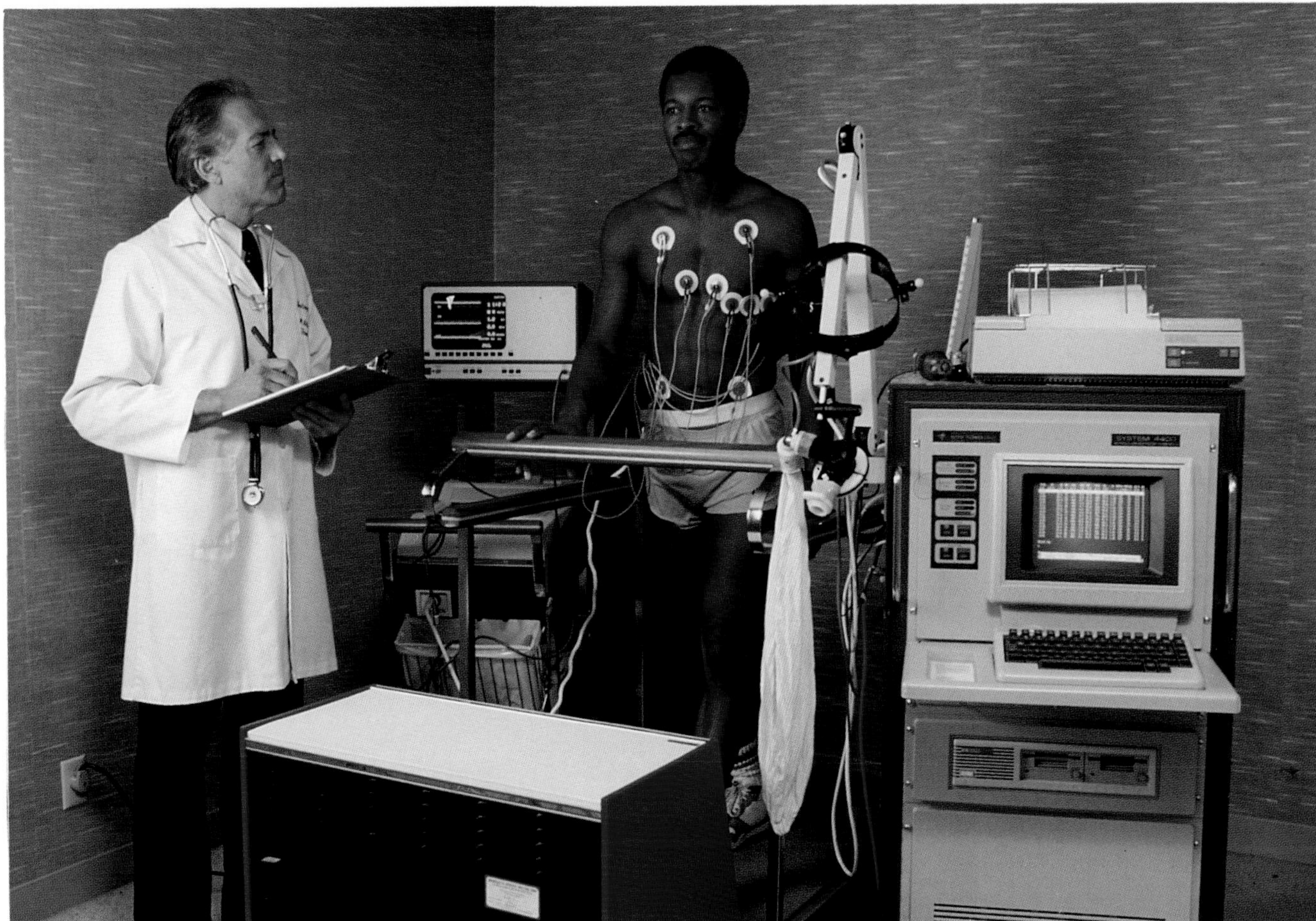

Preventive medicine, such as the stress test being administered here, is often the best insurance for maintaining good health. Westchester's health care facilities are well equipped to help residents stay fit. Photo by Pete Saloutos/TSW Click/Chicago Ltd.

efits packages that rivaled city hospitals. The hospitals show an interest in maintaining high morale among employees to encourage long-term employment in these growing fields.

People who want to maintain their health through proper diet, stress management, smoking cessation, and responsible behavior regarding drug or alcohol use have many quality programs available to them in local hospitals. Signing up for such programs can reduce the incidence of diseases that lead to long illness and the need for hospitalization, making the hospitals' preventative programs life- and money-saving alternatives for Westchester residents.

Revolution in medicine in the last decade has meant far more outpatient care by hospitals. A reduced length of stay for many types of surgery has been adopted as an alternative that has value for patients and frees beds for acute care.

According to 1989 statistics made available by the Hudson Valley Health Systems Agency, 809,913 patient days were spent in 2,752 hospital beds for medical and surgical procedures in the county's 14 hospitals.

The Westchester County Medical Center in Valhalla, built in 1979 and equipped with 439 beds, leads the area in size and the nature of its services, including highly advanced neonatal and burn treatment units. Following in bed capacity are New Rochelle Hospital, with 311 beds and a 150-bed skilled nursing facility, and the 280-bed Lawrence Hospital in Bronxville. Among the private hospitals, Saint John's Riverside Hospital in Yonkers plays a leading role in its capacity for obstetric and pediatric care.

Saint Agnes Hospital in White Plains, while serving as a 184-bed general care hospital, has played a supportive role in treating those with cerebral palsy and other disabling conditions, and aiding their adjustment in an unimpaired society. The 214-bed United Hospital in Port Chester has a skilled nursing care facility and the largest psychiatric unit among the five private general hospitals with such facilities.

In 1988, White Plains Hospital expanded 83,144 patient days in its 277-

Support personnel at Westchester's hospitals are attracted to the sophisticated working environments provided there. Photo by Smith-Baer, courtesy, White Plains Hospital

bed facility, offering every type of care. Northern Westchester Medical Center in Mount Kisco also provided every type of care to a far-reaching community base of several towns. The 466 volunteers on its roster in 1988 are among the thousands of volunteers in Westchester who aid hospitals daily in their mission of relieving suffering.

The 114-bed Peekskill Community Hospital is an incalculable asset to the northwest corner of the county and those who travel through it. Phelps Memorial Hospital Center in North Tarrytown, with 202 beds, manages to fulfill all of the medical tasks of a general hospital for Hudson River communities and continually seeks new ways to serve the public.

Lower Westchester has several resources. Yonkers General Hospital, with 190 medical and surgical beds and a 19-bed detoxification center, has served a widely divergent population for years. Nearby Saint Joseph's Hospital is a 165-bed facility in Yonkers which also has a 29-bed psychiatric unit. In addition to its service, Mount Vernon Hospital, with 243 beds for medical, surgical, obstetric, and pediatric care, is an asset as a major employer in the community.

The hospitals are part of the Northern Metropolitan Hospital Association, a group of 36 facilities in the lower Hudson Valley that represent major employers for many communities. In Westchester, hospitals account for employment of about 500 to 1,200 people in their communities. Together, hospitals encourage government interest in maintaining the high standards of health care in the region. The state Department of Labor predicts that the work of these facilities make up some of the fastest-growing occupational categories of the 1990s.

The hospitals of Westchester are prized for the sensitive, conscientious professionals and volunteers serving in home towns from birth to old age and for the powerful role they play in the economic well-being of the county.

WESTCHESTER SCHOOLS: PUBLIC EDUCATIONS

Westchester County's 40 school districts grace its diverse cities, towns, and villages with well-maintained buildings that are often set on pretty and spacious campuses. Communities historically support excellence in the districts and profit in the fine reputation of the schools. A key yardstick of the success of these systems is the fact that an overwhelming majority of Westchester students seek higher education and readily find places at the top schools in the nation. An estimated 105,000 youngsters were part of the Westchester County public school network in 1989.

Westchester public schools attract highly trained professionals who are certified under rigorous standards set by the State of New York. Many districts have teachers on staff who are educated to the masters level and beyond. In addition to seeking postgraduate credits, teachers are encouraged to engage in workshops at teachers' centers, and to participate in advisory partnerships with master teachers and in mentor programs—continually advancing in their fields.

County schools surpass other schools in the state in fulfilling the standards for curricula set by the New York State Board of Regents and Department of Education. The typical school day is packed with skills courses in reading, math, writing, history, languages, science, and computer literacy, and with music, art, gymnastics, critical thinking, and personal values courses. Westchester's public school students are so adept in required coursework that it is common for districts to report that more than 90 percent scored above the state average test scores when the districts file annual reviews in their required Comprehensive Assessment Reports.

The districts are united in promoting a comfortable environment for learning for the average child, the gifted, and the impaired. Districts developed special programs for the gifted and talented throughout the 1980s. Vocational and special education needs are met by the vast networkers of the New York State Board of Cooperative Educational Services that operate in different districts and in special centers in southern and northern Westchester. The student who wishes to enter the work force directly after high school may choose from a wide range of vocational courses—from horticulture to draftsmanship, car repair to secretarial training.

There is a special commitment at the Northern Westchester Hospital Center to the needs of the aging. Programs for senior citizens include Health Access, Coordinated Care, and the Care Givers Support Group, all run by Senior Care Services. Photo by Joseph Vericker, courtesy, Northern Westchester Hospital Center

POINTS OF PRIDE

Officials of Westchester's public school districts each year make note of the sources of their districts' pride in an annual guidebook prepared by the Westchester and Putnam School Boards Association. Among the finds in the 1988-1989 edition are items included in this overview:

—The Mount Vernon public school system, which educates students of all races and socio-economic levels, notes in a 1988-1989 guidebook of area public schools that its graduates are studying at Harvard, Yale, M.I.T., Duke, Brown, and Columbia.

—White Plains public schools enjoy one of the most favorable ratios of students to teachers in the state at 10.4 to 1. Parents Choice programs allow parents to select their children's elementary schools by preference rather than by typical neighborhood boundaries.

There are 40 school districts serving the diverse needs of Westchester's students with a talented corps of educators and administrators who are dedicated to providing quality education. Photo by Rich Zila

—Peekskill is pleased to have an ongoing relationship with its sister city, Asahikawa, Japan, which results in annual student exchange between their school systems.

—Yonkers, which operates programs to educate 18,000 students, has magnet schools drawing children to special courses, among them high-tech, computers, and the performing arts. From its early childhood center to its four high schools and three alternate programs, Yonkers' public education system offers options to suit the diverse needs of the city's wide-ranging populace.

—New Rochelle, (rated in 1989 as one of the 10 most livable cities for families in the state), provides its schoolchildren with a pre-kindergarten program, gifted and talented programs, computer education from grades K to 12, and a planetarium operating at its impressive high school campus.

—Rye City public school students enjoy a host of similar advantages plus a cable television station at the district high school, the top rung of its very strong college preparatory program.

—In all, 98 percent of the graduates of Edgemont High School attend college. The school's debate team has won major tournaments, its mathematicians compete in problem solving contests, and the district has a model United Nations program which has received national recognition. The district serves students from parts of Tuckahoe and Scarsdale.

— About 20 percent of Scarsdale's high school graduates are National Merit Semifinalists or commended in that academic classification, 40 percent are involved in advanced placement courses that require college-level scholarship, and many of the 98 percent who seek higher education attend prestigious institutions.

—Rye Neck offers a theater arts sequence of study in addition to the courses typically offered by Westchester schools. Serving part of Mamaroneck and part of the city of Rye, it was the first district in the area to offer an all-day kindergarten program.

—Eastchester prides itself on offering programs that welcome poets, artists, and writers into the classroom. It has been recognized as having one of the most extensive performing and creative arts programs in the county, including music programs with Lincoln Center in New York City and the Westchester Conservancy.

—Mount Pleasant School District includes Hawthorne, Thornwood, and parts of Valhalla and Pleasantville. Its Westlake High School has been designated one of the top secondary schools in New York State and its elementary and middle schools have been commended for innovative programs.

—Mamaroneck Union Free School District is among the districts in Westchester offering an extended day program for kindergarten students.

—Harrison's Parsons Elementary School was the first in New York State to institute a Japanese-English bilingual program.

—Blind Brook-Rye Neck Union Free School District in Rye Brook prides itself on educating a record number of international students who are the children of diplomats, professionals, and

Expansive grounds at New Rochelle High School allow room to roam and grow. Here students head into school after lunch. Photo by Rich Zila

businesspeople from abroad.

—Public Schools of the Tarrytowns serve an ethnically and culturally diverse population of about 1,850 students and runs a nationally acclaimed program for students whose native tongue is not English.

—Poncantico Hills School District serves a community of 2,000 in parts of Mount Pleasant, Greenburgh, and North Tarrytown with one kindergarten-to-eighth-grade school serving approximately 275 students. The facility is near the sprawling Rockefeller State Park Preserve and has an olympic-size pool and tennis courts on the campus.

—Bronxville prides itself on providing a rigorous college preparatory program and graduating students from its well-equipped public school system for higher education at top schools.

—Irvington public schools report that 95 percent of its class of 1987 went to college.

—Somers Central School District reported its high school students scored well above the state and national average on Scholastic Achievement Tests for college entrance. The 1988-1989 guide listed scores of 443 verbal and 468 math.

—Of the 90 percent of Briarcliff Manor students who sought higher education, 84 percent attend four-year colleges. The small district has a wealth of programs surpassing state guidelines.

—Pleasantville Public Schools include elementary, middle, and high schools for about 1,100 pupils. Its programs include extended-day kindergarten, an Olympics of the Mind, and college preparatory courses for the 85 to 90 percent of its students who plan to attend college.

—Ardsley's public school administra-

Young women don't have to stand on the sidelines when it comes to intramural sports. Here the John Jay High School's girls' lacrosse team, from Cross River, competes against the Scarsdale High School team. Photo by Geoffrey Kerrigan

tors report that the majority of its professional staff is rigorously educated, having accumulated 60 credits beyond the master's degree level.

—Yorktown Central School District's middle students are taught by a team-teaching method that is popular among Westchester educators. At the high school level, there is a skills options program offering enrichment and remedial choices beyond the general curriculum, and a career center and alternate school program.

—Byram Hills district in Armonk reports that its school board maintains a fund for 20 to 30 projects a year to be initiated by its staff in an effort to bring students to areas of study beyond a curriculum that also is strong in college preparation.

—The Croton Harmon School District has engaged in unique shared courses with neighboring Ossining. It also maintains a relationship and exchange programs with La Rochelle, France, and Salamanca, Spain.

—Greenburgh Central #7 in Ardsley has an Early Childhood program for pre-kindergarten children and all-day kindergarten programs.

—Valhalla Union Free School District's two elementary schools and junior high school operate on a non-graded basis that emphasizes mastery of skills and the development of personal responsibility.

—Bedford Central School District treats its nearly 3,000 students to education that is tailored to individual needs and parental wishes.

—Lakeland District maintains a Little Red School House as a lively historic resource for the students, who attend the district from Yorktown, Cortlandt, and parts of Putnam County.

—Tuckahoe Union Free School District boasts an average class size of

Good teamwork builds camaraderie among members of the Mamaroneck High School girls' field hockey team. Photo by Rich Zila

22 pupils and a full-day kindergarten program. Its high school has a Media Center, Computer Center, and modern science and language labs.

—The Elmsford district's Hamilton High School boys basketball team was hailed as the New York State champion in 1987 and 1988.

—Hastings on Hudson prides itself on ethnic diversity, academic achievement, and art and music programs that include band, orchestra, and choral and jazz groups.

—Administrators of the school district serving Port Chester note that its public high school is home to a nationally acclaimed marching band.

—Ossining's public high school was honored as one of the 10 best in the state in 1985.

—Just about every one of its 1,600 public school students walks to schools in the small southern Westchester community of Pelham, including to the high school where the art of communicating is learned at a cable television station, literary magazine, and school newspaper, and where honors and advanced placement programs are available in all academic areas.

—Katonah Lewisboro, a 55-square-mile district serving South Salem, Waccabuc, Cross River, Goldens Bridge, Katonah, and small parts of North Salem and Pound Ridge, has about 2,900 predominately college-bound students who consistently score in top percentiles in state tests of math, reading, writing, and science skills.

—Chappaqua Central School District noted in 1988-1989 that its Horace Greeley High School was listed among the top public high schools in the nation by *Money* and *Town & Country* magazines.

—In the Hendrick Hudson School District in Montrose, the Blue Mountain Middle School was a charter school in the first White House ceremony honoring schools of excellence for outstanding secondary schools.

—School board members, officials, and teachers from the North Salem Central School District have attended three such awards ceremonies in the Rose Garden of the White House in the 1980s. They accepted awards from former president Ronald Reagan and President George Bush that honored all three schools in their system as outstanding. In 1989, 218 schools were honored nationwide.

Children feel free to express their individuality in an ethnically and culturally diverse environment. Photo by Rich Zila

PRIVATE SCHOOLS

Private schools have played a special role in Westchester society since the 1800s, when military academies turned out officers and gentlemen for command posts in the Civil War and proper girls finishing schools polished the music, language, and social skills of young ladies who would be their wives.

Ossining High School's marching band strut their stuff at community parades and football games. Photo by Rich Zila

Today's private schools carry out a demanding academic mission for both male and female students, many of whom pursue further Ivy League education and leading roles in business, academia, government, and diplomacy. Before that leap into adulthood and leadership, private school students can count on facing challenging coursework, high expectations for academic excellence, opportunities to test themselves on athletic fields, and the chance to enhance their view of the world through friendships with out-of-state and foreign students, as well as with study abroad.

The late billionaire Malcolm Forbes is one of the distinguished alumni who attended The Hackley School in Tarrytown when it was a liberal arts school for boys. Founded in 1899, today Hackley is a kindergarten to 12th-grade coed institution educating 785 students in three schools. Boys from the seventh to 12th grades may board at the school, which is on a scenic, wooded 113-acre campus overlooking the Hudson River. About 65 percent of the staff lives on campus. In the high school class of 1989, all of its 93 graduates went on to college.

There are about 250 boys and girls educated annually in grades six through 12 at The Harvey School in Katonah. The school, which has boarding facilities for its predominantly male student body, is on a sprawling 100-acre campus in a historic area of Katonah. The school has an indoor ice skating rink that is the site of many area tournaments. The student-teacher ratio, a prized benefit of private school education, is reported to be 7 to 1 at The Harvey School.

At the Masters School in Dobbs Ferry, 60 percent of the 250 sixth- to 12th-grade female students board, including about 50 students from the Orient, Middle East, Europe, and Latin America. The school dates back to 1877 and today offers 100 college preparatory and honors classes and 13 advanced placement opportunities. Its performing arts program is one of the features prompting girls from 32 states and 16 countries to attend the school, which is on a 94-acre campus on the Hudson River.

America's First Lady, Barbara Bush, is one of the famed graduates of Rye County Day School in Rye. Playwright Edward Albee is another. Today the coed school has classes in pre-kindergarten to 12th grade and serves more than 750 students a year. The "Harvard Independent Insider's Guide to Prep Schools" 1987 edition describes Rye County Day as having "a well-packed 22-acre campus" with strong teams in soccer, ice hockey, and tennis "for some of the most promising students from

Connecticut, Westchester, and New York City."

PAROCHIAL AND CULTURE-BASED SCHOOLS

There are scores of academically strong, high-spirited schools operated under the auspices of the Roman Catholic Archdiocese of New York. Among the schools graduating students to win admission in the nation's most competitive colleges and universities are Iona Prep and Ursuline School in New Rochelle; Holy Child and Resurrection School in Rye; Maria Regina High School in Hartsdale; Good Counsel Academy and Archbishop Stepinac High School in White Plains; and John F. Kennedy High School in Somers.

Such schools may be college preparatory schools in which honors and advanced placement courses predominate, or high schools with a broad range of courses. The schools do not limit their enrollment to Roman Catholic students. They are run in a tradition in which spiritual values are underscored in the schools as they have been since various religious orders founded them.

A handful of yeshivas operate in Westchester County. The Solomon Schechter Day School in White Plains, where about 450 students study, is an institution in which an equally strong emphasis is placed on scholarship and the traditions of Judaism. Graduates of the school enter nationally acclaimed colleges and universities.

Keio University of Tokyo, Japan, laid the groundwork in 1989 for a new Japanese high school of the same name to open in Harrison in the 1990s. The Keio High School will retain many Japanese educational methods in its transition to the United States. The German School in White Plains and French American School in Larchmont pay similar attention to cultural heritage and educational standards.

Stately buildings, landscaped grounds, far-reaching athletic programs, and well-equipped research and study labs are hallmarks of Westchester County's independent schools. Enrollment in these private and parochial institutions represent the choice of families of an estimated 25,000 students in the county. Tuition varies at these schools and many provide scholarship opportunities. Some of the most expensive high schools offer curricula comparable to small colleges.

HIGHER EDUCATION

Executives in Westchester are known to skip the power breakfast so they can attend a unique series of morning lectures hosted by The College at Purchase, State University of New York. The college, which opened in 1967, regularly welcomes about 1,000 adults to the 8 a.m. lectures. They are sponsored by a dozen Westchester corporations and offer a variety of topics. An economics writer for the *New York Times,* a Northwestern University social policy expert, an ABC television commentator and media watcher, and a Princeton physicist gave the corporate crowds ample food for thought in the series that ran through the spring of 1990.

Thousands of people annually stroll through the ultramodern college's Neuberger Museum and explore the field of stark sculpture on the campus grounds. People of all ages attend the theatre, music, and dance programs presented at the school, which awards degrees in fine and performing arts.

Faculty members on the stately campus of Manhattanville College prepare special courses about changing career patterns that client company IBM has arranged for executives who opt for early retirement. The college, established in 1841 and housed at a castle-like former estate in Purchase, holds art exhibits and music programs for the general public throughout the year.

Manhattanville has blossoming ties with Keio University, a Japanese institution, which has begun a project to build an academy on land it purchased from Manhattanville. The alliance is expected to promote cultural and educational exchanges between the neighboring institutions, one of many indicators of the global view taken by Westchester educators today.

In Dobbs Ferry, Mercy College demographers gather data for local banks that are preparing to expand their market of services for newly emerging minority entrepreneurs of the area. The new Americans in Westchester have business ideas and markets that are novel. Discovering the extent of their customer base and forecasts for success are key ingredients being researched by the college, which has more than two dozen degree programs, including nursing and veterinary training.

Nearby Marymount College in Tarrytown keeps pace with a new educational market, reporting that within a three-year period it drew 3,000 adults to courses in computer technology. The college, which offers courses in personnel management, training and development, and information resources, prepares workshops for General Motors executives working at their Tarrytown headquarters.

Midcounty, at the New York Medical College in Valhalla, medical professionals train doctors at one of the oldest such institutions in the state. They also offer their expertise to local companies that seek to streamline health care benefits programs for employees. Doctors at the 130-year-old medical school teach a range of specialties, including health administration and tropical medicine. They also advise companies about setting up in-house services and programs for healthy life-styles.

At the Polytechnic University in Hawthorne, adults earn master's degrees in an array of engineering fields, including programs designed to equip executives with the knowledge to gauge the changing technological needs of their firms. The university regularly acts in an advisory capacity for private and public sector studies and has close ties with major firms in the county.

Westchester Community College in Valhalla, housed at the former Huntington Hartford estate, offers two-year degrees and one-year certificates in dozens of areas and professions. Its graduates continue their education in four-year institutions or join the county's office, health, and trades work force. The college serves small-business owners in the earliest phases of development through advisors who give practical information about financing and running businesses. It welcomes the public to events on campus throughout the year, and provides a showcase for its culinary students by hosting lectures and displays on food preparation and dining experiences, open to the public. It is among the top-rated community colleges in the U.S.A. and adds significantly to Westchester's quality of life.

Iona College in New Rochelle has a second campus, Elizabeth Seton College in Yonkers, and is at the half-century mark as a Westchester institution graduating students in the arts, sciences, and business. The college has a strong international focus and a growing technological emphasis which shows itself in required technology courses for all of its students. Its master's level program includes a pioneering and unique pastoral counseling program available to laity and clergy of all faiths who work in mental health capacities in the county.

The College of New Rochelle began as a Roman Catholic institution educating women in 1904. With the graystone Leland Castle at its center, it continues training area educators, nurses, and graduates in business, arts, and sciences.

Sarah Lawrence College, founded in 1926, is an institution known for high academic standards and an intellectually stimulating climate. Its program range includes the study of early music, human genetics, and health advocacy. Among its highly trained faculty is E.L. Doctorow, who in 1989 was declared the state writer by Governor Mario Cuomo.

Gracious settings are home to Concordia College in Bronxville and The King's College in Briarcliff Manor, which share a Christian mission and biblical emphasis in the two-year and four-year degree programs they offer.

Pace University has a bustling campus in White Plains and one in Pleasantville for a wide range of programs, including agricultural studies. The Pleasantville campus is unique in the county for its working farm and pampered livestock.

The Berkeley School, Monroe Business Institute, and Westchester Business Institute dominate the county's office technology training field. The institutions offer associate degrees in computer programming, secretarial, and accounting areas and have marketing and management programs.

Several New York City-based institutions offer courses in satellite schools in Westchester County. The Dobbs Ferry campus of Long Island University enrolled about 880 students in 1987 and New York University at Manhattanville attracted about 200 students.

There were 44,005 people enrolled in Westchester colleges and business schools in 1987. That year, Maryknoll School of Theology in Ossining was training 90 students at the school, located on the grounds of its world missionary headquarters. Saint Joseph's Seminary and College in Yonkers and Saint Vladimir's Orthodox Theological Seminary in Tuckahoe drew about 360 other students.

Administrators and educators at Manhattanville College in Purchase believe that students thrive on an education based on the following values: the personal and central relationship between student and teacher, a balance between social responsibility to the whole community and personal responsibility to one's self, and a commitment to an academic program that crosses all international boundaries. Photo by Rich Zila

5

SOME SERIOUS PLAY

Westchester County is a rewarding place for work, working out, relaxation, amusement, community involvement, and community traditions. It also is a place where an international executive touches down at corporate headquarters to report in, rest up, and get a change of clothes from home before again taking off. Today, as has been true for years, providing a life in Westchester is the best an executive can do for a family.

It is possible to find space for secluded living or for a socially active life in a close-knit planned residential community, in either case never having to step off the property. Private tennis courts, gardens, and swimming pools grace the landscape. Townhouse communities such as Heritage Hills in Somers and Half Moon Bay in Ossining have unique recreational amenities available to residents and thrive as choice places for the maintenance-free life-style busy people seek today.

Individual municipal recreation departments pride themselves on programs in their parks for team sports, camps, and crafts that attract families and active singles of all ages. The county throws open thousands of acres of parkland for fun. There are an estimated 16 recreational park acres for every Westchester resident, one of the highest recreational ratios in New York State's 61 counties.

Scenic natural resources surround residents in a dozen different ways. Landlocked and shoreline communities respond protectively to maintain beauty and space. For young and old, there are uncluttered places for activities and for competitive or solitary sports.

Recreation activities span all seasons. Children can hardly wait for the first snow so they can take their sleds to any one of the numerous hills of Westchester. Photo by Rich Zila

With open land and waterways come opportunities for all types of play. The quality of life continually lures people to set up shop close to the leisure action. Leisure as an economic force is growing as the county's upscale and sophisticated population matures and has more time and money to buy into the action and to accumulate the trappings of favorite sports. Though fewer children are being raised in America today than in the postwar boom, their growing years in Westchester readily qualify as wonder years.

And whether people are just beginning their lives here or have settled into comfortable routines in their home towns, indoor and outdoor, all year round, Westchester knows how to profit from fun.

SEASONS FOR FUN AND PROFIT

The Easter egg hunts popular in several Westchester towns signal spring as surely as a fresh round of house hunting. The house hunt is a popular local pastime for fun and profit, as people scour long-established neighborhoods for promising finds, and transform many older communities with renovations that are true to local historic character.

A 30-year-old banker from Briarcliff spends warm spring weekends with her husband scouting for Victorian houses to restore in Hudson River towns. When they find what they are after, the executive couple leaves the office behind on weekends to do the scraping, sanding, and staining to bring the luster back to such gems and put them on the pre-

Residents of the Half Moon Bay Condominiums in Croton-on-Hudson enjoy the simple beauty of the river, recreational amenities, and a maintenance-free life-style. Photo by Peter Britton

mium house market. They also lend their support to groups working for historic preservation of the Hudson region.

In this house-proud county, home improvement emporiums, lumber yards, and village hardware stores do brisk business year-round but heat up especially in the spring. The sound of hammering vies with the crack of baseball and softball against bat and the whistle of referees on the sidelines at soccer fields. Historically male chores and games are obviously the province of both sexes today, on ladders and on the playing field. There are antique shows, collectibles markets, and estate auctions to fill the new male or female homeowner's schedule.

Meticulous house and garden sprucing can wait for the 50ish hospital administrator who never misses the South Salem 10K race on Memorial Day and the chance it brings to mingle with other jogging executive neighbors and friends he nods to on daily runs. Memorial Day traditionally brings hundreds together in South Salem to race and be part of the parade that ends at Lewisboro Town Hall's patriotic ceremony. The crowd of boy and girl scouts, old soldiers, and families with baby carriages and pets breaks its silence and moves off to a nearby church fair where ragtime music and barbequed burgers compete for attention.

For hundreds of residents of Bronxville, there is a similar homey village tradition that kicks off the summer season, complete with race, parade, and chicken barbeque at the meadowy Bronxville High School field. Residential lakes, beaches, pools, and private country clubs draw their members into open spaces border to border with Memorial Day traditions of their own. The signs of the season are fixed to a club's iron gate or stone entrance columns, predictable and comforting facets of the leisure available to many people here.

A stroll along the scenic boardwalk at Playland in Rye is a treat any time of year. The park has three ice rinks, a casino, an Olympic-size swimming pool, a miniature golf course, a game arcade, and a restaurant among its many offerings. Photo by Barbara Brundage

Everyone can enjoy the Fourth of July fireworks that burst over the lake at New Rochelle High School, including a new generation that blankets the school's lawn. Young executive couples with growing families now inhabit the fine homes of the city and neighboring communities. Many carry their youngsters on backpacks through the holiday paces they knew growing up in Westchester, from the fireworks of July and the Thanksgiving Day parade to the best hills for sledding and the favorite local nurseries and tree farms to explore at Christmas. A recent summer tradition is taking hold at the July New Rochelle Waterfront Festival, where in 1988 an estimated 60,000 people saw fireworks and tall ships off shore.

By nightfall in summer, Rye Playland crowds are ready for fireworks and any of 48 head-spinning rides that whirl next to the Sound. Daytrips at Playland are packed with rides, musical entertainers, and other performers, from the stage to the high diving board. The amusement park's tree-lined boulevard is filled with flowers and benches, inviting a moment's rest. Rowers take rented boats out on an 80-acre lake, miniature golfers putt, and swimmers

Trick or treating in Sleepy Hollow territory must be especially spooky for these children. Although no one has reported seeing Washington Irving's headless horseman in more than 150 years, the legendary creature lives on in the imagination of the young. Photo by Rich Zila

take dips in an Olympic-size pool or at the Sound shore beach. In winter, the triple rinks for ice skating draw people to Playland. The 60-year-old amusement park has been spruced up and updated for expansion in coming years.

Stars flash overhead at the domed Andrus Planetarium of the Hudson River Museum in Yonkers to acquaint even the youngest child with natural wonder. Historic collections of furniture and artifacts fill the museum's nineteenth-century mansion section and modern art graces the museum's late twentieth-century quarters, where even the colorfully decorated gift shop stands as a charming work of contemporary art.

The eighteenth-century sloop *Clearwater* is a wooden ship with a 100-foot mast that welcomes aboard environmental students of all ages to cruise the Hudson and learn about the health of the river. Folk singer Pete Seeger has often climbed aboard for these journeys. The Clearwater organization draws crowds to Westchester in June for cultural festivals serving up folk food and music from around the world and raising money in support of local ecological programs.

On the Long Island Sound, a nineteenth-century Baltic Sea trading schooner carries on its own environmental education mission for a group called SoundWaters. The good ship *Ann Christine* has been enlisted as a floating classroom for the people of Westchester and Connecticut to use in the new decade.

BOOM SPORT

As the first American home of golf, Westchester is teeming with golf perfectionists who are ever refining their swings on the county's 40 private and five public courses. On the public courses alone, the sport brought over $400,000 in revenues to the Westchester County Department of Parks, Recreation and Conservation in 1988, when a quarter of a million rounds were played.

National attention focuses on the county during the year in three annual tournaments. Sleepy Hollow Country Club in Scarborough is well into a decade of hosting the Seniors Professional Golf Association Commemorative Tournament in late May.

Ahead of the game among longstanding tournaments, The Westchester County Club in Harrison hosts the Westchester Classic each June. In 1990, the first Ladies PGA Big Apple Classic welcomed 150 professional women golfers to compete for about $400,000 in winnings at Wykagyl County Club in New Rochelle in August. Local interclub tournaments, family competitions such as father and son, father and daughter tournaments, and in-club competitions complete the season.

The National Golf Foundation in Juniper, Florida, reported in 1989 that nearly 10 percent of the population of New York State plays golf. That's 1.6 million people. And in 1988 the national golfing public reportedly spent $15.6 billion, or $675 per person, on equipment, clothes, fees, lessons, and travel.

By March, Westchester's avid golfers have dusted off their array of holiday game gifts and are heading for the county's challenging courses. The play continues through November on public courses—dawn to dusk. Ninth-hole refreshment stands and restaurants are open in the high season. Some golfers bundle up and remain at play on private courses into December.

With more and more people age five and up playing the game, Westchester County has plans to develop a second course at Mohansic Golf Course in Yorktown Heights, adding to the field of play now found at Dunwoodie and Sprain Lake in Yonkers, Saxon Woods Golf Course in Scarsdale, and Maple Moor in White Plains.

Affection for the sport has far-reaching impact on many aspects of life in Westchester. Land near a golf course rivals the Hudson River, Long Island Sound, and numerous lakeshores as distinctive and highly prized real estate. A fund-raising charity auction can

One of America's favorite pastimes is practiced by this youngster. County athletic programs offer little league action throughout Westchester. Photo by Rich Zila

expect interested bidders when a day of golf at a renowned private club such as Winged Foot is put up on the auction block. Business and social life centered around the game in the county fill posh dining rooms of local clubs and challenge in-house chefs to continually explore new culinary heights to keep members satisfied. There is work for the professional golfer, pro-shop keeper, caddy, and grounds crew, and catering staff linked to the golf season. Club engagements for holiday and family celebrations are nearly year-round.

The County Chamber of Commerce, Inc., has seen interest in its annual golf outing grow steadily since it began hosting the event in 1986. At an October outing, 130 chamber members gathered for lunch, games of golf and tennis, and an awards dinner at the Westchester Hill Country Club in White Plains. The pinnacle "hole in one" play was not achieved, so chamber officials tucked away the $1,000 savings bond prize for another year. But golfers stood for the applause and ribbings, picking up their prizes for the lowest score, the longest drive, and heroic "Most Honest Golfer" or highest

This mother and baby enjoy the great food that Americans have been devouring at outdoor summertime gatherings for decades. Photo by Linda Zila

admitted score. Such an awards ceremony figures in hundreds of golf dinners across the hard-driving county. The tricky game is bound to keep its audience captive and the club industry in the county on course.

LANDED GENTRY

Hikers and leisurely horseback riders take to public trails that run through parts of Eastview in Tarrytown, Briarcliff Manor, Ossining, New Castle, Yorktown, and Cortlandt to the Blue Mountain Reservation in Peekskill. The mature hardwood forests and old stone walls of the area lend a sense of history and remarkable seclusion to trails that skirt residential neighborhoods and serve as a unique outdoor resource at their doorsteps.

The 750-acre Rockefeller State Preserve Park in Pocantico is a stunning space for riding and hiking. Across the county, public bridle paths restored along the Hutchinson River Parkway feed northeast from Eastchester to Purchase with access through property owned by the State University of New York at Purchase, Pepsico, and Texaco, and are used by bikers and hikers, too.

In the northeastern towns of the county, acres of private land are threaded by about 150 linear miles of trails and designated for use by local equestrians who are members of the Bedford Riding Lanes Association. According to Carol Bancel of South Salem, one of the 17 members of the board governing the association, the protected trails crisscross large parcels of rolling landscape and woods in Bedford, Mount Kisco, Katonah, and Pound Ridge.

Bancel said landowners have let local riders use the old trails on their property since the 1930s, when fox hunts were part of the Bedford scene. Today's area riders participate in a hunter pace competition, following a rigorous countryside course minus the fox. They can be spotted urging their horses across Route 22 at the Beaver Dam Sanctuary in Katonah on the hunter pace course in the late autumn.

New developers of the area's prime residential property tend to cooperate with the Bedford Riding Lanes Association in allowing old trails to stay open to riders and developing property in ways that enhance the highly prized farm landscape that newcomers seek, Bancel said.

"Our goal is always to open new trails and to maintain old ones and of course to prevent old ones from being closed," she said, adding, "A lot of people do move to Bedford and other towns because they want to ride."

The horse and hound set covers much ground in North Salem when members of the Goldens Bridge Hounds, Inc., convene for high-spirited seasonal rides across the countryside. Safety-conscious hunt officials peer across farmland from checkpoints on local

ABOVE: Members of the Archville fire department proudly display its collection of historic photographs and memorabilia at the St. Mary's Church Fair in Briarcliff Manor. Photo by Linda Zila

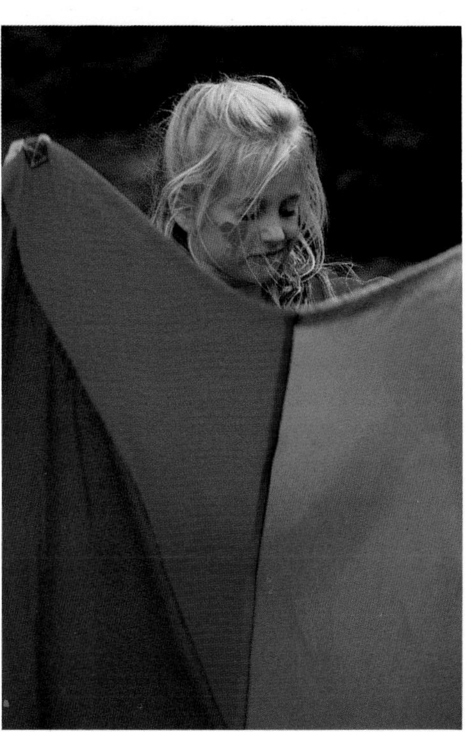

LEFT: This colorful youngster wears her heart on her cheek at the St. Mary's Church Fair. Photo by Rich Zila

roads and halt cars for the few moments it takes horses and their riders—in velvet hats, britches, and red coats—to cross the pavement from meadow to meadow, deliriously happy hounds at their sides. In North Salem, a group called the Open Land Foundation encourages donations of property in town where local riders and naturalists roam.

Golfers enjoy The Sleepy Hollow Country Club's velvety greens. The elaborate clubhouse, Woodlea, formerly a private residence, offers a restaurant, pro-shop, and bedrooms for members and their guests. Members also enjoy tennis, squash, and paddle courts, horseback riding, and a swimming pool. Photo by Rich Zila

The foundation's chairman, Carol Younghair Goldberg, said the group has been given 450 acres since 1974. Membership pays for upkeep on the property, pruning and maintaining trees, and mowing grassland for paths for riding and walking. The acreage includes a 117-acre flatland, complete with pond and rolling hillside outlined with stone walls. Blue bird houses made by schoolchildren dot the property, which has served as an outdoor science lab for North Salem children.

The Nature Conservancy, a national organization with a half-million members, has a Lower Hudson chapter based in Katonah that oversees 25 preserves in the area where people hike and explore. Individual benefactors have also given land to municipalities, adding to the general greenery that is a backdrop for Westchester people in motion.

GARDEN CLUBS, RIVER WATCHERS, AND TRADITIONALISTS

On a blustery November morning in 1989, the historic John Jay homestead in Katonah filled with area garden club members for an environmental program that included Robert F. Kennedy, Jr., as a guest speaker. Kennedy's talk about the Hudson River was hosted by the Bedford Garden Club and Rusticus, a second Bedford garden club, both affiliates of the Garden Club of America. Their special program reflects the global awareness of the Westchester woman.

"The words 'garden club' conjure up an image that no longer applies," said Candy Borner, a 15-year member of the Bedford Garden Club and chairman of its public relations. "Maybe a long time ago clubs attracted quiet little ladies who confined their interest to their own gardens but not anymore. We've been hammering on a lot of doors where the environment is at stake, not just taking care of flowers in our own gardens."

The Bedford Garden Club is nearly 80 years old and is one of the founding clubs of the Garden Club of America. Today, what matters to the Bedford club's 125 members and the 50 members of Rusticus is the quality of the entire earth's environment—from Westchester County to the Amazon rain forests.

"Think globally, act locally," said the son of the slain 1968 presidential candidate to the predominantly female gardening audience. They ranged in age from thirtysomething to eightysomething and are neighbors to the 35-year-old environmental lawyer and Mount Kisco father of two. In both professional and private life, Kennedy is involved in several environmental projects in Westchester. His strongest association is with the Hudson River and with groups of fishermen and residents who

ABOVE: Fox hunting is a serious spectator sport in Westchester's northern country. Members of the Goldens Bridge Hounds, Inc., shown here, conduct a hunter pace competition where riders attempt to cover a cross-country course in a predetermined time. Photo by Geoffrey Kerrigan

LEFT: The blessing of the hounds takes place each autumn as the Goldens Bridge Hounds mark the beginning of foxhunting season. Photo by Geoffrey Kerrigan

A show of "Hands Across the Hudson" on Earth Day 1990 at Bear Mountain demonstrates that power in numbers can make a lifesaving difference in the environment. Photo by Rich Zila

Earth Day at Bear Mountain on the Hudson River was celebrated by many of Westchester's citizens who are committed to preserving the environment. Here a participant paints his Landrover with inspirational messages. Photo by Barbara Brundage

watch over it. He termed the waterway "probably the most productive estuary on the face of the earth."

"We've managed to keep the system clean and green," Kennedy said about the Hudson. As a scuba diver on underwater sojourns in the Croton River, a tributary of the Hudson River, Kennedy has dived to the base of Quaker Rock to watch thousands of herring, anchovies, striped bass, blue crabs, giant eels, exotic species from the Caribbean, moongazers, blue fish, pumpkin seed sunfish, yellow perch, and 50-pound carp swim by.

So rich a spawning ground is the Hudson River that fishermen are cautioned to maneuver their craft slowly through key areas in the spring. The fish are so plentiful that Kennedy said he could "hear them bouncing off the bottoms of the boats."

In North Castle, strong forces for preserving local history and for developing residential property came together in a unique way to save a 1798 Quaker meeting house. Dory Finch Watson, a resident of the hamlet of Banksville and a founder of the North Castle Historical Society, and William Cavaliere, an Armonk developer, became allies in saving the fragile structure that stood on Cavaliere's property. After Cavaliere offered to give the meeting house to the organization, Watson and the historical society launched a fund-raising effort in late 1989 to move the meeting house to a site on Route 22. An old tavern, blacksmith shop, and one-room schoolhouse form a village there that draws young and old students of history.

History is a strong force in Westchester. Cavaliere said he "got swept up in the history of the meeting house" and that prompted him to want to preserve it. In Mount Vernon, the pre-Revolution Saint Paul's National Historic Site on South Columbus Avenue and the Bill of Rights Museum have their own hearty band of supporters. The church is forever linked to eighteenth-century patriot John Peter Zenger and his stand for freedom of the press. Like many historical structures in the county, it serves as a picturesque setting for historic readings, period music, and craft demonstrations in the height of the holiday season.

SEA, AIR, AND LANDSCAPES

Nearly 40 boating clubs have sprung up in the century after real estate magnates built elegant communities around the fashionable regatta life-style on Long Island Sound. In Rye, American Yacht Club members look back over a distinguished log of racing triumphs, including 1989, when the club hosted a half-century-old world championship regatta for International One Design sailboats.

The skilled sailors who congregate for such events and for the leisured social life are part of Westchester's upscale market for millions of dollars in boats and boating equipment. Corporate support for yachting events is increasing and is similar to the backing given to equestrian events that raise funds for county charities. The impact of yachting ripples from the sport to gracious homes to businesses serving a unique life-style. The silhouette of the county's yacht clubs and bobbing fleets of luxury boats highlight the quietly elegant Westchester scene as vividly as the county's serene horse pastures.

Today, a new flock of bird watchers heads to the shore and joins boaters squinting at the sunlight and deep blue waters. The tall grass and craggy coast of the Sound welcomes a host of seabirds at marshlands in Rye and Larchmont. In parkland and beaches in Mamaroneck and New Rochelle, the natives make it a habit to tempt waterfowl to delay migration and plod on the docks for daily bread. Seagulls, Canada geese, and mallards comply.

Inland, high-powered scopes are raised by seasoned bird watchers who fill a raptor viewing stand atop a hill at the Arthur Butler Memorial Sanctuary in Bedford. The bird watchers keep

Croton Park has been known for centuries as an excellent fishing ground. Shad, sturgeon, and bass are among the types of fish found in the Hudson River. This angler ends his business day at the edge of the river, looking for a bite. Photo by Linda Zila

Light streaming through the richly decorated stained glass windows of the United Methodist Church in Mamaroneck reflects off the geometric wall surfaces of this Gothic revival sanctuary. Photo by Rich Zila

count of the thousands of hawks, eagles, osprey, and falcons that use the air above Westchester as part of their north-south flyway during migrating seasons. An afternoon of sighting is a sociable time punctuated by calls to look up in every direction, including a quarter of a mile up where the raptors soar.

Nature lovers look down to follow a delicate path of light through the tall tulip trees that hug the side of the steep Mianus River Gorge in Bedford where mink and beaver are said to roam at dawn. A forest ranger leads nature walks here to the Hemlock Cathedral and to a mica-flaked outcrop where Indians quarried the rock they sharpened into arrowheads and tools. At the 142-acre Cranberry Lake Preserve in North White Plains, park rangers have always cautioned visitors to follow them closely on moonlight treks where the night creatures freeze in a flashlight's glare.

By day, nature and history buffs track the path that Indians took to little-known caves along the Hudson. Children rush to circle around live and lifelike exhibits at the well-known Greenburgh Nature Center in Greenburgh and at the Trailside Museum at the 4,700-acre Ward Pound Ridge Reservation at Cross River. In both places, the crafty taxidermist has set wildlife displays in brilliant still life. The path of Indians is easy to imagine along the trail by the museum in Pound Ridge, where an Indian village stands by a rocky stream.

In winter, cross-country skiing and sleigh riding lure visitors to the park's hills and meadows. In summer there are fiddlers, antique and crafts people, and hot air balloonists drawing county crowds. Across the county to the Hudson River towns, visitors find shade trees and placid vistas at Croton Point Park in Croton, Teatown Reservation in Cortlandt, and George's Island Park in Montrose.

Last year 60,000 people visited the nineteenth-century Muscoot Farm in Somers. The assorted farm animals on the nearly 800-acre site are accustomed to being lavishly petted. They press against fences to watch crowds gathered for harvest festivals and re-creations of historic programs at the

This synagogue's strong supporting columns symbolize the enduring traditions of Westchester's Jewish community. Larchmont Temple is one of the county's many places of worship. Photo by Linda Zila

gracefully columned Georgian manor house of Muscoot.

In 1989, Westchester County officials announced a proposal to link Muscoot Farm with the 200-acre former Lasdon estate in Yorktown. The county plan calls for building a walking bridge over the Amawalk River, a fly fishing stream which separates the two properties. Trails are planned for the Lasdon estate, which is the site of the county's Vietnam Memorial.

The acres of land given over to apple orchards and vineyards attract visitors to northern Westchester towns. Family rituals include the apple picking expe-

***FACING PAGE:* Muscoot Park, a 777-acre interpretive farm in northern Westchester's town of Somers, is restored to reflect the county's agricultural heritage. Friendly farm animals include cows, horses, donkeys, sheep, and chickens. Photo by Linda Zila**

dition, the wine and cheese outing, and excursions into the Octoberfest atmosphere of fairs held in various towns. At night, the stars are more brilliant than any other time of year as the season's constellations wind their way above the scanning telescopes of resident astronomers.

Westchester houses a highly educated and eclectic audience for all sorts of leisure activities and their accoutrements. Crossing from the Scarsdale train station, a dapper, 40ish man with a mustache and thick graying hair strode toward a string of shops, his cashmere overcoat flapping in the wind. He ducked into one shop entrance and asked the clerk for a reserved copy of the book, *In the Game of Golf,* then browsed around. Before the man left the store with his golf tome, he had found a second nonfiction book to his liking, an epic starting in the 1960s titled, *The Grateful Dead, A Family Album.*

Sea birds of all kinds can be spotted by bird watchers and nature lovers near Westchester's miles of coastline. Photo by Linda Zila

Caramoor in Katonah has a reputation for its classical summer music programs featuring the Orchestra of Saint Luke's, a group that performs subscription series at Carnegie Hall in New York City. The outdoor concerts attract thousands of guests to the 100-acre grounds to congregate under the tent at its Venetian Theater and in the Spanish Courtyard of the former Rosen estate.

Autumn performances in the music room of the mansion mark a revival of a unique Westchester cultural experience. For a fraction of the thousands who flock to summer concerts, attending performances in the music room recreates an intimate musical era of the 1930s and 1940s when the Rosens held court.

At a November 1989 concert, Russian emigre pianist Alexander Paley, winner of the 1988 New York Competition, commanded the keys of the baby grand in the music room at Caramoor for a hushed two hours. From memory, he played Chopin's Sonata no. 3 in D Minor, Opus 58, and the Four Mazurkas from Opus 41; Ravel's *Le Tombeau de Couperin;* and Rameau's Suite in E Minor. Paley's performance resonated in the antique-filled room as if the room itself was an instrument, and it left Caramoor director Howard Herring beaming for having brought Paley to the mansion.

It was at Caramoor that black opera singer Marian Anderson had sung in 1958 for the first performance at the Venetian Theater. The acclaimed singer had been stung by discrimination on other stages but was sought and prized by the Rosen family to inaugurate the public theater.

Alex Paley was the subject of applause by about 150 Caramoor guests in the music room. After his performance, the slight, wiry haired musician smiled shyly at the people who trooped to see him in an upper room of the house museum. In the crisp Katonah night, there were no street sounds to break his musical spell. It simply became part of Caramoor lore.

OPEN
APR

HOLIDAY NOTES

On Sundays in a typical month in December 1989, it was possible for a Westchester resident to sample the hot cider and music at Saint Paul's, attend a wreath making class at Washington Headquarters' Museum in North White Plains, see a bell exhibit and hear a bell performance at Smith Tavern museum in North Castle, and arrive in time for a candlelight tour of Van Cortlandt Manor in Cortlandt, the Old Dutch Church in Pocantico Hills, Philipsburg Manor, Upper Mills, North Tarrytown, or Lyndhurst Castle in Tarrytown.

December is a month to hear classical and popular music in the county's churches, synagogues, cultural centers, and music halls. Among the varied offerings on the Westchester calendar, the Emerson String Quartet performed at Congregation Emanu El of Westchester in Rye; violinist Benjamin Hudson played at the Pelham Arts Center; pop singer Andy Williams performed at the Westchester County Center in White Plains; and folk singer Arlo Guthrie performed at the Paramount Center for the Arts in Peekskill.

People were invited to make their own holiday music—caroling around a bonfire at Sunnyside in Tarrytown, by the town trees of Bedford Village, Somers, South Salem and North Salem, at the John Jay Homestead in Katonah, and in a Handel's Messiah Sing with the Pleasantville Cantata Singers at the United Methodist Church in Pleasantville.

Year-round, there are 23 bands and orchestras giving performances in the county, according to the Council for the Arts in Westchester. Voices raise for 20 chorale societies and thespians take to the stage in 28 community theater groups. The Westchester Chorale's 150 singers attracted 800 people to their winter concert at Concordia College in Bronxville. The Taghkanic Chorale has a strong following in northern Westchester performances at the Paramount Center for the Performing Arts in Peekskill.

WINTER MANEUVERS

On Bay Avenue in Larchmont, a rough-hewn wooden jungle gym stands between two white stucco mansions, the Long Island Sound lapping against the backyard lawn into winter. To the west near Weaver Street, youngsters check for the first sign of ice to form on the Larchmont Garden Lake on Myrtle Boulevard. Skating is the best way to reach the tiny island in the middle of the lake.

More skaters wait for the flag to fly over county-patrolled waters such as the sheltered inlet to Twin Lakes on California Road in Eastchester. A barrel fire crackles for warming the hands of tikes on twin-edged skates at lakeside, while serious teen ice hockey players regularly claim a portion of the outer ice field. More skaters will take a turn at the Village of Tarrytown facilities and on shallow Bronx River and

FACING PAGE: Northern Westchester is apple country. Many orchards feature pick-your-own apples or set up farm stands to sell their juicy apples and freshly milled cider. Photo by Victoria Lamas

Caramoor's widely acclaimed music festival takes place outdoors in the Venetian Theater, under a wonderful canopy, from June through August. The Rosens, who built the great house, had a love for music and for entertaining friends. Their musical evenings were the seeds of the music festival that has been pleasing audiences for 45 years. Photo by Peter Schaaf, courtesy, Caramoor

Hutchinson River ponds in the southern part of the county. Some head for the tented public rinks in Yonkers, Larchmont, and Rye.

In the dead of winter, hunting parties cross field and forest to thin the deer and pheasant stock in Westchester. The woodsmen converge on lodges run by private clubs in numerous locations. Permits allow seasonal bow-and-arrow hunting of deer and shooting of select fowl on private land. Local falconers train their birds to hunt in season on large estates with groups in Long Island and neighboring northern counties. The target range, trap and skeet shooting facilities, and archery range of the Sportsman Center in Peekskill are added attractions for precision target sports from April to November.

Cross-country skiers joke about having winter membership on the snow-covered golf courses of Westchester. Groups sign up for ski clinics and traverse public golf courses and parks while heated games in 30 platform tennis leagues get under way.

In Purchase, Port Chester, Yonkers, Peekskill, New Rochelle, and Mount Vernon, coaches in the Amateur Boxing Federation pace a new generation of kids through the discipline of the ring in programs run by the Police Athletic League, the Y, and community centers. Basketball clinics, volleyball games, and craft-oriented activities fill several winter hours in county-sponsored programs. Soccer and softball crowd the warm weather months for several age groups and inspire serious competition. School competition is strong in these sports and in sports such as track, swimming, tennis, and golf.

ON STAGE

Spectators can move from the ball court to the music hall for concert series at the Music Hall in Tarrytown and other community halls housed in libraries, colleges, historic sites, and conservatories. The Emelin Theater in Mamaroneck has a wide-ranging choice of intellectual and entertainment diversions and has long served as a gathering place for people in Sound towns. The East Coast Arts Theatre at Wildcliff is staging world premieres of dramatic works at a nineteenth-century mansion and former museum overlooking the Sound in New Rochelle. Across the county, the Elmsford Evening Dinner Theater is in its second decade offering popular musicals and other entertainment.

Westchester's proximity to New York City reverberates in the high quality of music one may hear year-round. The Chamber Music Society of Lincoln Center performed Mozart at Ossining High School in 1989—in the same season that the Colorado String Quartet played Beethoven. The eclectic Paramount Center for the Arts can boast of performances by the Philharmonia Virtuosi, Laura Nyro, and The Ink Spots within the 1989-1990 calendar season.

FOUR SEASONS FOR MIXING BUSINESS AND PLEASURE

The Westchester Marriott in Tarrytown is on a corridor flanked by several corporations. The hotel, which offers rooms to accommodate groups of 50 to 800, is the site of many unique local events, including an annual Westchester scuba divers exhibition in the spring, complete with a fashion show of underwater gear.

Special groups of all types congregate in the county. The Westchester County Center fills with booths for a baseball card show, a record collector's show, and a sportsman exposition. Across White Plains at the Holiday Inn, Crowne

Shown here is the stone manor house of Philipsburg Manor at Upper Mills in North Tarrytown. The property is owned and operated by Historic Hudson Valley, an organization which hosts many family programs including Pinkster, an annual spring festival originally celebrated by the Dutch and African-Americans of colonial New York. Photo by Rich Zila

Plaza, The County Chamber of Commerce, Inc., holds its annual luncheon and salutes the county's top 50 companies, many of which host business meetings and conferences at local facilities. At Stouffer Westchester Hotel, several chamber "Spotlight" cocktail parties are held throughout the year, bringing its newest members into contact with established area leaders, spurring a cycle of new meeting opportunities.

As a county that is both home and home for business, Westchester's penchant for mixing business and pleasure finds several elegant outlets. Serious business conducted in quiet meeting rooms are followed by poolside dinners in the setting sun at a glass-enclosed pool room at the Hudson River Inn and Conference Center in Ossining. The paneled conference rooms of the Tarrytown Executive Conference Center open to the landscape of a graceful old estate, modern sleeping quarters, and mansion dining rooms. At the Arrowwood Conference Center in Rye Brook, interior walkways span terraced space for lobbies and dining alcoves, and overlook green pockets of indoor gardens and stalwart swimmers doing laps in an indoor-outdoor pool.

The Rye Town Hilton easily accommodates guests for charity balls and business, offering quiet dining rooms, regal dining halls, and a portion of the 3,500 hotel rooms available to the county traveler.

WESTFAIR 2000—SHOOTING FOR THE NEW MARKETPLACE

This time it is not the circus or the Boston Pops packing the Westchester County Center bleachers. Not boxing and not basketball. It is work and the workplace that holds court at the annual Westfair 2000—an event spon-

Washington Irving, America's first successful commercial writer, created his delightful home, Sunnyside, in the area he called Sleepy Hollow. The property was opened to the public in 1947 and has been enjoyed by countless visitors and school groups who can experience nineteenth-century America through in-depth workshops. Photo by Rich Zila

sored by The County Chamber of Commerce, Inc. The expo attracts those who are based in Westchester or preparing to work in its peaceful, prosperous, and open surroundings with the latest advantages of the technical revolution.

Westchester tech and service buyers streamed steadily into the two-day event in 1989, pausing to ask questions in and collect hard copy on the more than 150 companies with booths at the exhibit. The exhibitors reflected the mobile life-style of Westchester County's executive, service, and sales force who wield cellular phones as they journey. On the other hand, many displays highlighted the stay-put attitude of office personnel who can have just about anything delivered to their door, including a bank teller.

The self-styled entrepreneur of the 1990s with a mind to make work fun could stroll through Westfair and find ideas for setting up a low-stress office place with the latest electronic tools, and information from inviting local financial service institutions and a host of auxiliary forces. Among the high-tech hardware displays were portable FAX machines, photo copiers, and telecommunication systems from top national companies. A number of new business ventures have sprung up around them, contributing to the changing face of work in Westchester. On the 1989 playing field:

A petite blonde, 30-year-old Christine Dowd, still bears the deep tan gained from living for a decade in Florida. In June 1989, she set up C & S Cellular Company, Inc., with Susan Strang, the company's vice president, in White Plains. The service is proving to be a boon to clients that range from Westchester executives to delivery boys, said Dowd, who is opening a second office in Yorktown. Her firm is linked to the Metro One service. In a nearby exhibit aisle at Westfair, potential customers gathered around NYNEX representatives who described their competitive communication network in the fast-growing cellular market.

At Westfair, gourmet desk lunch ideas were test marketed for Great Food to Go, a company formed by Antun Restaurant of Elmsford. Kaja Ross invited people to check the menu for favorites in individual lunches that more and more people are ordering for themselves and as business gifts. Corporate and private parties already keep her hopping in the county.

"I like my job because I get to be with people when they're happy," Ross said. "Weddings are very much back in style here. First time, second time, third time around. It's fun to arrange them."

Ross said some weddings are distinctively Westchester. At a recent one, the bride and groom, both avid county joggers, cut into a large sheet cake decorated with two running shoes, laces tied together in a knot.

Fewer and fewer people meet for more than a moment at the office coffee pot, and representatives from Filterfresh, a Rockland firm, offer a machine designed to brew individual cups with push panel precision. They report that several Westchester companies have dropped coffee making from the list of job requirements at the office. Union Carbide, Hewlitt Packard, United Parcel, and Dellwood Dairy are on their list. A Hewlitt Packard executive paused at Filterfresh's Westfair booth to offer his compliments and sample a fresh cup.

People stopped to eye the Brazilian beach scene on a television screen belonging to Jack Miller of Broadcast Video Productions in Armonk. Six years ago the retired New York City detective launched a second career in video. He now tapes corporate presentations. Miller showed how he links stock film footage of all kinds with business meeting and lecture coverage to achieve his concept of attention-getting

The Northern Westchester Center for the Arts in Goldens Bridge offers courses in both the visual and performing arts. Children and adults can pursue serious study under the direction of established educators and artists in the center's well-equipped facilities. Photo by Geoffrey Kerrigan

The newly restored Westchester County Center public assembly and entertainment facility offers more than 2,000 events annually including antique and collector shows, fairs, circuses, concerts, and athletic events. Photo by Rich Zila

corporate cinema—Brazilian beach scene so far not included.

There were displays of financial services and saving options available at a host of banks, among them Apple Bank, which offered copies of its 1988 annual report at its Westfair display table. In another aisle, Chemical Bank brought along its mobile teller unit, a trademark traveling bank of Chemical design that companies arrange to serve employees at major office sites in Westchester.

Chem bank executive Renee H. Norman said workers queue in front of the mobile teller unit in an office lobby or cafeteria to cash their checks on payday. The service is saving employees and employers time and travel. Among the Westchester firms offering this new benefit, Norman said, is Towers Perrin, a Valhalla consulting firm employing 600 people.

Scott Hall, a head engineering technician for Micro-Point in Mount Kisco, described the specialized computer packages that his 24-year-old company provides for small and medium-sized firms as well as departments in major institutions. Like other computer companies exhibiting at Westfair, Hall's innovative firm has captured a piece of the market by offering customized accounting packages.

Darrin Monaco is a young marketing exec with International Furniture Rental in Hawthorne and is manning a booth at Westfair. The IFR showroom is part of a network that tells its budding

The variety of weddings in Westchester is endless. Settings include outdoor landscaped parks, catered riverboat cruises, as well as traditional services. Photo by Linda Zila

business customers in America to rent suites of furniture and "Look Like You've Arrived Even When Your Office Furniture Hasn't." In Westchester, Monaco said several personnel firms have been opened by women who have taken advantage of the rental option to fill their offices. He said executives transferred from out of state and abroad also arrive in Westchester apartments, condos, and townhouses that are owned and completely furnished by their companies.

Adco/Federal of Port Chester, "The Company that Watches Over You," handed out brochures abut the security systems it develops and monitors for Westchester homes and businesses. Olga "Auggie" Mackin, sales representative for Poland Springs Natural Spring Water in White Plains, distributed information about the types of standing and table top coolers that today's water gourmets order for the home and office. Data Clean Corporation, a company "protecting computer room environments," gave away buttons to Westfair visitors. A handful of promotional companies displayed other advertising tools.

Noble Associates ran an exhibit table where it advertised office and warehouse space in Port Chester, a town that is slated for a major renaissance this decade. With thousands of acres of fresh space and revitalized waterfront property to be developed in a partnership between Port Chester government and private developers, the expectations for new business are high in the town.

Westchester itself is primed for the decade's new business players.

An antique B&O Railroad caboose and the old station of 1890 make up the Station Restaurant in Valhalla. Photo by Rich Zila

6

LOOKING TO THE FUTURE

In the 1770s, George Washington commented in his diary about his journey on horseback over the rocky roads of Westchester. Were he to return today, he could see how enterprising farmers had seized upon those pesky rocks after the Revolutionary War to fashion stone walls for dividing properties in the countryside. The rough-hewn walls are kept in place today in many parts of Westchester through the efforts of their staunch admirers—individual landowners, historical societies, and, in some cases, by local government decree.

If there are any obstacles to overcome in the county's path into the future, Westchester has shown itself to be brimming with people who are strong enough to grapple with the elements and come up with common sense ways of handling them. A sense of driving purpose and pragmatism is evident in its long-term planning for growth in business, housing, recreational amenities, cultural, social, and health programs, and educational opportunities for the people who live here.

MOVERS AND SHAKERS

Since the early 1980s, nearly 1,000 people engaged in county and municipal government, local and global business, real estate, law, the environment, the arts, health, education, and social service have been examining the elements of Westchester society that brought it to this pre-twenty-first-century turning point. Many of them have emerged from shirt sleeve meetings and forums with fresh answers for dealing with the new social, economic, and environmental reality that challenges people across the nation and around the world.

General Foods corporate office, located in Rye Brook, is one of Westchester's most impressive corporate structures. Designed by Kevin Roche John Dinkeloo and Associates and completed in 1983, the building, which is set off behind an artificial lake, incorporates a skylighted multilevel atrium courtyard. Photo by William Hubbell

Chef Robert poses proudly inside of La Petite Affaire, the restaurant that he co-owns. Westchester's restaurants are numerous and varied. Everything from Eastern, Middle Eastern, Continental, American, and other cultural cuisine can be savored. Photo by Rich Zila

Groups such as The County Chamber of Commerce, Inc., and the Westchester County Association represent a wide variety of interests and regularly volunteer expertise and time to conduct studies and issue reports that outline plans and update the progress of programs in action. In individual municipalities, citizens have been applying the same focus on the future.

Through its Office of the County Executive, various county departments, and a 17-member board of legislators, Westchester County concerns itself with creating, legislating, and executing steps to deal with the overall economic, development, services, social, and recreational picture affecting more than 800,000 people. The county provides municipalities, businesses, residents, and prospective investors with the data from studies undertaken about a host of topics. The county also comes forward to suggest scenarios for adding housing and new business opportunities through the cooperation of groups of municipalities.

BRINGING IN NEW BUSINESS

The County Chamber of Commerce, Inc., reported in its recent survey of achievements that it had offered information and assistance to 800 prospective investors. It directed people with existing businesses or business proposals to resources available through the Westchester Small Business Council and Westchester Venture Capital Network, a collective it had started in 1986. And as many as 10,000 people took advantage of the opportunity to exhibit their products and services and meet other businesspeople at the chamber's nine annual "Spotlights on Your Business."

The drive to be an entrepreneur is an enduring one in Westchester, where the climate for business favors large and small enterprises. The 350 branch offices of top banks, The County Chamber of Commerce, Inc., local chambers, the Westchester County Office of Economic Development, the Westchester Small Business Council, and S.C.O.R.E. (Service Corps of Retired Executives) are ready to nurture fresh enterprises and keep the county flourishing.

Women can find added networks through specialized women's business organizations. Men's and women's professions are in business in Westchester, offering all of the legal, accounting, insurance, advertising, marketing, and promotion services needed to launch a new venture. Among several services, the county economic development office works with the New York State Depart-

Anthony Camisa and Douglas Hammond (right), co-owners of Schmulmeyer's in Tarrytown, specialize in antique textiles and fabrics from the eighteenth century through 1950. The men travel twice a year to England and France to find the fabrics, and they count among their customers members of the international museum community as well as buyers for fashion designers in quest of inspiration for "new" designs. Photo by Barbara Brundage

ment of Economic Development to match Westchester companies in the Joint Venture program, promoting fresh overseas business development.

Business owners who convene at The County Chamber of Commerce, Inc., gatherings in White Plains are invited to learn different aspects of running a business in regularly scheduled workshops and seminars. The meetings cover topics from attracting employees to training them to developing benefits programs. Total attendance for such gatherings reached 4,000 members in 1988.

In White Plains and Peekskill, ideas became businesses after some novice businesspeople tapped the wisdom offered in one-on-one conversations with retired executives at S.C.O.R.E. offices. According to the records kept in the Peekskill office of S.C.O.R.E. from February 1989 to February 1990, about two people sat down on each available meeting day to talk with a retired executive and learn the ropes in new businesses and in expansion.

HOME AND WORKPLACE—THE LOCAL PROSPECTUS

Officials in towns and cities have carried out master planning for all types of development with an eye for local betterment. Long-established cities have been committed to reviving industrial areas that have new purpose and new possibilities while retaining the imprint of the past in their treasured

Town halls, such as the North Salem Town Hall, shown here, were Westchester's first public buildings. Photo by Rich Zila

The rich, fertile soil of northern Westchester still nourishes the agricultural businesses that remain. At Aronson Farm, a cow curiously examines a posted sign. Photo by Linda Zila

architecture. Today New Rochelle, Yonkers, Peekskill, and Port Chester are poised for dramatic housing and commercial advancement and for a revival of their waterfronts. White Plains is putting the finishing touches on its inviting central business district and transportation hub. To the north, picturesque small towns such as Pound Ridge and North Salem attend to the challenge of blending new housing, retail and office space into a rural, colonial backdrop. The mix of the large and small, the current and the quaint is part of the independent and complex character of Westchester.

For over a decade, upcounty Lewisboro has met success in encouraging the building of housing for middle-income citizens in new, market-priced townhouse and multifamily developments as part of its own master plan while meeting the overall county's needs. Lewisboro has a longstanding citizen's group committee to handle applications for middle-income housing and for maintaining its stock of such units. Town officials have reported that other municipalities routinely inquire about what works for Lewisboro and then fit the formula to their own needs.

Like many municipalities in today's Westchester, Yorktown invites developers to be mindful of its public servants and senior citizens in planning the profitable new housing units built within its borders for executives and professionals. The towns in the north also seek to maintain their pastoral appeal and the environment itself by enacting laws that allow landowners to build apartments in large homes, and renovate carriage houses and farm structures to serve single working peo-

Thriving local businesses on Parkway Street are part of Katonah's small-town charm. Photo by Rich Zila

ple and senior citizens.

Westchester municipalities tend to tailor their planning to suit their land, existing resources, and people. Rather than using massive urban water and sewer systems, many northern communities use underground water supplies and natural ground waste systems, which set natural parameters for growth. Interest in maintaining the beauty of a community has led to the creation of historic districts and preservation districts with laws that keep the lush canopy of trees over country lanes and eliminate the possibility of jarring architectural differences from property to property.

Westchester communities offer high-income executives a variety of housing possibilities—from manicured mansions to secluded upcounty woods to high-rise accommodations overlooking the Hudson. In 1989 the Westchester Housing Forum instituted new programs to assist builders with projects in all parts of the county that increase the county's housing stock for the average- and low-income family. The forum's programs and other incentive programs such as bonus building units, zoning changes to permit developing small lots, and tax abatements are solutions that have been suggested to add to Westchester's housing.

THE INTERNATIONAL CORPORATE SCENE

Westchester has already made a national name for building new office space at a strong pace throughout the 1980s. Westchester 2000 reported in its November 1989 report that four million square feet of office space is available for large and small firms. The financiers, realtors, and development companies responsible for these sparkling new workplaces also have added to the county's supply of community art and sculpture for the public's enjoyment and have supported many cultural and artistic events through involvement in the Council for the Arts in Westchester. The sense of Westchester as an enjoyable home and workplace emerges with the community-conscious realtor's eye for beauty.

The number of internationally known corporations grew in Westchester when Trans World Airlines arrived in Mount Kisco in the late 1980s and joined KLM Royal Dutch Airlines of Elmsford to open its headquarters in the county. They join Reader's Digest, IBM, General Foods, and Pepsico in making Westchester mailing addresses known throughout the world.

Such corporations show interest in the quality of life in the county itself. In Mamaroneck, the Flik International Corporations employ 650 people among many catering firms under contract to offer corporate employees the travel-saving benefit of on-site dining facilities.

When environmental questions were raised in the late 1980s about the effect of styrofoam production on the ozone layer, seven of the top nine companies in the county acted swiftly to curb the use of such products in their cafeterias. Their response, like their immaculate corporate campuses, show a deference to their host communities that help make the general climate for business a pleasant one.

Planting trees in Westchester is emerging as a preferred local antidote to the changing global ozone conditions now under study. Patricia Hotchkiss, a county legislator and former town supervisor, told an upcounty gardening group that support in the private and public sectors is gathering to plant five million trees in the county. The pro-active solution has captured support as a naturally beautiful answer to unwanted environmental changes evident around the world, Hotchkiss said.

International corporations of every ilk have been present in force since the 1950s and remain strongly positioned to seize the new economic moment that history is creating after the crumbling of the Berlin Wall and the turn to free

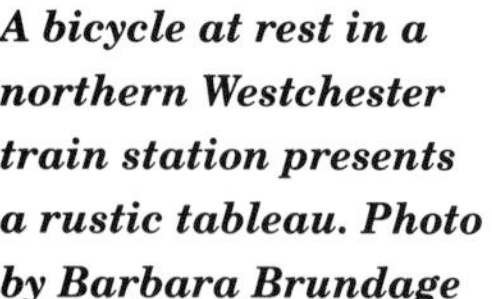

A bicycle at rest in a northern Westchester train station presents a rustic tableau. Photo by Barbara Brundage

The spillway at the New Croton Dam curves back into the reservoir to provide approximately 1,000 feet of spilling edge. The new Croton water system was constructed between 1892 and 1907 to meet the increasing water needs of Westchester and New York City. Photo by Rich Zila

enterprise by Eastern European nations. With its government and commercial support, its solid workplaces and educated work force, Westchester is up to any boom prospects that new European, African, Latin American, or Asian markets present in this decade. Westchester's public and private schools and colleges show a commitment to educating internationally aware and technically adept students to enter the corporate arena well into the next century. The county has made corporate world movers and shakers welcome as neighbors and businesspeople.

TRANSPORTATION AND UTILITIES

Populated since pre-Revolutionary days, the county is actively keeping its present-day roads in good condition and its future road system developing at a steady rate. The task covers improvements in interstate and state systems to resurfacing of city streets and country lanes in the 450-square-mile county.

The people running rails and bus systems are aggressive in their campaign to promote use of mass transit and prevent commuter traffic jams that can occur in metropolitan regions. For the Metropolitan Transportation Authority, ridership of the rails stands at more than 95,000 people per work day. It has undertaken projects to create new parking areas along its three rail lines. The county oversees the Bee Line system and counted its ridership in 1988 at 110,000 per day. Its annual ridership rose to 30 million in 1988, up from 21 million in 1977.

To ward off the daily gridlock that can plague any metropolitan location, in Westchester it has been recommended that the multiple occupancy of cars should be rewarded with special commuter driving lanes on its highways in the future, and that more park-and-drive lots be added to allow commuters to curb their single-occupancy driving. Solutions such as these, as well as pro-

Cluster housing in Westchester has been growing in popularity over the last two decades. This type of arrangement preserves more open land and requires less construction of access roads and parking areas than traditional separate housing. Photo by Rich Zila

The sparsely settled town of Somers is carefully zoned. Big old houses are set back on large lots of land and residents enjoy a secluded way of life. Photo by Rich Zila

posals for monorails to parallel present highways and truck lanes for the east-west I-287, are among proposals under consideration by county leaders.

The blueprints for a new Westchester County Airport are being spread before county legislators and planners who are scrutinizing suggested modernization. The airport that now serves more than 700,000 people a year is slated to have a fresh look and the latest in facilities for the traveler under a mansard-roof terminal.

Westchester's electric and gas utilities are run by Consolidated Edison Company of New York and New York State Electric and Gas Company. The basic infrastructures that allow fresh water to pour from a kitchen tap or garbage to be picked up, carted away, and safely disposed are under local and county scrutiny and the subject of proposed expansion. Westchester County, with its Yonkers and Peekskill sewer and refuse facilities, and a seven-town northern regional coalition support a cooperative solution to waste disposal.

Westchester has had time to mature and develop ways to tighten the nuts and bolts of smoothly operating such basic community services. The effort to maintain present structures and plan new ones has engaged the interest of engineers, state, county, and local officials, and residents who volunteer to serve on special local boards.

RECREATION

From 1979 to 1989, Westchester County itself spent $55 million on capital improvements of recreational land for all of its residents. It continues adding to a greenbelt of biking, hiking, and jogging trails which loops through several communities, which the county hopes will one day total 90 linear miles for its active residents. New golf courses are planned and programs in parks and other facilities are operating to heighten the public's awareness of its resources.

Programs are encouraged to educate the public about conservation, to promote recycling of paper, glass, and

Time-honored apartment houses are given a new lease on life as co-op condominiums. The Popham Hall Coops in Scarsdale serve many first-time homeowners. Photo by Rich Zila

IBM World Trade Americas/Far East Corporation, in the town of Mount Pleasant, is one of Westchester's most dramatic corporate structures. Furnished with an office landscape system—units rather than walls—the building is striking when viewed against the dark evening sky. Photo by Rich Zila

Shown here is the Peekskill passenger overpass with Indian Point power station in the background. Electricity produced at Indian Point is supplied to the Metropolitan Transportation Authority for commuter rail lines and mass transit facilities as well as other governmental customers. Photo by Rich Zila

metal, and to carry out cost effective leaf composting, making Westchester homeowners and residents environmentally active and aware.

E911

Paid police and both paid and volunteer fire and ambulance services are all aided in their operation to provide a swift response to emergencies by a county communication network that was developed in the last decade. The E911 telephone system of answering an emergency is enhanced by computerization of data and replaces the need to know local emergency phone numbers. It has been promoted by the county to serve even the smallest rural community police force with its telecommunication network and computerized method of spotting the location of an emergency. Cities, towns, and villages have their own corps of volunteers and paid employees aiding residents and supporting and maintaining their stock of modern life-saving apparatus.

LIBRARY SYSTEM

The county is served by an extensive library system that has 45 branches and four million books, videos, records, and other material to check out. The Westchester system is highly service oriented and operates everything from an Educational Brokering Service to a Homework Hotline. Literacy volunteers and volunteers who act as mentors to students can use the quiet corners of Westchester libraries to meet with people who have decided to improve their skills. Art work is displayed and cultural programs offered in the county's libraries. Computers swiftly identify the location of books in the system and residents may use any of the library branches in the county.

Pleasantville's Department of Recreation, located in this building, oversees the maintenance and improvement of recreational land in the area. Many recreational facilities offer residents access to weight room equipment and game rooms. Photo by Barbara Brundage

SPECIALIZED EDUCATIONAL RESOURCES

Westchester schools are served by the New York State Board of Cooperative Educational Services to provide vocational training and educational services for students with special needs. The programs lead vocationally directed students to learn in classrooms and an array of workplace settings. Its programs have won the support of many large and small companies that annually profit by gaining qualified entry-level workers in many technical, mechanical, service, clerical, and other specialized fields that are forecast to continue growing. B.O.C.E.S. facilities in northern and southern Westchester assess students and provide a range of training programs.

EDUCATION, BUSINESS, AND SOCIETY

With the travel, leisure, and tourist industries projected to hold top spots as growth industries in the year 2000, Westchester Community College educators are developing associate degree programs to train people for work in those fields. The courses would cover a range of employment options, from the work of the travel agent to the hotel keeper, according to college president Joseph N. Hankin.

The Valhalla-based institution already has a jump on training students in food preparation and hotel industries and in several health and service professions that also will dominate growth, Hankin said. Prospective employers in the health industry can tap trained

White Plains fire department's hook and ladder team poses proudly before their well-maintained fire engine. Photo by Rich Zila

graduates in radiology, respiration therapy, nursing, and home health courses. Electrical, mechanical, and civil engineering courses are strong at the college. In all, the college started the decade of the nineties with the highest enrollment ever: Hankin estimated that 9,000 students were registered for Westchester Community College classes.

For 15 years, WCC has had a cooperative program with General Motors in Tarrytown that satisfied the needs for trained mechanics now assembling mini-vans at the plant. In recent years, the college held English language classes in various communities for new Latin American and Asian immigrants. It houses the headquarters of the Literacy Volunteers of Westchester County at its Valhalla campus and backs the nonprofit organization that trains volunteers to teach reading to adults throughout the county.

As society changed, the college developed extra business programs and offered adult career planning to answer demands that mushroomed as families and female roles turned homemakers into full-time job hunters. The longer lifespan of the average American has added a new interest group of students to the campus. Hankin said 3,000 retired people have enrolled in special Elder Health courses, and many retirees are now seeking a whole new array of job skills for new careers.

EDUCATION'S MESSAGE TO TOMORROW'S WORK FORCE

As educators and business and government officials nationwide grapple with deficits in elementary level reading, math, and writing skills that hamper the success of young people entering higher education and the workplace,

Hankin said he wants to meet the problems early on. At a February 1990 interview, Hankin said he and a half-dozen other college presidents in Westchester were drafting an encouraging letter that he favors sending to very seventh grader in the county.

After the presidential letter committee finishes its work on the proposed letter, Hankin said a dozen local college presidents would have to decide if they would join in signing it, in effect telling the seventh graders to study hard, stay in school, and be assured of getting into one of the county's colleges. Those who commit themselves to studying and graduating from high school would be "guaranteed" admission to at least one of the participating institutions, according to the draft letter.

"We want to give them a view of their future that many of them may never have had," Hankin said. "We want to tell them to try hard, don't give up, graduate." He added that 25 percent nationally do not graduate.

Hankin said that high schools, corporations, and colleges should continue to work together to prepare students who will be employable for all types of professions, but that junior high school students are not too young to get encouragement from society.

"I believe you can't start early enough," he said.

THE ETERNAL SCHOLAR

It is never too late to learn, as well. As part of the effort to prepare Westchester for the next century, in the mid-1980s Hankin wrote about the technological changes that would increasingly expand people's ability to study in their homes and offices. The computer and phone modem, FAX and telecommunication equipment available now and in the future make it possible to offer courses far off campus and challenge educators to deliver those courses.

Officer Allison Lent of the White Plains police department is one of Westchester's finest. The municipal police departments work hard to keep neighborhoods safe. Photo by Rich Zila

Westchester educational leaders are advanced in their knowledge of technological developments and engaged in dialogues with corporate leaders to use the hardware and software that has been advancing so rapidly to provide creative instructional delivery systems. Hankin, with nearly 20 years as a Westchester college president, predicted that new systems may be designed with these tools, and with closed circuit television and interactive cable television systems, for time-saving and cost effective training at the workplace and to serve individuals in the county who want or must study at home.

BUILDING ON RESOURCES

Westchester County Industrial Development is a diverse resource of real estate, finance, engineering, law, and government specialists that assist in arranging long-term financing for desirable economic development. Local industrial development is available in several municipalities as well.

Builders and real estate developers envision new projects and are active in carrying their forward-looking message to the public. The Construction Industry Council of Westchester and Hudson

***RIGHT:** Westchester's libraries are well equipped to serve a multitude of information needs. The county system is a cooperative service agency made up of member libraries that bring residents access to more than four million books, video cassettes, records, compact-discs, magazines, and other data. Photo by Rich Zila*

Valley, Inc., boasted in 1989 of its membership of 500 contractors, materials and equipment suppliers, specialty and service firms doing business here in a $1.5-billion-dollar market for all types of construction projects.

Landscaping, environmental, engineering, and architectural businesses also abound in the county and an active Westchester Builders Institute, Inc., supports individual professionals carrying out their visions. The plans on the drawing board will translate into work in the future. The New York State Department of Labor in 1989 projected growth in construction industry jobs in the Hudson Valley Region, which includes Westchester. By 1991, the department predicts a need for 10,000 new workers in the extractive and building segments of the construction business in the Hudson Valley. This increases the number of people in these occupations from about 75,000 in 1987, not counting special trade occupations such as electricians, plumbers, carpenters, etc.

SOCIETY

Westchester's archipelago of municipalities engage the interest of many of their residents in volunteering for quality of life and beautification ventures close to home. Like the Revolution-era farmer, today's Westchester resident readily deals with the world outside his or her door. As a result of large and small individual efforts, communities remain functional and beautiful.

It was reported that an elder Dewitt Wallace, who with his wife, Lila, founded *Reader's Digest,* was so committed to personal action for the general good that one Saturday morning in the 1970s he enlisted a dozen top *Digest* executives and board members to help him pick up papers and other litter tossed by the train track at the Mount Kisco train station. The same couple acted as benefactors by creating parks, health care, and recreational facilities for the public.

Today, celebrities living in Westchester lead quiet lives and still take time to give of themselves. Actress Jill Clayburgh, a Mount Kisco resident, devotes her time to a Croton Falls organization, "Friends of Karen," that aids families of critically ill children. Actor E.G. Marshall has quietly waited with

***BELOW:** These young members of an ice hockey team take time out from their game to pose for a group portrait in Tarrytown Park. Westchester's Hispanic community is flourishing with more than 250 of its own businesses, according to Hector Garced, founder of The Hispanic Chamber of Commerce. Photo by Rich Zila*

his neighbors for his turn to speak at Bedford Town Hall when environmental issues crop up.

Actress Colleen Dewhurst, fashion designer Calvin Klein, and business magnate Carl Icahn stand behind the efforts of nonprofit groups to ensure that historic and cultural treasures sparkle with lively events in the county. Opera great Robert Merrill has been devoted to New Rochelle and singing its praises for years. They are but a handful of giants in their fields who are involved in the county and they are regularly joined by media, publishing, sports, and business greats in creating a sophisticated corps of benefactors in Westchester.

The county has active Rotary Clubs, Lions Clubs, Junior Leagues, garden clubs, and a variety of associations that bring people from all walks of life together to balance the requirements of a healthy economy, a healthy environment, social order, and peace and prosperity for individual home and business owners. Exhibits, galas, dinners, and country fairs fill the Westchester calendar of events that such groups offer for the general good.

Individuals can volunteer their time and talents in programs that offer aid to families in crisis, the elderly, and the young operated by religious organizations and by public and private initiatives. People who set out to change the direction of their lives can call the Westchester Self Help Clearing House to link with 250 mutual support groups that meet in the county, or they can tap the resources available through helping professionals in private practice and in the offices of the Westchester County Mental Health Department.

A PROFITABLE FUTURE

Left to its own devices, the more than 300-year-old county has blossomed with a harvest of homes and businesses that is to be prized by its citizens. The 450-square-mile county of Westchester has a healthly heartbeat and a well-earned knack for doing good business as it prepares to put another century under its greenbelt. Given all the historic landmarks of its proud past that are still here for residents and visitors to enjoy, Westchester's people stand on solid enterprising ground, willing and highly able to build a profitable future.

The guiding values set by Dewitt and Lila Wallace, founders of **Reader's Digest** *in Pleasantville, include a concern for employees, and a commitment to high ethical standards. Shown here are company executives arriving at work in the morning. Photo by Rich Zila*

The Chevrolet Lumina, the Pontiac Trans Sport, and the Oldsmobile Silhouette are the current ATVs manufactured at the General Motors plant in North Tarrytown. Directly across the Hudson River are the rolling hills of Rockland County. Photo by Rich Zila

PART 2

WESTCHESTER COUNTY'S ENTERPRISES

Photo by Rich Zila

7

NETWORKS

Westchester County's role as a modern, thriving metropolitan center is made possible by its network of communication, transportation, and energy providers.

AT&T

One of Westchester's largest employers, American Telephone & Telegraph is in the business of moving and managing information both domestically and globally. The company's 2,700 employees in White Plains and 14 other county locations serve business, government, and consumers. For these customers, AT&T designs, manufactures, sells, rents, and services a variety of sophisticated communications products, ranging from telephones and facsimile machines to computer-based operations systems.

The need for a local switching center to handle the county's growing number of long-distance telephone calls was what brought AT&T to Westchester in 1954. Then headquartered in New York City, the firm moved 450 employees to White Plains, into the building it still occupies. AT&T retains its signature building in New York, 550 Madison Avenue, but has relocated its headquarters to Basking Ridge, New Jersey.

In Westchester, AT&T offers large and small businesses as well as county and state governments a diversity of voice and data transmission services as well as communications, computer, and data networking products and systems. The company also provides customized data networking solutions that connect otherwise incompatible and widely dispersed computer systems into integrated networks. Its products for business and government also include PBX equipment, key telephone systems, fax machines, and related equipment and services.

Several specialized groups meet the unique requirements of these customers. The data systems group designs, develops, and markets computer and data networking products. The business markets group serves the voice and data communications needs of large- and medium-size businesses, emphasizing solutions that integrate communications products and services. The general business systems office provides systems, products, and maintenance services keyed to smaller businesses' individual situations.

For the telecommunications industry, the network systems group offers not only Integrated Services Digital Network (ISDN) products and services, but also switching, transmission, and computer-based operations systems. Through its national organization, this group manufactures, markets, and installs these systems.

Consumers also merit special treatment. For them, AT&T supplies long-distance services and quality telephones and related products. The operator services group handles long-distance calls for which person-to-person service or special billing is required. Three AT&T phone centers in the county carry both a wide selection of consumer products and an assortment of telephone systems and fax machines suitable for the at-home business.

Still another specialized unit, the network operations group, services and supports company activities in all markets. In addition to designing, maintaining, and managing AT&T's Worldwide Intelligent Network, this group installs and maintains telephones, PBXs, and computer equipment and systems for large customers. It is also responsible for managing AT&T's access to local telephone networks. The White Plains Regional Network Operations Center is one of six centers in the nation that remain open 24 hours per day to monitor approximately 80 million calls per day, ensuring that customer calls are processed quickly and accurately.

AT&T offers more to the Westchester community than even its long list of innovative products and services would indicate. The

Three AT&T phone centers in the county carry a wide selection of telephone systems and fax machines for the home or office.

company and its employees are deeply involved in a multiplicity of local civic and charitable causes. The involvement includes board memberships and financial and in-kind support.

Executives sit on the boards of a wide variety of associations, such as American Red Cross, Better Business Bureau of Westchester, Girl Scouts, Junior Achievement, Metropool, Private Industry Council, The County Chamber of Commerce, Westchester Coalition, Westchester County Association, SUNY-Purchase Executive Board, United Way of Westchester, and Volunteer Service Bureau

The list of organizations supported by AT&T and its employees is still longer. It includes hospitals, such as St. Agnes, St. Jude's, Vassar Brothers, and White Plains, and health-related groups such as the American Heart Association, the Cystic Fibrosis Foundation, the Diabetes Association, and the Mental Health Association. It also includes minority-support groups, such as Affirmative Action Program, Inc., INROADS, and the National Association for the Advancement of Colored People, and cultural organizations such as Caramoor, the Historic Hudson Valley and Neuberger museums, the New Orchestra of Westchester, and Philharmonia Virtuosi. Children, schools and colleges, veterans, the blind, the elderly, and the handicapped are among other beneficiaries of company and employee contributions of money and time. The value of the financial contributions is complemented by the many generous hours of work the employees donate.

Much of the employee effort is channeled through two volunteer arms. Many employees, including retirees, belong to the long-established Telephone Pioneers of America. Under the auspices of this group they work for such organizations as Children's Village and New York School for the Deaf, serve in the battle against such diseases as cerebral palsy, and engage in such tasks as collecting food and clothing for the needy.

Exactly 100 employees belong to the Century Club, formed in 1987 by AT&T to encourage greater volunteer activity by its own staff and to serve as a model for other companies sharing that goal. These employees, assigned to the club and given one day of training by AT&T, represent every level and department of the company. While they receive the support of their supervisors, they perform their volunteer tasks mainly on their own time. A variety of cultural, civic, and charitable organizations benefit from Century Club activities.

American Telephone & Telegraph is well-known as a socially responsible citizen as well as a major employer. In that light, the firm's long-term commitment to the county and its people is clear.

AT&T is in the business of moving and managing information both domestically and globally.

At AT&T, friendly, quality service to both callers and clients is the number-one priority.

WZFM

Long an integral part of the Westchester community, WZFM, 107.1 FM, has strengthened its involvement since its purchase by West-Land Communicators, Inc., in 1989. As an early sign, a new morning program was introduced in 1990 to fill the 6 a.m. to 10 a.m. spot. The program, "Morning Express," emanates from WZFM's van, which cuts a wide path around the area, stopping to broadcast from offices, shopping centers, gyms—wherever the hosts and programmers locate active county people at work or play. The station wants its audience to participate in the broadcasting as well as the listening end.

The audience has proved willing, responding warmly to WZFM's outreach efforts. That becomes evident on tuning into the rock-based, adult-contemporary music station's call-in programs. Its 7 p.m.-to-midnight "Saturday Night Specialty Show," which plays requests for hits from the 1950s and 1960s, has drawn large numbers of interested callers ever since it went on the air in 1982. They call from all over the WZFM listening area, which extends throughout Westchester and Rockland counties and into northern New Jersey and southern Connecticut.

To make sure its listeners get not only their favorite music but also the best possible sound, the 24-hour station went all compact disc early in 1990. In preparation it spent $50,000 to install a studio full of state-of-the-art equipment, from radio boards to compact disc players.

The third ingredient of the WZFM mix is top-notch on-air personalities. Talking to and not at the radio audience, they complement the musical format by coming across as up-front and involved broadcasters.

While playing pop hit music mainly from the 1960s to today's favorites to entertain its audience, the station has also staked out a position of service to the community. Its watchword: "If it's important to WZFM listeners, it will be on WZFM first." The station offers local, regional, and national news, the most accurate local weather reports, and, with its own traffic reporters, frequent updates on road and rail conditions. It features exclusive, up-to-the-second traffic reports from the Texaco Samaritan Van. In addition, WZFM works with the local oil company to provide a unique public service—helping to keep traffic on the Cross Westchester Expressway flowing smoothly.

Another WZFM public service is an information line, available from any touch-tone phone 24 hours per day. Named Information Telephone, the service extends to movies, cultural and family events, weather, sports scores and highlights, and lottery results.

WZFM's distinctive programming and services attract a coterie of devoted, young, upscale listen-

On the air with the "Morning Express": WZFM adds news, traffic, and weather to the best morning music mix.

The WZFM van traverses the county to bring live life-style remotes to listeners.

ers. A demographic profile shows the vast majority are 25 to 49 years old, have household incomes of more than $30,000 per year, and tune in four or more hours every day. These listeners dine out frequently, own two or three cars, and regularly attend movies, concerts, sporting events, and the theater. More than three-quarters of them report that the station's advertisements help them make their buying decisions.

The ads themselves are frequent prize winners. Prepared with the expert assistance of WZFM personnel, they have earned top awards for several years in a row from such professional groups as the New York State Broadcasters Association and the Advertising Club of Westchester.

WZFM's files attest to the effectiveness of both its advertising and its support for a variety of civic and charitable causes. Letters from satisfied advertisers of all kinds—automobile dealers, retailers, health care providers, large corporations, and small companies—praise the station for helping them increase sales.

Letters from such public-service advertisers as towns, schools, colleges, and charities take the same tone. Among them, the Leukemia Society of America commended WZFM for its generosity in running frequent public service announcements and for efficacy in producing contributions. Other expressions of gratitude bear the names of the White Plains Public Schools, Village of Ossining, and Dominican College.

Many more nonprofit organizations are also the beneficiaries of WZFM's helping hand. In 1988, when the county set out to put teddy bears in every ambulance and police car for the reassurance of frightened children, WZFM joined in enthusiastically. The station broadcast appeals to the public for donations of the stuffed animals and served as a drop-off place. It helped the county collect more than 3,000 teddy bears. In addition, WZFM serves as the official station for the March of Dimes Walk America project, which fights birth defects, and WZFM provides major support for the Arthritis Foundation and Lighthouse for the Blind.

For WZFM, such activities are as much a part of its mission as providing enjoyable listening for people of all ages. Looking ahead to an exciting future, it anticipates enhancing its service to Westchester while also becoming an integral part of Rockland County, which lacks a radio station. At the same time WZFM intends to deliver unique programming. West-Land Communicators promises that it will be like no other station in the metropolitan area. The station presents listeners with the chance to win something virtually every hour.

The essence of 107.1 will remain music that offers depth, variety, and texture, in a bright and fresh blend, with tempo and balance custom mixed for the different times of the day and the changing activities and moods of the audience.

GANNETT WESTCHESTER ROCKLAND NEWSPAPERS

The Gannett Westchester Rockland Newspapers are driving forces in the communities they serve and trend-setters in the communications industry.

A subsidiary of Gannett Co. Inc. since their acquisition in 1964, the Westchester-Rockland group consists of nine daily and two weekly newspapers located in Westchester, Rockland, and Putnam counties.

A stone's throw from New York City, these suburbs are thriving residential, corporate, and commercial centers with their own distinct identities. The city of White Plains, the seat of Westchester County government, is home to dozens of major retailers—Neiman-Marcus, Saks Fifth Avenue, Bloomingdale's, Macy's, and A&S among them. Westchester's corporate tenants include the world headquarters of Texaco Inc., Pepsico Inc., Reader's Digest, TWA, and International Paper, as well as the United States headquarters of General Foods U.S.A., KLM, Fuji, and Hitachi. IBM's world and United States headquarters are located in Westchester.

Here, residents place a premium on the quality of local schools, services, and government. They also place a premium on news about their hometowns, which the local Gannett newspapers emphasize.

Westchester Rockland Newspapers serves the surrounding area from its modern, state-of-the-art facility at One Gannett Drive, White Plains.

The newspaper group dates back to 1883, when the county's first daily, *The Statesman,* began publication. Renamed *The Heralds Statesman,* that newspaper delivers news to the city of Yonkers and the villages of Dobbs Ferry and Hastings.

Serving the nearby city of Mount Vernon is *The Daily Argus,* while the central and northern communities of Westchester as well as Putnam County are served by *The Reporter Dispatch.*

Along the Long Island Sound, the communities of Mamaroneck and Larchmont are served by *The Daily Times.* Port Chester, Harrison, Rye Brook, and Rye are served by *The Daily Item,* while residents of New Rochelle and Pelham read *The Standard Star.* Hudson River communities are served by *The Citizen Register* in the Ossining/Briarcliff area; *The Daily News* in the Tarrytown, North Tarrytown, and Irvington area; and *The Star* in the city of Peekskill.

Rockland County, Westchester's neighbor to the west, is served by the *Rockland Journal-News.* The newspaper group's weeklies are *The Review Press-Reporter,* serving the village of Bronxville, and *Fairpress,* which serves nearby Connecticut communities.

The newspapers continue to operate under a time-honored tradition: providing complete local news. While local coverage is clearly their strength, the newspapers also provide news of New York City, the world, nation, and state, along with complete coverage of business, sports, health, the arts, and lifestyles.

The group is headquartered in Harrison, near Interstates 287 and 684, and has four satellite offices in Westchester and one in Carmel, Putnam County. The Rockland County newspaper has its own office and printing facility in West Nyack, while *Fairpress* has offices in Norwalk, Connecticut. The Harrison operation has the distinction of being the first newsroom in the country to introduce video display terminals for reporters and editors as well as an electronic pagination system for laying out its news pages.

Sixteen communities are covered by Westchester Rockland Newspapers, providing local as well as national and international news.

In addition to its technological advances, the newspaper group has been singled out for numerous journalism awards, including Columbia University's distinguished 1900 Mike Berger Award and numerous state and national awards. Its sports pages have been ranked among the 10 best in the country for the last two years by the Associated Press Sports Editors Association.

The group's commitment to the local community includes contributions through the Gannett Foundation to such local agencies as United Way and Westchester Council for the Arts. The company, in partnership with other corporations, funds the operation of a day-care center for employees and the public, runs a Newspaper-in-Education program for local schools, and sponsors a high school journalism contest.

WHUD-FM/WLNA-AM

As entities of Radio Terrace Inc., WHUD-FM and WLNA-AM reach out to Westchester County and the greater Hudson Valley marketing area.

On the air since St. Valentine's Day 1972, WHUD, at 100.7 FM, broadcasts 24 hours per day, seven days per week, with 50,000 watts of bright and easy music. The station's adult appeal is a function of its upbeat sound creatively mixed with well-known radio personalities who lend the New York City experience to suburban radio.

WHUD starts the day, Monday through Friday, from 5:30 a.m. to 10 a.m., with "The Ed Baer Affair." Special programming culminates on Sunday evening beginning at 8 p.m. with "The Joe O'Brien Concert Hall." Simulcast on WLNA, the concert hall plays the cream of the classics, Puccini to Prokofiev, Rameau to Rachmaninoff.

More than music, WHUD is also up-to-the-minute news and Wall Street updates, traffic, sports, and weather reports for Westchester, Rockland, Putnam, Dutchess, Orange, and Ulster counties.

WLNA, 1420 AM, went on the air on Thanksgiving Day 1948 as northern Westchester's local counterpart of WHUD's regionalism. Broadcasting daily from 5 p.m. to midnight, WLNA is full-service radio with adult-contemporary music, expanded news, and a variety of life-style features. "Good Morning, Hudson Valley" and "Noon Edition" are live news and information shows where current issues and events are discussed with guest news makers who provide lively dialogue with listeners who call in. Also unique is WLNA's "Buy and Sell," the free classified advertisements of the airwaves.

Sports, both national and local, get thorough coverage on WLNA, which broadcasts area high school games from September to June. Outstanding Westchester student athletes are highlighted weekly on "The Con Ed Sports Award Show."

And, nearly every week, the stations' van and WLNA's mascot, D.J. the Dog, take the show on the road, broadcasting live from businesses, hospitals, senior citizens' centers, schools, fairs, and festivals.

WHUD/WLNA, a powerful combination dedicated to giving and caring, supports many charities. On-air personalities have swam, run, and talked nonstop in radiothons for Northern Westchester/Putnam Special Olympics, Westchester Heart Fund, Peekskill Area Health Center, and a legion of other charities.

More than $100,000 has been raised for children through the sale of Fleetweather Calendars, 14-month, long-range, weather-prediction calendars sold under the auspices of the WHUD/WLNA Fleetweather Travel Foundation, Inc., and promoted by WHUD/WLNA. Such groups as the national Ronald McDonald House and the local Friends of Karen, which serves terminally ill children and their families, benefit from this annual endeavor. The entire community benefits, too, from WHUD/WLNA's ongoing commitment to meeting its needs every day of the year.

WHUD/WLNA reaches out to the community in every possible way—D.J. the Dog, mascot and "LNA team" regular, lends a hand to a little visitor at Peekskill's Riverfront Green during the broadcast of the Peekskill Area Health Center's Twelfth Annual Culinary Arts Festival. WHUD/WLNA's promotional efforts bolster fund-raising throughout the region for organizations such as the Health Center. Photo by David Basta

NORTHERN TELECOM INC.

In the business of moving and managing information, Northern Telecom Inc. provides a full range of products and systems to the telecommunications industry, businesses, universities, governments, and other institutions. The company's products are sold worldwide.

The development, manufacture, and sale of products are only part of Northern Telecom's total service concept. That concept also includes financing, training, consulting, and joint planning, as well as sophisticated system support. Its customer service function, in the hands of highly trained professionals, is concentrated in 13 regional offices. Spread nationwide from Westchester to California, these offices also handle sales and marketing. About 110 service and support people and 60 sales and marketing people staff the Tarrytown regional office.

Well into its second century, Northern Telecom was established in 1884 as a small manufacturing workshop to make telephone instruments. Today it is the nation's second-largest manufacturer of telecommunications equipment. Its products, which include integrated office systems, are used in more than 90 countries; its manufacturing, research, marketing, and service facilities are located worldwide.

In the United States, Northern Telecom's payroll exceeds 22,000 people. In addition to the regional offices, these employees work in its Nashville, Tennessee, headquarters and in 12 manufacturing plants and 13 research and development centers nationwide. The multibillion-dollar company's manufacturing and research and development facilities alone occupy more than 4 million square feet of floor space.

Northern Telecom's product portfolio falls into two broad categories: equipment designed for public telecommunications networks, sold to local and long-distance communications carriers, and office communications systems, sold to public and private users. The company makes virtually everything that goes into a telecommunications system. That includes telephones and terminals, the wire and cable connecting them to the network, switching systems that route information, transmission systems that transport it through the network, and operational and maintenance systems needed to manage the network.

The switching systems are the heart of the networks. Northern Telecom's Digital Multiplex System (DMS), a family of digital switches, is used by nearly every major telephone company in the United States, including all the Bell operating companies and the major independents. DMS systems are in use worldwide.

The counterpart to the DMS in the public network is Northern Telecom's SL family of switching systems, designed for use in large corporations, universities, and government offices as private telephone systems. SL systems are also manufactured and in service all over the world.

For its success, Northern Telecom credits scientific and engineering breadth, manufacturing depth, and market-driven research and

BELOW and FACING PAGE: Northern Telecom Inc. is the nation's second largest manufacturer of telecommunications equipment. With 13 principal region offices nationwide, including one in Tarrytown, New York, Northern Telecom is committed to customer service and satisfaction.

development. About 10 percent of employees are involved in applied research conducted at the company's research and development affiliate, Bell-Northern Research Ltd. (BNR), headquartered in Ontario. BNR, which also has laboratories in the United States, is responsible for developing the technologies, products, and systems that are marketed worldwide.

A major portion of today's research and development expenditures goes to products and systems for Northern Telecom's OPEN World program. Announced in 1982, OPEN, an acronym for Open Protocol Enhanced Networks, is the firm's committed approach to bringing order out of the information chaos rooted in the versatility of digital technology. That versatility, however, also prevents computers and other equipment, developed independently for specific purposes and made by different manufacturers, from communicating with each other. OPEN World removes the obstacles, enabling many different products to work together in an integrated system. Northern Telecom believes such interconnection is essential to realizing the full potential of the new information tools becoming available.

The company is also a leader in voice-recognition technology. It introduced that technology in the United States with a first-of-its-kind billing service, revolutionizing long-distance calling by eliminating the need for a human operator on most calls. The service "listens" to callers' responses and generates prompts that ask them to select requested service for collect, credit-card, or third-party billing.

Northern Telecom was also the first company in the world to introduce a telephone with an integrated display for use with Caller ID services. Called Maestro, it heralded a new era for the telephone, which can now let a customer know who is calling before he or she answers a call. The firm also developed and manufactures the sophisticated software that allows telephone companies to offer the Caller ID service.

These products, among others, are sold, installed, and serviced out of the Tarrytown regional office. That office is also known for participation in a variety of Westchester civic, cultural, and charitable activities. Beneficiaries include the Westchester County Council for the Arts and the Cystic Fibrosis Association.

Northern Telecom's commitment to United Way has been recognized many times, with awards for both support and level of donations. The company is also a leading backer of Inroads, the cooperative work-study program that provides special incentives for minority students. Northern Telecom is the nation's third-largest contributor to the program; its president sits on the Inroads board. The International Association for Students in Economics and Business is still another Northern Telecom cause. In a joint project with Pace University, the company employs trainees in its economics and marketing functions, giving them the opportunity to interface with executives.

In late 1989 Northern Telecom introduced a major new product: Fiberworld. Designed to improve the performance, capacity, and value of virtually every piece of communications equipment, Fiberworld is an advanced fiber-optic telecommunications network. Northern Telecom Inc. believes it will change the way people live and work over the next decade, leading the company—and the world—into the twenty-first century.

METRO-NORTH COMMUTER RAILROAD

Committed to providing safe, comfortable, reliable transportation, Metro-North Commuter Railroad has its objectives well in hand. On-time performance, low costs per passenger, a large number of riders, good condition of equipment, and increasing efficiency of operation—by any measure the railroad, which serves Westchester County and six other New York and Connecticut counties, has come a long way since its founding in 1983.

At that time Metro-North announced an ambitious mission: "To preserve and enhance the quality of life and economic health of the region through the efficient provision of transportation service of the highest quality." The public benefit corporation did not expect fulfilling that mission to be easy.

While tracing its roots to the New York and Harlem Railroad Company, begun in 1832 as a Lower Manhattan horse-car line, Metro-North counts its modern forerunners as the New York Central and Pennsylvania railroads, which merged in 1968 to become Penn Central Corp. One year later the privately held New York, New Haven & Hartford Railroad was merged with the new line by government order.

The mergers solved no problems. In 1972 Penn Central went into bankruptcy. The federal government stepped in and, in 1976, merged seven bankrupt railroads to form Consolidated Rail Corp., divesting it of its passenger business.

Metro-North inherited a railroad that did not work. Trains were late, heating and air conditioning did not operate, equipment was old and in poor repair, and maintenance had long been neglected. Metro-North moved quickly to turn things around, adding new employees and developing its own systems for accountability and other major functions. Funded through its capital program by the states of New York and Connecticut, the company brought many system components to a state of good repair. It bought new cars, laid new track, and set out to replace the entire signal system.

All that effort was directed toward the first priority: assuring every passenger of a seat and a comfortable ride. That accomplished, Metro-North moved to make getting to and from trains easier and more comfortable. In 1988 it announced a $20-million parking program to add several thousand spaces at stations throughout the route. A $35.5-million program, completed in early 1991, renovated eight Westchester stations. Further station improvements are under way, introducing amenities such as directional signs.

Continuing to address its prime concerns of safety, reliability, and customer comfort, Metro-North completed the installation of new electrical power supply lines on the

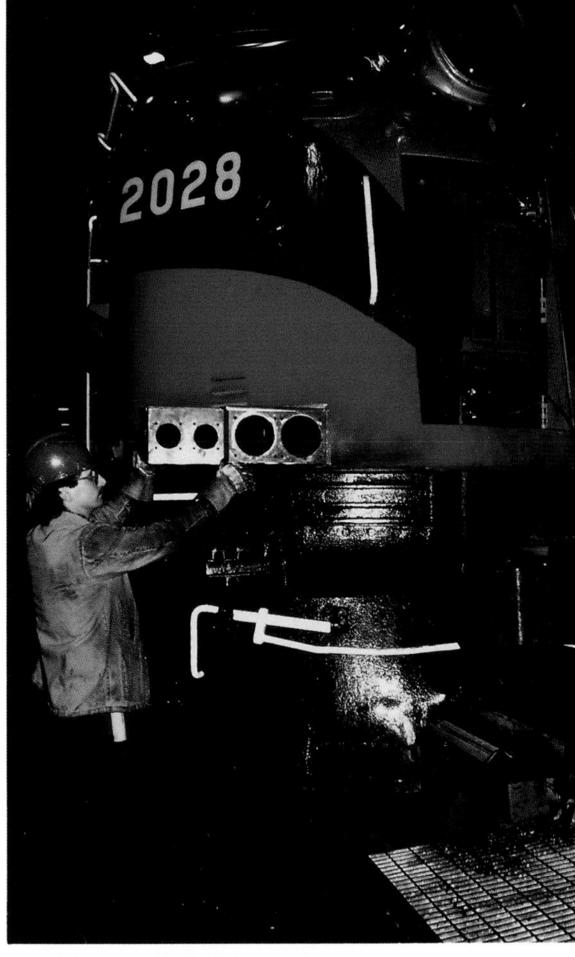

A skilled mechanic services a Hudson Line locomotive at Metro-North's Harmon shop. Photo by Frank English

Metro-North's Harlem and Hudson lines are equipped with electric, multiple-unit passenger cars. Photo by Frank English

Harlem and Hudson lines in 1989. The old third rail was replaced with bigger, heavier rail that reduces power loss between substations. As part of its modernization program, the last old substation, a 1910 holdover at Marble Hill, was replaced in 1989.

Still under way is the restoration of the Park Avenue tunnel, major segments of which are 75 to 150 years old. The project—replacing all four tracks and rebuilding the tunnel roof, which supports Park Avenue—will ensure continued safe, reliable service. The railroad views the $144-million restoration as one of its most important capital projects.

ABOVE: A sleek new station with large expanses of glass serves Croton-Harmon passengers. Photo by William Goidell

Although still in an early stage, the revitalization of Grand Central Terminal is Metro-North's most exciting project. Opened in 1913, the station, with its French beaux-arts and Roman bath architecture, is widely recognized as one of the nation's most significant buildings. It is listed on the National Register of Historic Places.

ABOVE: A statue of Mercury stands atop Grand Central Terminal, which is listed in the National Register of Historic Places. Photo by Frank English

While handling more than 500,000 people each day—100 million each year—the terminal remains underused. That will change as its antiquated infrastructure is replaced and its low-level retail activity is enhanced. Still owned by Penn Central but operated by Metro-North under a lease that runs to 2032, Grand Central will be restored to its original grandeur and function as both civic center and gateway to New York.

At the heart of all Metro-North's plans and programs are its customers. For their immediate benefit, the railroad has improved on-time performance to 90 percent or better. Trains are cleaned more often, and most complaints about lack of heat and air conditioning have been eliminated. To meet its goal of courteous treatment, Metro-North has instituted various training programs for customer-service employees. It monitors progress by having its own employees ride the trains and by periodically seeking passengers' comments.

The service-oriented commuter line adjusts its schedules to customers' needs. It conducts discussions with employers in its service area to ascertain their employee's needs and consults with the Westchester Department of Transportation for such purposes as coordinating trains with county buses. Metro-North also offers special arrangements for customers with cultural and entertainment destinations such as the Bronx Zoo, Caramoor, and Rye Playland.

Metro-North Commuter Railroad plans to intensify efforts to encourage people to leave their cars at home and take the train. This will help relieve congestion and pollution, improving the quality of life for all. Metro-North will also further enhance the region's economic life by making its fast, efficient, high-quality transportation available to growing numbers of residents.

NEW YORK POWER AUTHORITY

ABOVE: The Indian Point 3 Nuclear Power Plant in Buchanan reliably provides economical power to Westchester and outlying areas. Much of its output goes to government agencies in Westchester and New York City to power public buildings, streetlights, and commuter trains.

RIGHT: The Theodore Hill, Jr., Training Center in Buchanan provides state-of-the-art training facilities for staff members at the Indian Point 3 Nuclear Power Plant and other Power Authority sites in southern New York.

The nation's largest nonfederal supplier of public power, the New York Power Authority provides about one-third of all electricity used in New York State. Its 11 generating plants, including two in Westchester County, produce more than 6.8 million kilowatts. It also purchases large amounts of electricity from Canada for its customers' use.

Government agencies in Westchester and New York City are among those customers. Others include municipal electric systems, rural cooperatives, and distribution agencies; private utilities such as Consolidated Edison Co., which resell the electricity without profit; and designated industries.

In serving all those customers, the nonprofit Power Authority addresses its primary mission: to provide low-cost, reliable power for the people of New York State. It is increasingly successful in fulfilling that mission. In the dozen years between 1976 and 1988, the Power Authority saved Westchester and New York City consumers and businesses more than $2 billion. By 1996 savings will climb to $3 billion.

The steps that result in these savings also ensure ample power supplies for the area's growing needs. The Power Authority goes outside the state to look for new sources of power, runs its plants with great efficiency, and initiates conservation efforts with big and small customers alike.

Its transmission line between Marcy, New York, and Quebec, completed in 1978, allows the purchase of additional hydroelectric power. More such power will soon be purchased under the Power Authority's new 21-year contract with Hydro-Quebec, which takes effect in 1995.

Another source of savings is the agreement with Consolidated Edison Co. to create an unprecedented public power franchise area within the utility's service territory. The agreement calls for the Power Authority to supply all the electricity for subway and commuter trains, public buildings, streetlights, and other public facilities in Westchester and New York City through the turn of the century and beyond. Projected savings of $1.4 billion will result in part from the Power Authority's assuming responsibility for future load growth.

The company was created to achieve just such savings in 1931 and was authorized to develop the U.S. share of St. Lawrence River power. But decades of delays followed, and it was not until 1954 that President Dwight D. Eisenhower signed the St. Lawrence Seaway Bill, enabling the original project to get under way. That same year Robert Moses was appointed chairman. Under his leadership, the project, a joint effort with Canada's Ontario Hydro, at last began to move ahead.

"What keeps us going is sheer stubbornness," Moses said as the project began to take shape. "For we are pitting against the rush of a mighty stream, clogged with ice in winter, with little more than audacious brains and brawn, ant-like men and toy machinery, the vaulting ambitions of two democracies." In 1958 the project produced its first power.

By that time a new U.S.-Canada project was under way: the redevelopment of the Niagara River's hydroelectric power potential. Completed in 1961, the Niagara Project can produce 2.4 million kilowatts of electricity in peak periods.

At both the St. Lawrence and Niagara projects, as well as at other centers, the Power Authority has significantly enhanced the surrounding areas with superb facilities for recreation and environmental conservation. These facilities include parks, marinas, beaches, a geological museum, and a performing arts center.

Richard M. Flynn has been Power Authority chairman since June 1985.

In 1974 the Power Authority acquired its first Westchester plant, the 965,000-kilowatt Indian Point 3 Nuclear Plant at Buchanan, which was being built by Consolidated Edison. A second Westchester plant, the 3,000-kilowatt hydroelectric Kensico Project, started producing electricity in 1985.

The Power Authority's nuclear plants, which produce electricity more economically than fossil-fuel plants, are among the nation's best run. Both opened new employee training facilities in 1988, and their programs meet the rigorous standards of the National Academy for Nuclear Training, qualifying the Power Authority for academy membership.

With 1,220 Westchester employees, concentrated at Indian Point and at the White Plains headquarters, the Power Authority takes a hand in a wide variety of community and civic activities. Beneficiaries include volunteer fire departments and ambulance squads, school boards, Little Leagues, Boy Scout and Girl Scout leadership programs, 4-H, Toys for Tots, Jobs for Youth, Big Brothers, Big Sisters, Rotary Clubs, Lions Clubs, and chambers of commerce.

The Power Authority also performs a unique community service—it saves jobs. It has protected 4,600 Westchester jobs by allocating electricity to General Motors, North Tarrytown; Hudson International Conductors, Ossining; Precision Value Corp., Yonkers; and Mearl Corp., Peekskill.

Today, under chairman Richard M. Flynn, the Power Authority is pioneering the restructuring of the utility industry, increasing competition to provide the lowest-possible rates for consumers while averting shortages. At the same time, emphasis is going to conservation, which Flynn believes can lower the nation's total electricity bill for the final eight years of this century by $40 billion to $70 billion, while eliminating the need to build $30 billion to $40 billion worth of additional power plants.

Another Flynn priority is a major expansion of the Niagara Project. On completion in 1998, this will add 330,000 kilowatts to its generating capability, for service to Westchester and other downstate customers. Such activities are what make the New York Power Authority a nationally recognized leader in the electric utility industry.

The New York Power Authority maintains a large headquarters staff in this building in downtown White Plains.

WFAS AM & FM

WFAS staffers take a break in the station's lobby between shows.

WFAS-AM 1230 began in Yonkers as WCOH in the 1920s, but moved to White Plains as WFAS following the Communications Act of 1932. Serving a small market (mostly White Plains and Yonkers), WFAS contented itself with providing local information to the rural population, summer residents, and early suburban migration.

As the population grew, WFAS became best known as Westchester's "Storm Center" station for winter school and business closings. Local news became increasingly vital to this expanding area.

By the 1980s, with Westchester's population over a half-million, WFAS saw the need for a 24-hour news/information/talk format. WFAS is now one of the nation's leading, award-winning, suburban radio stations. With a newsgathering force equaled in size by only three New York City stations, WFAS-AM 1230s news format pulls the four corners of Westchester together.

In addition to news, WFAS' Traffic Network Center produces one of the nation's best traffic reporting systems. Supported by Westchester's exclusive "Eye in the Sky" fixed-wing surveillance airplane, plus a network of 100 other traffic sources, both private and public, the WFAS Traffic Network Center provides the most in-depth and complete traffic and train reports available to the Westchester public.

Local and international news, traffic, weather, and commentary are all hosted by Westchester's top-rated personalities. Locally produced shows cover financial advice, psychology, legal issues, and health problems.

WFAS-FM, Bright 104, has grown to become the leading adult-contemporary music station in Westchester. Since 1986 WFAS-FM has been playing the most familiar adult hits of yesterday and today, and it can now be heard in cars, stores, and offices countywide.

Music is the message on FM, and Bright 104 invested heavily to bring Westchester listeners the most advanced technology possible. The first all-compact-disc station in the New York metro area, WFAS-FM also produces all commercials from a CD production library. The station's state-of-the-art equipment is designed to reproduce the original music precisely.

In addition to superb music and engineering reproduction, Bright 104 benefits from the WFAS news department, the Traffic Network Center, Accuweather, plus a 24-hour lineup of professional disc jockeys.

WFAS AM & FM has also worked hand-in-hand with the business community, helping to sell its goods and services with good marketing strategies and professional commercial production. More than 500 advertisers benefit from WFAS' large listening audiences each year.

Just as important as the profit-making segment of the community is the nonprofit segment. WFAS-AM and Bright 104 FM devote many hours each week promoting hundreds of worthy causes. Whether it is active participation in bike-a-thons on the Bronx River Parkway, 5K runs around Cross County Shopping Center, Day in the Country in Cross River, or just announcing nonprofit events and fund-raising activities, WFAS-AM and Bright 104 FM have contributed more than their fair share of community service to Westchester.

WFAS-AM and Bright 104 FM now reach more than 100,000 adult listeners in Westchester each week, more than most New York City stations. As Westchester continues to develop its own independent social and economic structure, this listenership will continue to grow, and WFAS AM & FM will continue to be a vital information and entertainment center for the "Golden Apple" of New York.

WFAS-AM broadcasts news and information 24 hours per day from this state-of-the-art studio.

Photo by Rich Zila

Photo by Rich Zila

8

MANUFACTURING

Producing and distributing goods for individuals and industry, manufacturing firms provide employment for many Westchester County residents.

J.F. JELENKO & CO.

A leading manufacturer in the dental health industry, J.F. Jelenko & Co., in Armonk, sells a broad range of quality products in the United States and overseas. The company is known for its sophisticated dental alloys and technologically advanced laboratory equipment; it has a dominant share of the U.S. dental-alloy and dental equipment markets. Underlying these impressive figures is Jelenko's commitment to supplying the finest products and customer services available anywhere, a pledge made by founder Jess Jelenko, Sr., in 1912 and honored by his successors to this day.

Jelenko was a 28-year-old salesman of dental alloys when he decided to go into business for himself. His start was modest. Renting a 1,200-square-foot loft at One Union Square in Lower Manhattan, he began making alloys and, with just one salesman, began to sell them locally.

ABOVE: Jess Jelenko, Sr., started with one room, one salesman, and a dream. He built a company that, for more than 77 years, has continued to respond to the needs of the dental health industry.

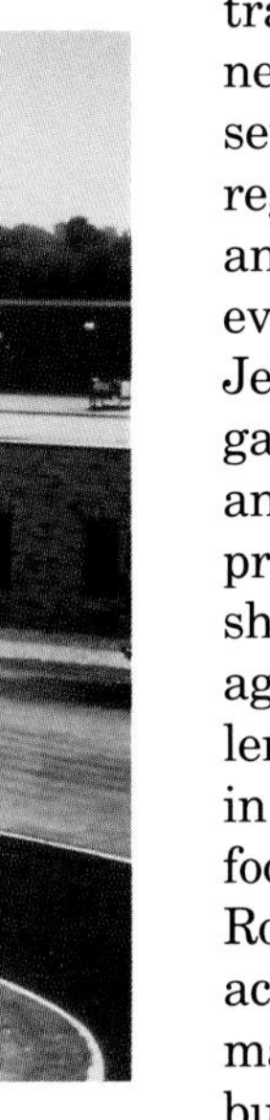

ABOVE: Jelenko's research, manufacturing, warehouse, and general office facilities are all housed under one roof in the Armonk building.

Although business was slow at first, Jelenko's dedication to quality and service eventually paid dividends. By 1927 the company was selling its dental gold alloys nationally, and it moved uptown to 52nd Street, tripling its space. One year later the farsighted founder took two crucial steps. He began to plan for expansion into foreign markets—today a major factor in the business—and he established a research and development function, putting the company in the forefront of the industry's advancing technology. Jelenko owes much of its growth and progress over the years since then to research and development's contributions to alloy manufacturing.

The first major breakthrough came in 1938, when the company introduced an electrical precision casting machine with critical temperature controls. The new Thermotrol Casting Machine revolutionized the process, producing stronger and tougher castings than had ever before been possible and helping to make the name of Jelenko synonymous with dental research and development. Since then the company has followed a steady course of product-line expansion while retaining its lead in technology. It now manufactures 25 different pieces of equipment, including burnout ovens, porcelain furnaces, and hand pieces. A complete dental lab can be outfitted with its equipment line.

In 1948 the Jelenko Education Department was established to train dentists and technicians in new products and techniques. That set the stage for the series of major regional educational symposiums and seminars that are still held every year. Two years later Jess Jelenko, Jr., became president. He gave added emphasis to research and development and educational programs, and, under his leadership, the company prospered, once again outgrowing its quarters. Jelenko moved to Westchester County in 1964, building a 25,000-square-foot, campus-type facility in New Rochelle. The new facility not only accommodated the expansion of manufacturing and administration but also housed a specially designed educational facility, reflecting the firm's professional image.

Four years after the move, the Jelenko family sold the business to Pennwalt Corp., a prominent name in health care. About the same time the company strengthened its international sales department, becoming a growing presence in Canada, where it now has a distribution center, as well as Europe,

Latin America, Southeast Asia, the Middle East, and Far East. On the home front, Jelenko opened new avenues of distribution, initiating direct sales to government, universities, dental dealers and laboratories, and dentists.

Once more, in 1980, growth spurred relocation. In seeking a new and larger site, Jelenko looked to the convenience of its highly valued employees, many of whom lived in lower Westchester's cities. About 70 percent of today's 160 employees are county residents; more than 30 percent have been with the company 10 years or longer. The site selected in Armonk, considered an easy commute, is a 7.5-acre tract on which Jelenko constructed a 75,000-square-foot facility. Its size permits all manufacturing processes to be consolidated under one roof, improving both product availability and quality control.

To design its campus, Jelenko chose educational, not industrial, architects. The idea was that a school-like facility would foster the company's ability to conduct extensive teaching, one of its major functions. In addition to product and process training, Jelenko runs seminars to keep customers abreast of changing techniques and products and opens its doors to various other educational users. Study groups from the dental programs of nearby colleges and professional associations, including the Metropolitan Study Club and the Westchester Dental Society, take advantage of Jelenko's facilities for lectures and practical demonstrations.

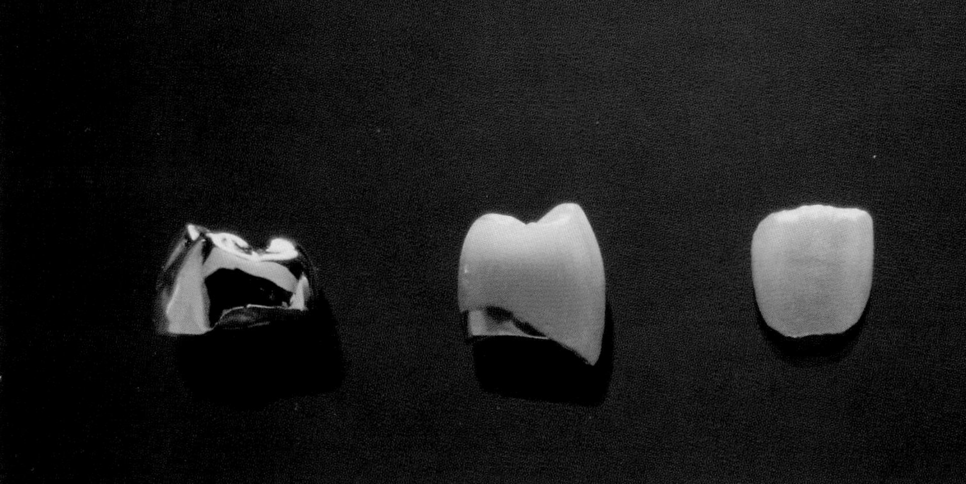

From 1912, when Jelenko entered the dental market with precious metal crowns, to the 1960s, when porcelain applied to metal frameworks was introduced, to the present-day porcelain veneers of cosmetic dentistry, Jelenko is at the forefront of serving the dental health industry.

Jelenko also supports many other community groups, including the County Chamber of Commerce, Inc., the Armonk Fire Department, the Westchester County March of Dimes, and the United Way. With company encouragement, employees engage in various charitable activities, including walk-a-thons, annual baseball games to raise money for Easter Seals, and clothing drives for homeless children.

In 1986 Jelenko was acquired by management and investors committed to the standards of excellence established by the Jelenko family.

To maintain its leadership in the industry, the firm is moving in new directions while continuing to produce dental attachments, porcelain, consumable merchandise, and accessories, as well as 50 different alloys and equipment with microprocessor capabilities. As the dental market becomes increasingly want driven rather than need driven, Jelenko is advancing into the exciting new field of cosmetic dentistry. In September 1988 it acquired controlling interests in two companies engaged in the development and marketing of porcelain veneer systems. These new products offer consumers an easy way to a perfect smile. This new direction for product development exemplifies Jelenko's ongoing determination to be first and best in its field.

Jelenko will continue to lead the way to the future of dental health with cosmetic dentistry by making a "perfect smile" a possibility for everyone.

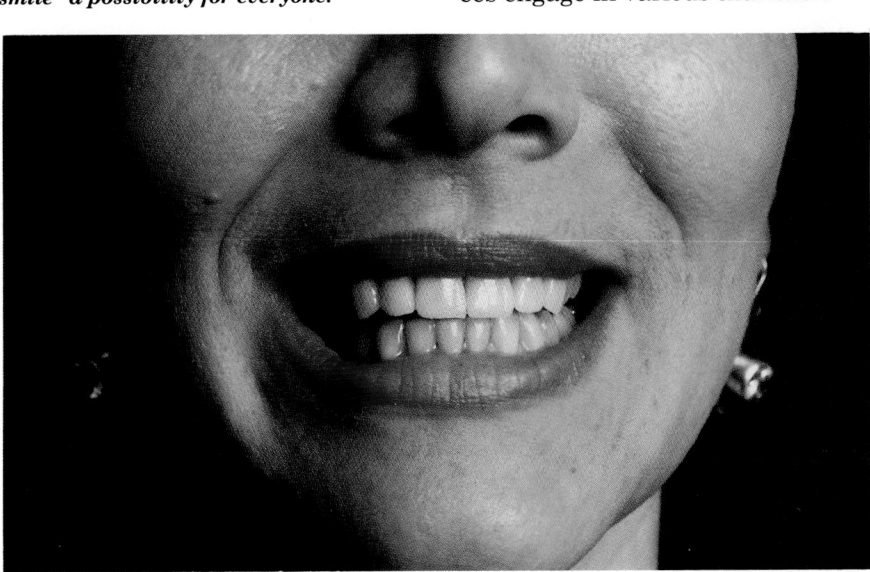

TEXACO INC.

On prominent display at the Harrison headquarters of Texaco Inc. is a seven-foot-high sculpture made out of building blocks. From the front it appears to be simply a rendering of the familiar red "T" inside its star and circle. But closer inspection reveals the words "Ours to Build," while a look at the back of the sculpture shows that each block bears the name of a department and its employees' signatures—nearly 1,300 in all. This sculpture stands as the tangible symbol of the critical role of employees of the newly restructured company.

The new Texaco, a different company from the traditionally centralized old one, has emerged with the solution to problems experienced in the 1980s. Texaco is a long-established multinational corporation with interests in petrochemicals, natural gas, and industrial lubricants and additives as well as oil.

Founded in 1902, The Texas Company made rapid strides in its first decade. It began European operations and extended domestic sales nationwide, adopting "Texaco" as its trademark. In 1911 the firm opened its first gas station, in Brooklyn, New York. After supplying the government's needs through two world wars, Texaco converted to peacetime production and entered a long period of steady growth. The oil crisis of the 1970s redirected that growth, as the company undertook tremendous capital investments to expand and develop the various operations of its worldwide enterprise.

By the 1980s Texaco had made several major acquisitions, worldwide as well as in the United States, and encompassed several operating divisions. But its 1984 purchase of Getty Oil Co. resulted in litigation. Extended by appeals, the litigation threatened to become a roadblock when, in 1987, Texaco decided to settle and get back to business. The restructuring that followed Texaco's settlement included selling foreign and domestic assets, cutting overhead, refocusing its debt management program, and an ongoing process of striving for maximum value and improved profitability.

Today Texaco is a company on the move—more competitive and entrepreneurial than ever before. Operating in some 150 countries and territories, it ranks among the top 10 *Fortune* 500 companies. Texaco can cite a progression of broad achievements over the past few years. They range from reducing debt and improving operating earnings to paying special dividends and completing a successful restructuring of assets.

Coming out of the restructuring, the dynamic new company challenged its employees to perform and found them quick to respond. Front-line employees began to take the calculated and informed risks that lead to enhanced profitability. Employee-driven quality-improvement programs created better products, fostered teamwork, and engendered aggressive marketing plans to win new business.

With their commitment to the creed of "Ours to Build," employees have come to share a vision of Texaco as a competitive leader in the industry, striving to be one of the most admired companies in the nation. Ingrained in the Texaco culture are the values to realize this vision. They include guiding principles as old as the company: quality, customer service, inspired

Quality products and the appealing and convenient System 2000 retail outlets are building sales in the United States and abroad.

Oil-rig platforms, which become second homes to workers on 12-hour shifts, are where Texaco's commitment to excellence begins.

LEFT & RIGHT: The new Texaco and its employees salute each other in this sculpture, unveiled at a company picnic and now permanently installed at the Harrison headquarters.

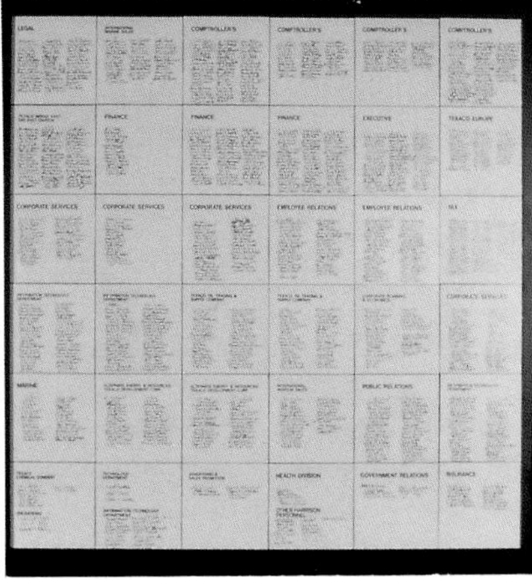

leadership, corporate responsibility, respect for the individual, and high ethical standards.

The values also include business objectives: "To become the leader in our industry, we will concentrate on doing things right the first time, on time, throughout the company; refine superior products, using the best available technology; supply customers with the highest quality, competitively priced products; and conduct our affairs as a good corporate citizen, with concern and respect for the individual and the environment."

The emphasis on good corporate citizenship is widely recognized. Considering that Texaco employees are a major homeowner group in the neighborhood, Texaco tries to improve quality of life by lending its expertise in solving problems of transportation, health, and environment, among other civic concerns. It supports 79 local nonprofit organizations, in addition to United Way, and it is particularly proud of four affiliations.

In a long-standing relationship, Texaco people serve on the Westchester Lighthouse Board and work on various committees. Texaco's support for the Hudson River Museum, which has the county's only public planetarium, permits free admission to the star show one evening per week.

Sponsored by Texaco, the Samaritan Van patrols county highways six hours per day, Monday through Friday, to assist stranded motorists. The driver is an emergency medical technician as well as a skilled mechanic, typically helping more than 400 people each month. Harrison schoolchildren benefit from Texaco's Adopt-a-School effort, which opens up company facilities for tours, provides films and speakers, and sponsors various school activities. The White House has honored Texaco for this program.

A community activist with abundant resources, Texaco makes a variety of far-reaching cultural contributions. In the county, Texaco works with Caramoor on concert broadcasts. Nationwide, the firm is renowned for more than 50 years of sponsoring live radio broadcasts of the Metropolitan Opera's Saturday afternoon performances. Internationally, Texaco is the founding sponsor of the three-year celebration, 1991-1993, of the 500th anniversary of Columbus' discovery of the New World.

Since moving to Westchester in 1977, Texaco has experienced many changes. Today, as a smaller company after the major restructuring, Texaco Inc. puts its faith in progressive vision and quality service, performance, and product.

Texaco's Harrison facility, built on a 107-acre site, is three football fields long and one football field wide.

AIN PLASTICS, INC.

A matchless inventory and dedication to personalized service distinguish Ain Plastics, Inc., Mt. Vernon. Those characteristics, plus a reputation for quality and integrity, have powered Ain's growth from a single small store to the most comprehensive plastics supplier in the United States.

The distributor was founded in Lower Manhattan in 1970 by Norman Drucker and Alex Gabay, who remain president and vice president, respectively. Although neither was experienced in plastics, both were accomplished salesmen. Drucker and Gabay, by choice, still spend most of their time selling as well as managing the company.

Within two years they needed bigger quarters and relocated to Mt. Vernon. When the city began offering low-cost building loans to industry in 1981, Ain was first to respond. It had again outgrown its space, but was reluctant, for its employees' sake, to leave the community. Keeping up morale is a prime company objective, evidenced by its roster of long-term people. With the loan, Ain built a 60,000-square-foot facility and, at the same time, doubled its local work force, now about 70 people.

Offices are on the second floor; the warehouse is on the first. "A lumberyard for plastics," by Drucker's description, the warehouse contains hundreds of items, each stocked in depth to fulfill Ain's promise of immediate availability. Products include plastic sheets, rods, tubes, and film, as well as such accessories as tools, adhesives, and polishes. Ain's catalog runs more than 200 pages; all major manufacturers are represented. A cutting room with state-of-the-art equipment allows the company to meet precise customer specifications. The services also include polishing.

Ain Plastics' headquarters, a sleek white stucco building, contains 1.5 acres of floor space.

Ain's customers include businesses, industry, schools, arts institutions, the professions, and the military. Its 10 service centers nationwide, in addition to Westchester, are located in New York, New York; Norwood, Massachusetts; Lancaster, Pennsylvania; Norfolk, Virginia; Chicago, Illinois; Southfield, Michigan; and Santa Clara, Berkeley, and Santa Fe Springs, California. Some of them specialize: The Michigan branch is geared to serving the automobile industry; the Virginia branch serves the U.S. Navy. The Westchester operation has a broader customer base, including many *Fortune* 500 companies, but finds display makers—department stores, museums, and theaters—are among its major buyers.

The same concern Ain shows for its customers and employees extends to the community. The company supports such Mt. Vernon services as the police and fire departments and the schools. Ain also contributes to the American Cancer Society, among other causes, and makes in-kind donations to various nonprofit groups.

Ain Plastics, Inc., is determined to be everyone's plastic supplier by offering the best products and service available. Looking forward to continued growth, it plans to open five more distribution outlets.

LEFT & RIGHT: The warehouse stocks vast quantities of plastics in rod, tube, and sheet forms used in a variety of applications.

UNION CARBIDE CORPORATION

Since moving into Westchester County in the 1950s, Union Carbide Corporation has become a highly valued corporate citizen. Its Tarrytown Technical Center employs more than 600 scientists, engineers, and technicians who are engaged in product and process research, development, and technical service in support of three corporate units. These units, Linde Industrial Gases, Specialty Chemicals, and UOP, supply sophisticated products and systems to a wide variety of industries worldwide.

ABOVE: Research and development on silicones is carried out in this modern, glass and steel building.

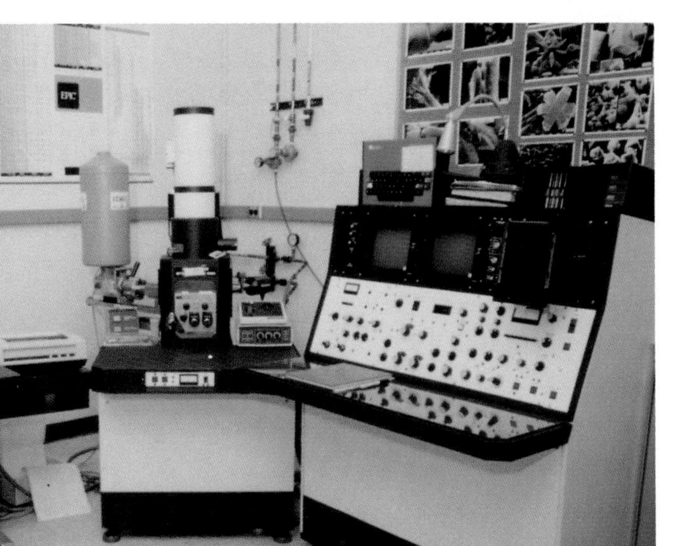

ABOVE: Analytical lab equipment is state of the art at Union Carbide's Tarrytown Technical Center.

Union Carbide's Linde Industrial Gases operation is one of the three largest worldwide. Its main products are oxygen, nitrogen, and argon, which are separated from the air and purified. Specialty Chemicals is recognized as an international leader in the technology, manufacturing, and marketing of silicone fluids, surfactants, and organo-functional silanes. UOP, established in 1988 as a joint venture with Allied-Signal Inc., provides catalysts, adsorbents, molecular sieves, and technical and engineering products, processes, and design services to the oil, gas, and energy industries.

On the cutting edge of technology in all these areas, Union Carbide traces its roots back to 1892, when Thomas L. Willson and Major James T. Morehead produced calcium carbide while trying to make aluminum in an electric furnace. In 1898 Union Carbide Company was formed to manufacture calcium carbide. It became Union Carbide Corporation in 1917, after acquiring the Linde Air Products Company.

Today Union Carbide, headquartered in Danbury, Connecticut, is an $8.5-billion corporation with 44,000 employees worldwide and customers in more than 100 countries. In 1989 the firm reorganized, forming a holding company that kept the corporate name and several subsidiaries. According to chairman Robert D. Kennedy, the reorganization was designed "to give our business leadership maximum flexibility and a clear view of strategic options, and permit them to focus on their external competitive environments."

In Tarrytown, Union Carbide is known as a good neighbor. Many employees are active in United Way; one is a former president. Employees who belong to company rescue squads tend to carry over their experience to their home communities, often serving as volunteer firefighters and emergency medical technicians.

In 1988 Union Carbide sold its buildings and 275 acres to Keren Developments Inc., leasing back 400,000 square feet in a lease that runs to the end of the century. Union Carbide also retained a 25 percent share in any new development on the site, beginning with the 450 condominium units and 2 million square feet of office space to be built in the 1990s. That assures Union Carbide Corporation, an established Westchester company, a long-term future in the county.

SAFE FLIGHT INSTRUMENT CORPORATION

Many of the products that make flying safe today were originated by Safe Flight Instrument Corporation, White Plains. The company's long list of inventions begins with the product it was launched to market, the stall-warning indicator, developed by Leonard M. Greene in 1946. Greene, whose scientific background extends to chemistry, physics, and aeronautics, had witnessed an airplane accident caused by stall and realized the pilot had never known he was in danger. Greene's invention made sure that need not happen again.

Since the 1950s the device has been standard equipment for aircraft worldwide. Greene was recognized for the achievement by the Flight Safety Foundation, which presented him with its first Air Safety Award. He was honored again in 1983, during Westchester's tricentennial celebration, when the stall-warning indicator was named one of the 10 outstanding engineering achievements in the county's history.

Many more inventions and honors have marked Greene's tenure as president of the company he founded. His more than 60 patents for aviation and related technology include automatic throttle systems, landing and approach indicators, and wind shear warning and recovery guidance devices. The wind shear protection equipment, invented by Greene in 1975 and fine-tuned by him over the years, will become mandatory for all U.S. air transport-type aircraft in 1992, under a Federal Aviation Administration directive.

Safe Flight's entire product line consists of equipment to improve the safety and performance of all types of fixed-wing aircraft—general aviation, corporate, commercial, and military. The firm's customers include the majority of the world's aircraft manufacturers, more than 50 airlines, many operators of corporate jet aircraft, and all the U.S. armed forces.

Thanks to the dedication of Safe Flight's employees, the company is a leader in quality as well as technology. Both government and industry attest to that. In 1982 the firm received the Department of Defense's Award for Quality Excellence. One year later an unprecedented second Quality Excellence Award was presented to Safe Flight by the Pentagon—no company had ever before received the

***RIGHT:* Leonard M. Greene, founder and president of Safe Flight Instrument Corporation.**

***BELOW:* The award-winning landscape design of Safe Flight's modern headquarters in White Plains enhances the company's working environment.**

Electronic assembly and in-line inspection proceed with meticulous care in Safe Flight's clean, well-lighted computer production area.

award for two years running. Also in 1982 Safe Flight won the Small Business Administration's designation as Prime Contractor of the Year in its region of New York, New Jersey, Puerto Rico, and the Virgin Islands.

Its emphasis on quality control continues to attract notice. In 1989 the McDonnell Douglas Corp. invited Safe Flight to join its exclusive Total Quality Supplier Team Program. Fewer than three dozen of McDonnell Douglas' hundreds of suppliers have earned a place in this program, which gives suppliers final responsibility for their own product quality.

Greene views Safe Flight's success as a function of his employees' dedication. For them, he has established a unique physical and psychological working environment. The premises, well lighted and ventilated, are fitted with the latest in ergonomically designed work benches. All areas where electrostatically sensitive devices are handled are equipped with such protective devices as wrist straps, mats, and shielded bags.

Since Greene is reluctant to terminate employees, the company does not staff up for major contracts. Instead, it hires part-time workers. Safe Flight also makes special efforts to employ the handicapped and to facilitate careers for older workers. Greene does not believe in mandatory retirement. When he learned that a large area employer was insisting on early retirements, Safe Flight ran advertisements inviting applications from those forced out. Such activities have won him a variety of honors. Among them, he has been nominated for New York State Employer of the Year, cited by the New York State Governor's Committee to Employ the Handicapped, and commended by the Secretary of the U.S. Department of Health, Education, and Welfare.

Greene's concern extends to the community and the nation. The Institute for Socioeconomic Studies, which he founded in the early 1970s, conducts seminars on major policy issues, attracting the participation of outstanding international figures. Closer to home, Greene has served on the boards of the Blythedale Children's Hospital and the Urban League of Westchester. He also cofounded the Corporate Angel Network, which coordinates the travel needs of cancer patients with the flight plans of corporate aircraft. Greene personally piloted the program's first flight, in 1981, and its 1,000th flight five years later. For these activities, too, he has been recognized, with such honors as the Distinguished Service Award of the Human Rights Commission of White Plains and the Albert Gallatin Award for Civic Leadership in the northeastern states.

Safe Flight's gifts to the community often focus on family- and child-oriented activities. The company has made significant contributions to the Hudson River Museum of Westchester and, in 1989, underwrote the costs of free Sunday admission to the museum for children under 12 years of age. "As a local firm of long standing, Safe Flight has a particular interest in local cultural resources. Admission to the Hudson River Museum is part of the benefits package we offer our employees, to make living in Westchester County more enjoyable to them and their families," says Greene.

From its beginnings in a one-room schoolhouse on Russell Street to its present status as a 150-employee company with spacious new quarters, Safe Flight Instrument Corporation has produced aviation safety and performance equipment to the highest standards. It remains an innovative company, oriented to research and development, and continues to explore new instrumentation concepts that will find their place in tomorrow's aircraft.

CIBA-GEIGY CORPORATION

CIBA-GEIGY Corporation, headquartered in Ardsley, is a leading developer and manufacturer of agricultural and specialty chemicals, pharmaceuticals, dyes, plastics, and vision-care products. It is a wholly owned subsidiary of CIBA-GEIGY Limited in Basel, Switzerland, the seventh-largest chemical company in the world.

CIBA-GEIGY had its beginnings in 1758 when Johann Rudolph Geigy started the Geigy Chemical Corporation in Basel, Switzerland, a company that traded in the colonial goods of the day. CIBA, an acronym for the Society of Chemical Industry in Basel, was established a century later.

The Geigy Chemical Corporation moved to Ardsley from its Manhattan headquarters in 1956. It was the second major corporation to relocate to Westchester County. In 1970 CIBA Corporation and the Geigy Chemical Corporation merged, creating CIBA-GEIGY Corporation.

CIBA-GEIGY's corporate headquarters is located on a 60-acre site in Ardsley. Its 11 buildings house research facilities and administrative offices for the Pharmaceuticals, Plastics, Pigments, and Additives divisions, as well as for corporate staff. In 1980 the corporation expanded to Hawthorne, where the Additives, Pigments, and Plastics divisions, in addition to several corporate departments, currently reside. Together, CIBA-GEIGY's Ardsley and Hawthorne sites have approximately 1,300 employees.

CIBA-GEIGY has 17,000 employees nationwide. Besides the one in Ardsley, major research and manufacturing facilities are located in Suffern, New York; Greensboro, North Carolina; Summit, New Jersey; Atlanta, Georgia; McIntosh, Alabama; and St. Gabriel, Louisiana.

CIBA-GEIGY is at the forefront of scientific innovation. The corporation is a leader in the research and development of psychothera-

ABOVE: A technician conducts tests on turbine oils with CIBA-GEIGY additives in a research facility at the corporation's Ardsley, New York, site.

BELOW: CIBA-GEIGY's corporate headquarters in Ardsley, New York.

peutic drugs to treat mental depression and obsessive compulsive disorder. CIBA-GEIGY's Voltaren (diclofenac sodium) is one of the most widely prescribed antiarthritics in the world. CIBA Vision Corporation, a subsidiary of CIBA-GEIGY Corporation, manufactures and markets soft contact lenses and a wide range of vision care products for consumers. The corporation's specialty chemicals serve important segments of the industrial and consumer markets. CIBA-GEIGY dyes add color to fabrics, and its agricultural products strengthen food production worldwide.

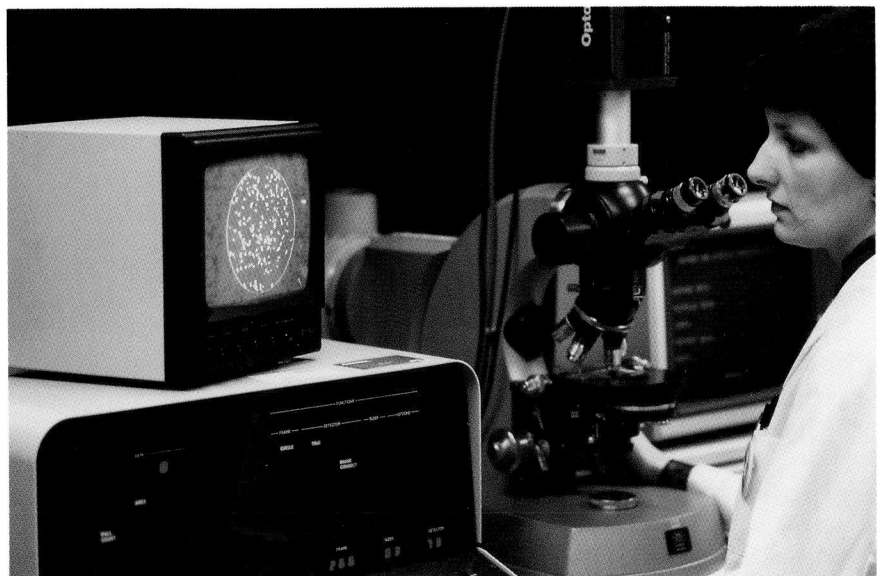

***ABOVE:** An image analyzer is used by a scientist in CIBA-GEIGY's Pharmaceuticals Division to study cells that contribute to joint inflammation in patients with arthritis.*

***BELOW:** Scientists from CIBA-GEIGY's Additives Division work together to create products for the plastics, coatings, and oil industries.*

CIBA-GEIGY also reaches out to the community. It is a major supporter of the United Way, the Westchester County Council for the Arts, the New Orchestra of Westchester, and the Philharmonia Virtuosi. CIBA-GEIGY's Volunteer Council organizes food drives, craft fairs, and holiday gift drives for Westchester's needy. Employees also volunteer at many charitable organizations, including the St. Cabrini Nursing Home and Children's Village.

CIBA-GEIGY recognizes the importance of education and has developed a variety of programs with professional and educational organizations in Westchester to provide students with valuable work experience.

The company is an active participant in the Yonkers School and Business Alliance Mentoring Program. Over a six-week period, high school juniors meet with CIBA-GEIGY employees to learn about careers in science, business, art, and computers. The firm's Westchester facility has a three-month summer college research assistantship program that enables students from local colleges to work with scientists in the laboratory. The company also has a summer intern program for high school seniors. Both programs provide students with valuable laboratory experience.

The corporation also sponsors the Natural Sciences Student Symposium at the State University of New York at Purchase. This event gives outstanding students in the school's natural sciences division the opportunity to present their senior theses before an audience of professors and community members. In addition, CIBA-GEIGY has provided support to several colleges in Westchester County, including Iona and Pace University.

CIBA-GEIGY's interest in the arts is portrayed through its corporate art collection. Since its inception in 1959, the collection has grown to more than 500 works, consisting primarily of pieces from artists of the New York School of Abstract Expressionism. The majority of the collection is exhibited at the Ardsley site, with several major works at other CIBA-GEIGY facilities. The collection has helped make CIBA-GEIGY a three-time recipient of the Business in the Arts Award. The corporation has also acquired a noteworthy collection of Swiss posters representing the culture, products, and landscapes of Switzerland from 1900 to the present.

As a diverse, research-oriented company, CIBA-GEIGY Corporation touches the lives of nearly everyone. It strives to meet society's changing needs through the discovery of new products and the creation of novel uses for existing products.

AEROTECH WORLD TRADE CORP.

A high-technology company with an entrepreneurial flair, Aerotech World Trade Corp. is an aerospace marketing and distribution company headquarted in Purchase, New York. Aerotech was created to serve as a vital export link between aviation/aerospace-related manufacturers and the international marketplace.

The company's marketing and distribution expertise is found in the following key areas: airline aftermarket spare parts, high-technology systems and components for new commercial and military aircraft, ground support equipment, airport systems engineering, and helicopter SAR equipment and accessories.

Aerotech is a family-owned and operated business, founded in January 1976 by Berg and Jan Endresen, a father and son team. Today, Jan R. Endresen, president and chief executive officer of Aerotech, is actively involved in the company's day-to-day business. Bergthor Endresen is chairman of the board, and Christopher Endresen, Jan's brother, is a product manager. But it is not only the Endresens who are family—Jan Endresen's management style encourages all employees to share the family feeling.

Aerotech's initial staff consisted of 20 employees, many of whom are still working for the Endresen family, and today the company has more than 130 employees worldwide. Technical sales offices are located in Italy, Germany, Holland, France, Israel, the United Kingdom, Portugal, Singapore, and the United States. The underlying business strategy of successfully integrating experienced professionals with superior product lines throughout specified regions around the world continues to give Aerotech the leading edge over the competition.

Success came rather rapidly for Aerotech. The company's sales climbed from $4 million in 1976 to in excess of $100 million in 1989. Key financial investments and acquisitions continue to expand Aerotech's resources and increase market share in key areas of the business. The acquisition of Aviquipo Inc. positioned the company as the number-two airline aftermarket spare-parts supplier. A vertical integration move to invest in a key manufacturer secured an exclusive international distributorship for Aerotech. Other acquisitions and financial investments the company is currently pursuing will increase the company's product offerings, expand the staff of highly qualified sales engineers, and give Aerotech penetration into key market regions worldwide, including a new joint venture in Beijing and new initiatives into Eastern Europe and the USSR.

BELOW & RIGHT: ***Aerotech's headquarters is in a wooded country setting adjacent to the Westchester County Airport.***

Aerotech is the recipient of several awards as a result of the company's achievements. In 1983 the company was honored with the Department of Commerce "E" award for excellence in exports. In 1990, as a result of its continuous export expansion efforts, Aerotech received the President's "E Star" award. Jan Endresen accepted the award from President George Bush at a White House Rose Garden ceremony.

Many employees take part in various civic activities, led by Jan Endresen, whose own activities include the Westchester County

World Trade Club, the New York District Export Council, a Department of Commerce appointment, and the board of trustees of Rye County Day School.

Looking ahead, Jan Endresen sees "extraordinary opportunities" with no change in the ambience that keeps turnover at Aerotech very low. "As Aerotech grows," he says, "the definition of the company may change to fit the needs of the market, but we will do our best to preserve the character that has defined Aerotech."

UNIVERSAL VOLTRONICS CORPORATION

This computer-controlled instrumentation and control system was designed by UVC for fusion energy research applications.

Serving both science and industry, Universal Voltronics Corporation designs and manufactures high-voltage power conversion systems, modulators, and related equipment. Its early products played a fundamental part in the development of the CAT scanner. Its newest products are changing the nature of open-heart surgery as well as furthering the superconducting super-collider project.

The company's start, in 1960, was modest. It opened on the second floor of a small loft building in downtown White Plains. Nine years later, when the loft was torn down to make way for The Galleria, UVC relocated to Mt. Kisco, constructing its own building in Radio Circle. A 1975 expansion doubled the size of the building, reflecting company growth.

The high voltage X-ray power supply system, which UVC produced for the CAT scanner, was its main product for a number of years. "We were the only company that could meet the exacting requirements demanded by manufacturers of medical imaging equipment," says Barry Ressler, who has been chairman and chief executive officer since 1983. Today the UVC system is displayed at the Smithsonian Institution's Museum of Natural History in Washington, as part of a permanent exhibit of the world's first whole-body CAT scanner.

The firm moved into fusion-energy research when CAT-scan installations declined. It has installed high-voltage fusion systems at many institutions, including Oak Ridge, Los Alamos, and Lawrence Livermore national laboratories, and it has won praise from the Department of Energy and its prime contractors. Overseas installations include Culham Laboratory in England, Fontenay Aux Roses in France, and JAERI in Japan. UVC is active as part of an international fusion energy consortium, including the USSR, Japan, Western Europe, and the United States, with the goal of developing a fusion energy experimental reactor. During the initial phase of this program,UVC delivered power supplies to the Lawrence Berkeley Laboratory in California and the Garching Laboratory in West Germany. In April 1990 UVC was awarded a contract from a laboratory in the United Kingdom to extend the injection voltage level for this project.

UVC's major products also include components of surgical lasers, airport security systems, particle accelerators, and various Department of Defense devices. Its work for a leading supplier of surgical carbon-dioxide lasers is a key component of a radical new way to treat heart patients.

In its community the company is especially active in United Way and the public schools. In a 1990 commendation, which was followed by an award, United Way cited Universal Voltronics Corporation for its "continuing commitment to improving the quality of life in our community." A participant in the Mt. Kisco schools' Shadow Program, the firm is host to high-school students who spend a few days "shadowing" a department manager to get an idea of what work is like.

"Since 1960," says Ressler, "UVC has addressed a range of medical, scientific, industrial, and defense applications unmatched by another company in our industry. We look forward to the new challenges, new applications, and the exciting years ahead."

TOP: This Universal Voltronics system generates more than a half-million volts of precision-pulsed power for use with free-electron laser research projects conducted for the U.S. Navy and Air Force.

BELOW: UVC built this high-energy storage capacitor bank for the Department of Energy's Lawrence Livermore National Laboratory mirror fusion project.

Photo by Rich Zila

9

BUSINESS AND PROFESSIONS

Greater Westchester County's professional community brings a wealth of service, ability, and insight to the area.

THE COUNTY CHAMBER OF COMMERCE, INC.

The only nationally accredited business organization in Westchester, The County Chamber of Commerce, Inc., is also the area's largest broad-based business group. It has been an outspoken advocate of orderly growth for more than 75 years, convinced that such growth is the engine that drives the economy.

Tracing its roots back to 1904, when its ancestor, the White Plains Board of Trade, was established, the organization went through a series of mergers and name changes over the years until, on March 18, 1981, it adopted its present name and format. The County Chamber states its purpose in a formal mission statement: "To advance the economic vitality, development, orderly community growth, and expansion interests of the Westchester County community."

In fulfilling that mission, the chamber initiates a variety of projects, provides a raft of services, and works closely with some 25 specialized agencies. Ongoing projects include support for affordable housing, for which the chamber has developed a comprehensive action plan, and transportation improvements, especially the reconstruction and expansion of the Cross Westchester Expressway (Interstate 287) and implementation of the Westchester County Airport Master Plan.

Encouraging new business investments, the County Chamber annually provides economic, demographic, and market information to several thousand local and outside companies. To enhance the growth opportunities for existing businesses, the chamber offers a series of networking, exposure, and referral programs. More than 10,000 businesspeople take part in these

LEFT: The offices of The County Chamber of Commerce, Inc., are situated in the central business district of the city of White Plains, the Westchester County government seat.

BELOW: The County Chamber's Area and Economic Development councils are presented a proposal for the development of a $120-million mixed-use office complex in the city of White Plains, a partnership venture between a private developer and one of the city's churches.

programs every year.

Chamber services begin with its magazine, *Westchester Commerce*. The monthly magazine is filled with substantive business articles and contains news of local people and companies as well as timely and special editorial features on pertinent business news, issues, and actions.

The chamber also sponsors special events. In addition to regular seminars and networking functions, the organization's premier event is the business-to-business Westfair Office 2000, an annual trade fair that qualifies as a "complete business shopping center under one roof."

Widening its influence, the chamber works with colleges and universities in the Westchester community; county groups, such as the Westchester Department of Social Services and the Westchester Library System; job councils, including Jobtrac-Westchester Private Industry Council and Senior Personnel Employment Council; and national business groups, including the U.S. Department of Commerce, the Small Business Administration, and the Chamber of Commerce of the United States.

Looking ahead, The County Chamber of Commerce, Inc., plans to continue its emphasis on area development, concentrating on waste-disposal planning and land use; environment, energy, and water resources; as well as housing and transportation. It will also continue to address economic development and small business affairs while reinforcing its affiliate relationships with such groups as the White Plains Chamber of Commerce, Roundtable on Westchester Health Care, Westchester Convention and Visitors Bureau, Ltd., S.C.O.R.E., and Building Owners and Managers Association of Westchester County, Inc.

***RIGHT:** County Chamber of Commerce members are given the opportunity to attend many business networking programs and receptions each year.*

***BELOW:** Business leaders from around Westchester County gather at one of the many special program luncheons and dinners sponsored by various County Chamber entities each year.*

TRANSAMERICA LEASING

Nearly as old as its industry, Transamerica Leasing of White Plains celebrated its 25th anniversary in 1988. The company, the world's largest lessor of multimodal transportation equipment, had its best year ever in that anniversary year, but it easily surpassed its own record in the next 12 months, with an 83 percent increase in operating income.

Transamerica Leasing is the industry's high-service specialist. Part of the $30-billion Transamerica Corporation, Transamerica Leasing is the descendant of Integrated Container Service, founded in 1963. The corporate name was changed to Transamerica Leasing in 1988. At the same time the company's three operating units, each a leader in its industry, were renamed. One unit leases containers and chassis to the steamship industry worldwide through 21 offices and 322 depots in 48 countries. The company offers a diversified inventory of equipment—marine cargo containers and chassis—built to its own strict specifications, and it continues to develop new products and services to meet its customers' needs.

Transamerica's trailer leasing units, among the nation's largest providers of lease and rental over-the-road trailers, has a fleet of more than 20,000 trailers, available in all configurations. A coast-to-coast network of 45 branch locations manages the fleet while more than 1,300 authorized locations provide service and repairs. In addition to leasing trailers, the firm is a pacesetter in supplying financing for customers who prefer to own instead of lease their equipment.

***ABOVE:* Transamerica Leasing equipment being loaded on a vessel in the Finnish port of Kotka.**

***LEFT:* Transamerica trailers are a familiar sight on the roads of the United States and Europe.**

A third Transamerica unit, one of the country's largest lessors of rail (intermodal) trailers and domestic containers, operates more geographic pools than any other lessor, making it easy for customers to pick up and drop off equipment in many locations within the United States. It also maintains an interchange system, which includes both rail and water carriers and helps minimize shipment delays.

Through these three units Transamerica Leasing seeks out opportunities to apply its expertise and resources to changing market conditions. For international freight movement it provides multimodal services that enable goods to move expeditiously from origin to destination via ship, rail, or highway. Within the United States it also helps achieve transportation efficiency through the provision of chassis pools and new-technology domestic containers.

In addition to its main business of leasing equipment, Transamerica Leasing manages other investors' equipment and expects a significant portion of its growth to come from new management agreements. The company's first major container fleet-management arrangement, with NIC Leasing, Japan's largest container leasing company, was so successful that it was soon followed by a second, with the New Zealand Meat Producers' Board. The board took advantage of Transamerica Leasing's proven management expertise and financial strength to complete a deal of its own—a unique multimillion-dollar containers-for-meat counter trade agreement with Poland.

The arrangement benefited all parties. "Transamerica provided the New Zealand group with a creative solution to the problem of trading with nations strapped for convertible currency," explains president Charles E. Tingley.

In its own community, Transamerica Leasing, which moved from New York City to Westchester County in 1985, is active in a variety of projects. In addition to regular blood drives, holiday toy drives are organized for needy and handicapped children. Children living in welfare hotels and shelters also gain from programs launched by Transamerica Leasing employees and assisted by the company. In 1986 several employees got together to buy school wardrobes for 10 homeless children. Each year more employees joined in, outfitting 120 children in 1988. With the assistance of the firm's legal department, the group has organized as a nonprofit, tax-exempt corporation, Back-to-School Clothes for Kids, and it expects to double the number of children it serves. A $5,000 contribution from Transamerica Leasing in 1989 put the campaign on target.

The company is also a major backer of performing arts groups in the region, including the internationally known New York City Opera and American Ballet Theatre. For more than a decade the opera company has stored and transported its costumes and sets in trailers leased from Transamerica, which returns the lease payments as donations, amounting to more than $100,000 annually.

Transamerica Leasing's economic contribution to the community takes many forms, starting with the 400 full-time jobs it provides. In addition, it offers valuable summer internships in its finance and legal departments to graduating university students. The program, begun when the company was still in New York City, now benefits local students and gives participants an edge in launching their careers in business and finance. They work part time during the school year and full time in the summer; some stay with the firm after graduation.

With an outstanding track record and a dedicated staff, including many long-term employees, Transamerica Leasing is committed to being the standard by which others in the industry are measured.

LEFT: Transamerica piggyback (intermodal) trailers are loaded onto a double-stack train in Cicero, Illinois.

BELOW: A 20-foot refrigerated cargo container. Transamerica Leasing has a significant presence in this specialized equipment area.

JACKSON, LEWIS, SCHNITZLER & KRUPMAN

Since 1958 Jackson, Lewis, Schnitzler & Krupman has counseled and represented clients in the increasingly complex field of labor, human resource, employment law, and litigation. Over that period it has become the preeminent U.S. law firm engaged exclusively in this practice.

Guided by the principles of preventive labor relations, Jackson, Lewis attorneys counsel both unionized and nonunion clients to resolve employment relations problems before they result in grievances, union organizing, governmental agency proceedings, or employment litigation. The firm's objective is to avoid the costly defense of employment-related complaints and the unproductive diversion of management time and energy. Should such defense become necessary, however, Jackson, Lewis is fully equipped to handle all aspects of litigation and administrative agency proceedings.

The Jackson, Lewis preventive approach assists clients in complying with the wide array of federal, state, and local labor and employment laws and regulations while maintaining management's right to take effective employee-relations actions.

Committed to the concept of client education and management development, Jackson, Lewis strives to keep clients and their management representatives informed of new developments. It uses in-house presentations, area conferences, and annual symposia and conferences as well as monthly newsletters and special bulletins. *Winning NLRB Elections: Management's Strategy and Preventive Programs* is a leading text written by members of the firm and reflects its commitment to a preventive practice.

Started in New York City, Jackson, Lewis expanded to White Plains to effectively serve its growing clientele in Westchester and the mid-Hudson area as well as in Fairfield County, Connecticut. In September 1981 managing partner Patrick L. Vaccaro opened a small office with six attorneys in the Sears Plaza Building. By 1990 the professional staff had grown to 24, and the Westchester location had become one of the firm's largest and most active regional offices. Standing alone, it is considered the largest labor and employment law firm between New York City and the Canadian border.

In addition to providing legal services to many county corporations, Jackson, Lewis is committed to the continuing growth and development of the community. For many years the firm has served as labor and employment law counsel to the Westchester County Chamber of Commerce. As a member of the chamber's board of directors, Vaccaro has been an active participant in the planning, direction, and leadership of the business group's activities.

Just as Jackson, Lewis, Schnitzler & Krupman supports the communities of its other regional offices—Boston; Washington, D.C.; Atlanta; Chicago; San Francisco; Los Angeles; Jericho, New York; Morristown, New Jersey; Greenville, South Carolina; and Pittsburgh—the firm will continue to make its White Plains office the hub of activity for client and community service and development in Westchester.

The professional staff of the White Plains office of Jackson, Lewis, Schnitzler & Krupman.

Photo by Rich Zila

Photo by Linda Zila

10

QUALITY OF LIFE

Medical and educational institutions contribute to the quality of life of Westchester County area residents. Southern Westchester Board of Cooperative Educational Services, 162; Empire Blue Cross and Blue Shield, 163; Yonkers General Hospital, 164; Saint Joseph's Medical Center, 164; St. John's Riverside Hospital, 165; Pace University, 166; College of New Rochelle, 167; United Hospital Medical Center, 168; New York Medical College, 170

SOUTHERN WESTCHESTER BOARD OF COOPERATIVE EDUCATIONAL SERVICES

The Board of Cooperative Educational Services is a pooling of resources that meets hundreds of the common educational needs of local school districts.

Southern Westchester BOCES, one of 41 BOCES in New York State, serves 35 local districts in a 184-square-mile area. Thirty-two of these districts are component members, participating in specific BOCES programs and services on a cost-sharing basis. They are eligible for special state aid to reimburse them for approximately 50 percent of their expenditures on BOCES services. The other three districts are non-components, paying a surcharge to use some BOCES services, and are ineligible for state aid.

The central administrative offices of Southern Westchester BOCES are in Rye Brook, but other offices are spread throughout southern and central Westchester County.

Culinary Arts is one of 17 program areas for high-school students at the Mid-Western Center for Occupational Education, a division of Southern Westchester BOCES located in Valhalla, New York. Adults can also attend daytime and evening career training programs at BOCES and choose from about 70 continuing education courses in fall, winter, spring, and summer terms.

The Mid-Westchester Occupational Education Center, Valhalla, offers varied programs for high-school students, a continuing education program for adults, and a complete career-training program.

The Instructional Services Division in Elmsford plans enrichment activities for students from many local districts. It also coordinates dozens of staff and professional development programs for school personnel.

The Regional Information (computer) Center, Elmsford, serves 63 school districts in three counties with comprehensive technological support for managerial and instructional use.

BOCES provides unique special education instructional programs for disabled students with multiple handicaps, autism, hearing impairment, learning disabilities, or emotional difficulties. Most classes meet locally, although severely disabled students up to age 21 attend the BOCES Rye Lake Campus, North White Plains.

BOCES' assessment and intervention services include evaluations on referral of handicapped and nonhandicapped students. The Interscholastic Athletics Department annually schedules more than 15,000 contests for about 80 school districts in Westchester, Putnam, and Rockland counties. The Transportation Department brings students to and from BOCES program sites.

Several dynamic BOCES programs focus on students at risk of not completing high school. At the Regional Alternative High School, students learn to achieve educational and personal goals in a setting of consistency, support, and encouragement. The Teenage Pregnancy/Parenting Program provides full days of academic and vocational courses for young mothers and a child-care center for their children. West-Prep, an academic treatment program, serves students with chemical dependency problems. The Incarcerated Youth Program enables students to work toward high school diplomas in BOCES classrooms at the Westchester County Correctional Facility.

The Regional Information Center of Southern Westchester BOCES provides computer services for school information management and student instruction to 62 school districts in Westchester, Putnam, and Rockland counties. BOCES offers programs for students of all ages, as well as for teachers and school administrators, in areas that also include Special Education and Instructional Services.

The business of BOCES is to make education work better for people of all ages. Southern Westchester Board of Cooperative Education Services has a $54-million annual budget, a farsighted governing board, and more than 800 talented employees who are committed to excellence and cooperation in education.

EMPIRE BLUE CROSS AND BLUE SHIELD

Empire Blue Cross and Blue Shield, the nation's largest private, not-for-profit health insurance company, serves 10 million policyholders under various programs, providing hospital and/or basic medical, major medical, dental, prescription drug, Health Maintenance Organization, and Medicare Supplemental benefits.

Empire Blue Cross and Blue Shield was formed in 1985 through the merger of Blue Cross and Blue Shield of Greater New York and Blue Cross of Northeastern New York. Today the organization serves the 28 eastern counties of New York State, which include the five boroughs of New York City, Nassau, Suffolk, Westchester, Rockland, Orange, Putnam, Dutchess, Ulster, Sullivan, Columbia, Greene, Delaware, Rensselaer, Albany, Schoharie, Schenectady, Montgomery, Saratoga, Fulton, Washington, Warren, Essex, and Clinton.

The organization's roots go back to the early 1930s, when medical care for the working classes was infrequent and expensive. After study by the United Hospital Fund and other hospital groups and health experts, legislation for a group hospital plan was passed in 1934. By the following year the Associated Hospital Service (AHS) of New York was opened. The first contracts offered individual coverage for group members. In 1936 family contracts were offered. By 1949 AHS had enrolled in excess of 4 million customers.

Empire's Yorktown Heights facility processes more than 3,000 claims daily.

As the Blue Cross system grew it fueled interest in a prepayment planfor doctor services—which came to be known as Blue Shield. In 1940 Medical Expense Fund was incorporated, and it provided up to $500 per year for services by a participating physician. The following year the Associated Hospital Service started its own physician prepayment plan—Community Medical Care, Inc. A merger of the two plans in 1944 formed United Medical Service. In 1949 UMS adopted the Blue Shield insignia; by then it had more than 1.5 million customers.

Empire's new telephone system permits the electronic routing of incoming calls for faster service.

Growth continued through the 1950s and 1960s. With the inception of the federal Medicare program in 1966, AHS and UMS served as the financial intermediary for the administration of Medicare benefits in New York State.

The early 1970s brought more changes and additions in benefits to keep pace with an evolving medical technology and society. In 1973 AHS started its first Health Maintenance Organization (HMO). AHS and UMS were separate corporations, but in 1974 the two companies merged to create Blue Cross and Blue Shield of Greater New York.

Health care cost management has always been a top priority at Empire Blue Cross and Blue Shield, and the corporation has pioneered many innovative cost-containment strategies, including managed care, ongoing utilization review programs, coordination of benefits between insurers, and encouraging the delivery of medical care in the most appropriate and cost-effective setting.

With more than five decades of experience, Empire Blue Cross and Blue Shield has the capacity and expertise to underwrite and administer the health insurance needs of large national corporations with multi-location facilities, small businesses with as few as three employees, and individuals without access to group health insurance coverage

YONKERS GENERAL HOSPITAL/SAINT JOSEPH'S MEDICAL CENTER/ ST. JOHN'S RIVERSIDE HOSPITAL

Residents of the city of Yonkers in need of health care consider themselves very lucky because they have three hospitals to choose from. Each offers very specific services, allowing the community total care within the city limits. The services of Yonkers General Hospital, Saint Joseph's Medical Center, and St. John's Riverside Hospital also attract patients from outside Yonkers, including New York City and other areas in Westchester County. While each facility retains its own mission and philosophy, a basic goal for all is to provide patients with the best health care possible.

YONKERS GENERAL HOSPITAL

Incorporated in 1896, Yonkers General Hospital, a 190-bed, voluntary health care facility, offers a full range of service to Westchester County and its environs. Originally named the Homeopathic Home and Maternity, Yonkers General was begun for the express purpose of providing care for maternity patients and sick infants and for the practice of homeopathic medicine as well as allopathic medicine.

Indeed, for more than 35 years, Yonkers General Hospital held the distinction of being one of the very few hospitals in the United States to have been begun by women and for women and to have been managed solely by women. The hospital's dedication to high-quality care has long been exemplified by its initiative in addressing the needs of the community and by pioneering programs to meet those needs.

More than a quarter-century ago, Yonkers General was one of the first hospitals in the country to provide cobalt teletherapy for the treatment of cancer. This unit is part of the city's first fully comprehensive cancer care program, which includes a satellite pharmacy for chemotherapy.

Among the hospital's long list of initiatives are the inclusion of occupational therapy, the only alcohol and drug detoxification program in southern Westchester, and the only full-service blood donor bank in the city.

Yonkers General Hospital also pioneered the treatment of heroin abuse in Westchester County and established the first methadone clinic outside of New York City. In addition, Yonkers' completed wing for ambulatory surgery includes an expanded microsurgery unit for ophthalmology.

Recognized by the state for its charitable care, Yonkers General Hospital has been the recipient of energy conservation grants as well as awards for its alcohol detoxification unit.

Certified by the state Department of Health and the American Association of Blood Banks, approved by the College of American Pathologists, the hospital is also affiliated with 10 universities.

Yonkers General Hospital has complete emergency medical service, and its emergency room is staffed 24 hours a day by fully licensed house physicians.

SAINT JOSEPH'S MEDICAL CENTER

An ambitious building program, undertaken with widespread community support in the 1970s, changed the face of Saint Joseph's Medical Center, but its mission has remained constant since its founding in 1888: to provide diagnostic and treatment services to its neighbors in a way that recognizes and preserves the dignity of each patient and his or her family members.

Today, Saint Joseph's combines a full-service, 194-bed general hospital with a 200-bed nursing home and a full range of outpatient service, including a busy Family Health Center. The medical center has retained its home-like atmosphere, despite the fact that it boasts the latest technology in all major medical specialties. The hospital is fully computerized, which allows physicians to access patient histories and test results from terminals on each floor.

Saint Joseph's accredited family practice residency program produces seven specialists each year, and studying alongside its residents are other employees who are availing themselves of tuition reimbursement and on-site courses that will result in certificates and diplomas ranging from high school equivalency to registered nurse and graduate degrees. The medical center serves as an important community health education resource

Yonkers General Hospital

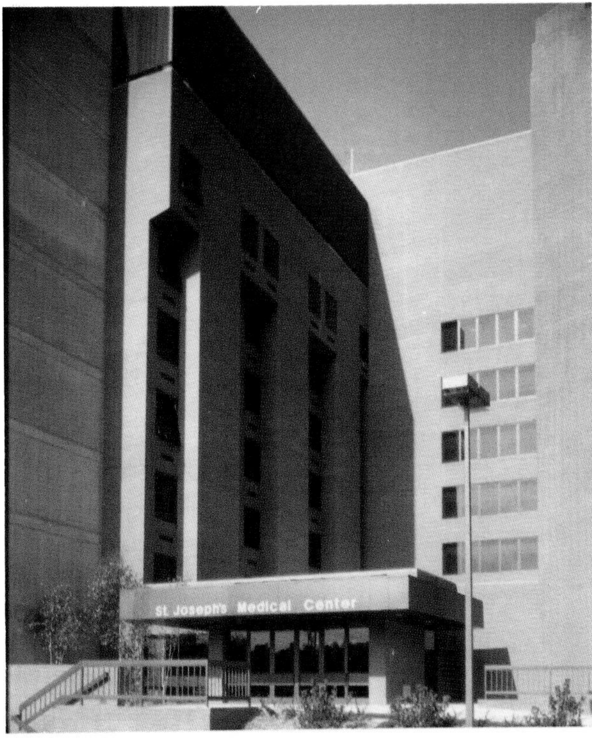

Saint Joseph's Medical Center.

and sponsors a diabetes club, a heart club, and special seminars throughout the year. It also provides care for several programs for the homeless in Yonkers.

Saint Joseph's Medical Center, located at 127 South Broadway, is operated under the guidance of the Sisters of Charity of Saint Vincent de Paul of New York, an order well-known for its excellence in health care. It serves Yonkers, Riverdale, and Kingsbridge, but its reputation extends well beyond this area. During 1989 almost 200,000 patients came to Saint Joseph's Medical Center; 28,000 people come to the emergency room alone.

ST. JOHN'S RIVERSIDE HOSPITAL

Like the Hudson River at its back, St. John's Riverside Hospital plays a vital and varied role in Westchester. St. John's is a progressive, full-service, nonprofit, nondenominational community hospital that has been providing high-quality health care and services since 1869.

St. John's was the first hospital in the county and, for a time, the only hospital on the river between New York City and Albany. St. John's also operates the oldest nursing school in Westchester, the Cochran School of Nursing.

Today St. John's, situated on 16 acres on North Broadway, is known for its excellence in health care as well as panoramic views of the river. With an outstanding professional staff, St. John's is committed to staying in the forefront of medical care. In 1989 the hospital completed a major building and renovation program designed to expand its services and keep up with changes in health care.

St. John's is at the cutting edge of technology in laser surgery, radiology, and emergency and critical care. Sophisticated services also include cardiac rehabilitation, physical medicine, occupational therapy, respiratory therapy, and laboratories. The corporate health department provides services designed exclusively for businesses to improve employee health and reduce health care costs.

St. John's provides the only maternity services in Yonkers and offers specialized care for women. Generations of Westchester residents have started life at St. John's and returned when their families needed medical care. It is not unusual for several generations of the same family to pass through its doors. St. John's prides itself on personal, family-oriented and technologically advanced care.

St. John's is able to maintain that strong tradition, in part, with its nursing school. The Cochran School of Nursing is an accredited two-year program, leading to an associate degree in nursing. Students receive their classroom and clinical training at St. John's, and many stay on to join its professional nursing staff.

Also a resource for community health education, St. John's sponsors health promotion programs, ranging from CPR classes to health fairs.

St. John's Riverside Hospital has a long history of proactive programs to respond to changing needs in the community. St. John's is dedicated to remaining a leader in health care in the county and a vital force in the Westchester community.

St. John's Riverside Hospital.

PACE UNIVERSITY

From its very beginnings in Manhattan's financial district in 1906 to its establishment as the foremost higher educational institution in Westchester in 1963, Pace University has maintained a pioneering spirit that makes it a special educational presence in Westchester County.

Pace was one of the very first major urban colleges and universities to reach out to the suburbs. From the start Pace tailored its academic programs to the special needs of the local and regional population. And, with the assistance of some of the county's most illustrious figures as well as today's dedicated leaders, it has developed new and exciting programs to service a varied and changing constituency.

ABOVE: Pace University attracts students from all over the world to its beautiful White Plains campus.

RIGHT: The innovative $12-million Evelyn & Joseph I. Lubin Graduate Center opened in White Plains in 1987.

Pace's Michaelian Institute for Sub/Urban Governance is providing local government officials with the intensive education they must have to keep up with a changing world. The institute's Law Resource Center is helping solve critical regional issues. Pace's School of Law is in the forefront of environmental law study and application. State-of-the-art computer facilities are preparing students as well as professionals with the latest advances in computer technology to meet the challenges of the next century.

Pace's world-renowned business schools are not only providing the coursework for tomorrow's corporate leaders, but also providing a host of special institutes, programs, and conferences focused on specific segments of the financial and business communities. Pace's School of Education is working with local school districts to keep youngsters in school and help maintain Westchester's educational leadership.

Pace students in its Cooperative Education programs—the largest of any four-year college in the metropolitan area—have become a significant source of manpower both for business and nonprofit agencies. The school's Environmental Center draws hundreds of schoolchildren and adults to the Pleasantville campus each year for hands-on nature studies. And Pace's Lienhard School of Nursing is providing both the education and training necessary for today's health care professional, while delivering urgently needed services to various segments of the population.

Pace and Westchester have indeed thrived. From the donation of the first 12 acres of land on Bedford Road in Pleasantville, which has grown to today's 200-acre campus, to the consolidation in 1975 with the College of White Plains, the acquisition of the Briarcliff campus in 1977, and the innovative $12-million Evelyn and Joseph I. Lubin Graduate Center, opened in White Plains in 1987, Pace University has maintained a steady momentum, placing quality education side by side with dynamic programming and service to the community.

Whether it was establishing a law school in White Plains in 1976, working with IBM to broadcast special managerial courses via satellite from Pace's Briarcliff campus, or fielding championship athletic teams in Pleasantville, Pace lends itself beautifully to the Westchester landscape. And, as bright as the past has been, the future looks even better.

Today Pace University draws students from the four corners of the earth. They join a remarkably diverse regional student body who have come to learn and live in an environment that is both rich in tradition and attuned to the challenges of tomorrow. The Pace experience is one that remains with them the rest of their lives.

COLLEGE OF NEW ROCHELLE

A forward-looking institution, the College of New Rochelle is "very well prepared to meet the future with confidence and enthusiasm," says its president, Sister Dorothy Ann Kelly, O.S.U.

The college's growth over the past two decades demonstrates this vitality. Three new coeducational schools have been added to the original women's School of Arts and Sciences, and recently a comprehensive support system of facilities, technology, and services has been developed in the newly renovated College-Center.

One of the oldest colleges in Westchester County, the College of New Rochelle was founded in 1904 by Mother Irene Gill, O.S.U., as the first Catholic college for women in New York State. The college, now independent, has sustained its mission and traditions while providing a curriculum that is contemporary and responsive to the needs of today's students.

To carry out the college's mission, three new schools were added: the Graduate School in 1969, the School of New Resources in 1972, and the School of Nursing in 1976. The Graduate School's 1,400-plus students pursue master of science and master of arts degrees in the fields of education, communications, gerontology, career development, counseling, and art. The School of New Resources enrolls approximately 3,000 adult learners in a nontraditional baccalaureate program that takes student maturity, personalities, and career commitments seriously. Six of its seven campuses are in New York City. The School of Nursing offers graduate, undergraduate, and continuing education programs.

In 1988 the College of New Rochelle opened the College-Center, which is designed to serve the needs of students in today's technological world. The College-Center combines research, career planning, networking, and mentoring opportunities with facilities that include communications technology, television, photography, and art studios. The center also includes the H.W. Taylor Institute for Entrepreneurial Studies, which provides professional expertise, technology, and resources specific to the needs of women in business.

The college serves its community as well as its students. In addition to educating women and men for a lifetime of personal and professional growth, it offers a wealth of cultural opportunities, such as lectures, discussions, art exhibits, and theatrical performances. In 1980 the college opened the Castle Gallery, which enjoys an excellent reputation for the quality and diversity of its professionally mounted exhibitions.

Sister Dorothy Ann Kelly, O.S.U., president since 1972, is personally dedicated to community service—a hallmark of the college's mission—holding office in a wide variety of local and national groups such as the Interreligious Council of the City of New Rochelle, the National Conference of Christians and Jews, the New Rochelle Hospital Medical Center, the Westchester County Association, and the Ursuline School of New Rochelle, among others.

With its multimillion-dollar investment in the College-Center and its commitment to access, the College of New Rochelle demonstrates its hopes for the future and looks forward with renewed commitment to the education of its students.

Leland Castle, the original home of the College of New Rochelle, is now a National Historic Site and houses administrative offices, the Castle Gallery, and reception rooms.

The Strawberry Festival at the College of New Rochelle is an annual spring event planned by students.

UNITED HOSPITAL MEDICAL CENTER

Proud of a rich heritage, the 100-year-old United Hospital Medical Center in Port Chester still honors its founders' pledge to "serve humanity, save lives, and relieve suffering." At the same time, the hospital remains in the forefront of modern technology.

It took the founders, 14 strong-minded local women, several months of running bake sales, fairs, and parties to raise money to meet a need they alone perceived—a hospital dedicated to healing the poor and infirm. In July 1889 they achieved their goal, opening the Ladies Hospital Association in two upstairs rooms on the corner of North Main Street and Willett Avenue. Three physicians and one nurse made up the medical staff of the two-bed hospital.

Within one year the hospital moved to double the number of beds, and just a few years later the women of the association initiated a building fund to purchase their own larger space. They bought the Jared Peck Estate, whose 14-room Victorian house seemed ample for the hospital's needs. But that soon changed, and around the turn of the century a new building campaign was launched. In 1909 the Ladies Hospital Association purchased the George A. Read Estate, 10 acres on the Boston Post Road, where the hospital still stands.

That same year the villages of Rye and Harrison joined Port Chester in acknowledging their mutual need for the services the pioneering hospital provided. As its charter was rewritten and mission expanded to reflect the broader coverage, its name was changed to United Hospital.

Today the hospital's constituency extends across the Sound shore area and beyond: south to Rye, Harrison, Mamaroneck, and Larchmont; northwest to Rye Brook, Purchase, and White Plains; and northeast to Port Chester and Greenwich, Connecticut. With 254 beds, 40 skilled-nursing beds, and 17 bassinets, the not-for-profit, voluntary community hospital is positioned to serve virtually all needs of all age groups.

The hospital has 600 staff members in medical areas. United offers the full range of medical and surgical specialties and the newest equipment available. Fully accredited by the Joint Commission on Accreditation of Hospitals, United also offers a variety of special services and therapies and has an impressive list of firsts to its credit.

Since 1961 its home care department, the only hospital-based program in the county, has sent United's own nurses into the homes of patients discharged from the medical and surgical units. In 1989 the hospital was awarded a grant to extend the service to patients discharged from the 22-bed psychiatric facility.

Its New Rochelle Alcoholism Clinic, a satellite unit, runs a nationally recognized program against drunk drivers. Operated in conjunction with the Westchester

United Hospital Medical Center constantly updates its equipment in order to remain in the forefront of modern technology.

Council on Alcoholism, the program is considered a model of its kind. United has a short-term inpatient substance-abuse unit and an outpatient program for recovering alcoholics and substance abusers. Unique in the county, the recovery program is geared to the needs of people who cannot take extended time away from their responsible positions.

In 1979 United established a hospice program to provide comprehensive services and support for the terminally ill and their families. Over the years the program has fulfilled its mission and extended its services to other Westchester hospitals and communities.

United also opened the county's first ambulatory-surgery department in 1981. After several expansions, the unit now accounts for nearly 65 percent of all surgical procedures. Among the users are both elective surgery and in vitro fertilization patients. In 1986 United introduced this new fertilization method, developed in Australia, to the county. It has been cited in a congressional report for administering one of the tri-state area's two most successful clinics.

In community outreach, too, United leads the way. In 1988 the hospital outfitted a van with mammography equipment and began taking the procedure to the community. Large corporations, small businesses, school districts, and shopping malls utilize this service.

A pacesetter in the prevention of AIDS, United is the only hospital in the county with an organized AIDS-care program that includes patient care, support, and education. To meet its objective of keeping AIDS patients on the job as long as possible, the hospital takes an educational program out to area employers and business groups.

An institution begun by volunteers, United Hospital remains dependent on them. The board of managers, Twig organization, volunteer services department, and Mayfair—all its dedicated volunteer workers contribute countless hours to fund-raising activities, hospital tasks, and patient support. With their help, the hospital embarked on an ambitious capital campaign in 1989, its centennial year, in keeping with its 100-year tradition of looking to the community for sustenance. Seeking a minimum of $5 million for the short-term and $10 million for the long-term, the campaign will fund three major projects: a centennial commemorative health facility for the improvement and expansion of outpatient services, new housing options to assist in retention and recruitment of staff, and a stronger fiscal foundation for the institution.

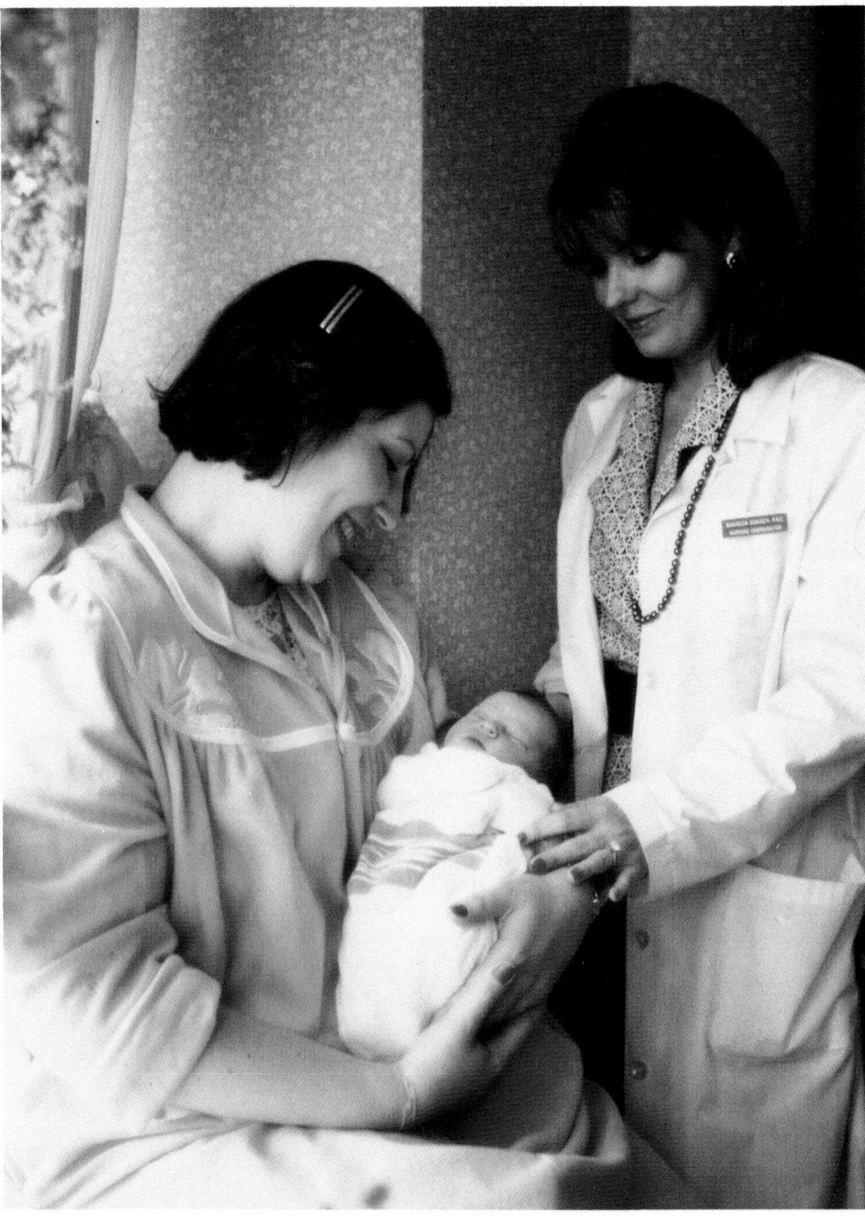

United, a not-for-profit, voluntary community hospital, is positioned to serve virtually all the needs of all age groups with a variety of services and therapies.

As it moves into the second century, United Hospital Medical Center is resolved to enhance its programs and services, keeping faith with all who take comfort in the knowledge that quality health care is close at hand.

NEW YORK MEDICAL COLLEGE

The largest private medical college in the state, New York Medical College, Valhalla, is several decades into its second century of service to a growing community.

The college, the first in the nation to have its own hospital, traces it roots back to pre-Civil War days. Through the efforts of William Cullen Bryant, noted civic leader and poet, and others, the college, then known as the New York Homeopathic Medical College, opened its doors in 1860 over a grocery on 20th Street and Third Avenue in New York City. With an initial roster of 59 students and eight faculty members, the new medical school was one of the first to offer a formal, graded curriculum.

Many changes, expansions, and innovations marked the college's early years. It linked up with hospitals as they were founded, built its own teaching hospital, and moved uptown to larger quarters. Expansion continued well into this century, and the college's renown spread. Still in the city and assuming an ever greater responsibility for urban health care, the college was invited to extend its reach to Westchester County in 1968.

The faculty of the college is comprised of more than 2,800 experienced physicians and researchers, many of whom are of international reputation. One out of three physicians in the mid-Hudson Valley region is a faculty member or alumnus of New York Medical College.

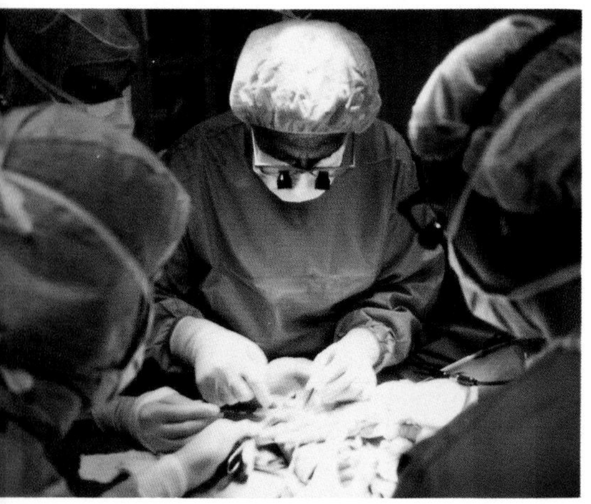

In response to the official invitation, the college began planning its Valhalla campus and joined the county in developing the adjacent Westchester County Medical Center. The first of the new college buildings to open for classes in 1972 was the $11-million Basic Sciences Building. This 4.5-acre facility houses the only academic biomedical research program in the Hudson Valley region.

At the medical center the college and its faculty are responsible for the education and supervision of the center's residents and the organization of research and medical administration. In this capacity the college has participated in the medical center's growth from a general county hospital to a tertiary-care regional medical center of outstanding reputation.

In 1978 the college was strengthened by establishing formal ties with the Archdiocese of New York. This relationship broadened the college's range of clinical affiliations through the Catholic-sponsored hospitals in New York City and the metropolitan region.

Today a preeminent medical university in the Catholic tradition, the school enrolls 760 medical students and nearly 700 graduate students pursuing M.S., M.P.H., and Ph.D. degrees at its Graduate School of Basic Medical Sciences and Graduate School of Health Sciences. The full-time faculty of more than 1,000 M.D.s and Ph.D.s is reinforced by a part-time staff of 1,800 physicians and researchers. But the best gauge of the college's enormous impact is that one out of every three physicians in the region, which includes five other counties in addition to Westchester, is a faculty member or graduate of New York Medical College.

The college is also a growing economic factor in the county, with a total budget in fiscal year 1988-1989 of $140 million. New York Medical College is a leader among medical schools in forging cooperative relations with the private sector. The college's program to transfer scientific results to industry is developing rapidly to enable new vaccines, diagnostic tests, therapeutic drugs, and devices to reach the marketplace and become available for public use. The college receives an increasing amount of public and private funds for its more than 300 research projects ranging from cancer and hypertension to arthritis and Lyme disease. In the 1978 to 1988 decade, the college advanced 13 places to rank 67th among the 126 medical schools receiving National Institutes of Health funding. This advancement in research was a

Today New York Medical College, a private institution, and Westchester County Medical Center, which is public, are joined in an unusual partnership forming an academic medical center.

singular achievement unequaled by any other medical school.

New York Medical College is deeply involved in planning and providing responsive health care programs for the people and communities it serves. Through its continuing medical education programs, the college keeps area physicians up to date with medical knowledge and advances. About one-third of the college's 30 affiliated hospitals, including the university hospital, Westchester County Medical Center, are in Westchester County. In New York City, the college is the largest provider of physician services in the city's public hospitals. Three of its four university hospital affiliations are located in the city: Lincoln Medical and Mental Health Center, Metropolitan Hospital Center, and St. Vincent's Hospital and Medical Center of New York.

RIGHT: The college is the only academic biomedical research institution between New York City and Albany. Scientists at the college are conducting more than 300 research projects ranging from fundamental investigations in molecular biology to investigations of potential new drugs used in the treatment of patients.

BELOW: With 760 medical students and nearly 700 graduate students enrolled, New York Medical College ranks as the third-largest private medical school in the nation and the largest in New York State.

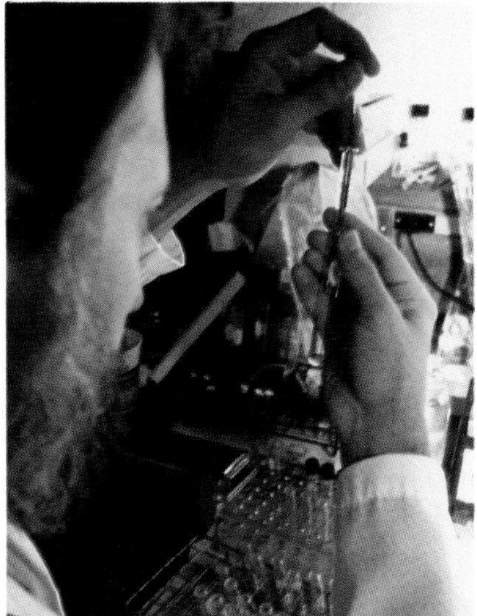

This network enables New York Medical College to offer students the widest variety of patient care experiences in the country. New York Medical College ranks first in the United States and third in the world with regard to the number of hospital beds (more than 12,000) available for teaching purposes through its network of affiliations.

To meet its continually expanding responsibilities, the college will soon embark on a capital campaign called "The Campaign for New York Medical College: To Teach and to Heal—Worldwide." The campaign, the first major fund-raising effort in the college's history, had a goal of $50 million.

For the future, New York Medical College plans to build on its tradition of providing good physicians and serving as a resource for them. The college also intends to respond to the growing international challenge by providing health professionals with M.P.H., Ph.D., and M.S. degrees to work in developing countries.

Photo by Rich Zila

11

THE MARKETPLACE

Westchester County's retail establishments, service industries, and products are enjoyed by residents and visitors to the area.

ARROWWOOD

For quality in design and function, Arrowwood, Rye Brook, sets the standard in its class. The resort conference center, located on 114 acres of rolling countryside, incorporates every amenity its varied guest list could fancy. County people out for a festive day or evening, tri-state residents on a refreshing weekend break, and corporate executives convening on important business all find Arrowwood tailored just for them.

The grounds—playing fields, ponds, and gardens—have all the earmarks of an exclusive country club. Taking advantage of the sloping terrain, the cedar building is set into the landscape at five levels; large windows in all public and private spaces afford panoramic views. Arrowwood's elegant lobby, displays of sculpture and painting, gourmet restaurants, and luxurious guest rooms bespeak a world-class hotel. The state-of-the-art conference facilities are a realm apart, delivering comfort and service along with technology.

Spanning the acreage, a par-35, nine-hole golf course is lined by evergreens. The challenging course is complemented by a 35-tee driving range, two putting greens, and a pro shop. Tennis and paddle-tennis courts with lights for evening play, a heated indoor/outdoor swimming pool that is usable year-round, and miles of trails for jogging, bicycling, cross-country skiing, and strolling entice even the sedentary out into the fresh air.

Another inventory of active sports facilities is on hand indoors. It includes tennis, squash, and racquetball courts; a swimming pool giving underwater access to the outdoor pool; and a sports and fitness center offering workout equipment, saunas, steam baths, a whirlpool, and massage.

Arrowwood's three restaurants, acclaimed by area critics, provide atmosphere along with fine food. Provare, "A Trattoria," features a northern Italian menu in a relaxed, open, sunlit setting. "We felt the demand from the Westchester community and our guests for a casual, spontaneous atmosphere," remarks John Wilderman, vice president and general manager of Arrowwood. Provare offers fresh regional ingredients, an antipasto bar, and a unique wood-burning pizza oven.

Large windows afford panoramic views—even from Arrowwood's heated indoor/outdoor pool, which is usable year-round.

The Atrium, set out on three tiers to overlook woods and water, specializes in classic American and nouveau cuisines. Fresh fish and aged beef and other choice meats are grilled to diners' tastes and accompanied by gourmet sauces. Open for all meals, the Atrium is especially favored by local people for its Saturday candlelight buffets with dancing and Sunday brunches with live jazz.

The Pub, a casual, country-style restaurant, serves soups and salads, hot and cold sandwiches, imaginative appetizers and rich desserts, along with a bounteous selection of drinks.

Holidays are special occasions at Arrowwood's restaurants. The Atrium is known for its Thanksgiving and Christmas dinners comprised of all the traditional specialties freshly made in its own kitchen. On Mother's Day and Father's Day, crowds come for the lavish brunches. A major event is the black-tie New Year's Eve gala, which features a cocktail dinner dance and winds up with a sumptuous 2 a.m. breakfast. Many celebrants stay the night in one of the resort's commodious guest rooms.

Designed for optimum comfort and privacy, many of Arrowwood's 274 guest rooms have private balconies or walk-out patios; duplex suites feature working fireplaces and wet bars. Guests are further indulged with bath sheets instead of ordinary towels, triple-sheeted beds with nightly turn-down service, remote-control television, newspapers at the door each morning, and chocolates on the pillow each evening.

Such amenities please not only guests on weekend getaways but also the demanding corporate executives drawn to Arrowwood for its renowned conference facilities. Precision-engineered to the most exacting requirements, the facilities include 36 meeting rooms, accommodating from five to 500 people. The rooms have soundproofed acoustics, individual temperature controls, pinnable wall surfaces, and glare-free lighting. They are equipped with the latest technology, from overhead projectors for slide, film, and video to sophisticated programming of multi-image systems and teleconferencing facilities. Meetings can be recorded, with audiovisual cassettes ready for replay within hours. Simultaneous translation, Panafax electronic boards, computer hookups, remote television camera pickup—Arrowwood has every technical capability any group might need.

Nó detail has been overlooked. Lengthy sessions? Chairs are especially made for long hours of seating comfort. Large groups breaking out into small ones? Smaller rooms adjoin meeting rooms. Short respites for refreshment? Each meeting room has a refreshment break area providing all-day buffet service of fresh fruit, pastry, soft drinks, and coffee.

Arrowwood's conference and resort facilities have proved an unbeatable combination. Occupancy rates have held steady at 80 percent, far above average, virtually since opening day in 1983. Built by Citicorp, Arrowwood was sold in December 1986 to Doral Hotels and Resorts Management, owner of resorts, hotels, and spas mainly in New York and Florida. Doral has since spent several million dollars to renovate guest and meeting rooms, the ballroom, and public areas for the satisfaction of conference and community clients alike.

For Westchester, Arrowwood offers added benefits in its multitude of civic and charitable activities. The resort conference center supports such cultural groups as the New Orchestra of Westchester and East Coast Arts. It also frequently donates in-kind services, including dinners and weekend stays, to diverse nonprofit organizations to be auctioned off or used as raffle prizes. In addition, Arrowwood maintains a close relationship with Rye High School under the business community's Adopt-a-School program.

A corporate and county resource, Arrowwood maintains an uncompromising standard of excellence throughout its facilities and services while meeting all its constituencies' needs.

Arrowwood's state-of-the-art conference facilities and meeting rooms deliver technology in comfort.

JCPENNEY

"To serve the public, as nearly as we can, to its complete satisfaction"—that was James Cash Penney's first rule for success in retailing, and the company he founded early in the twentieth century has never forgotten it. Now one of the nation's largest department stores, JCPenney has more than 1,300 stores nationwide and in Puerto Rico.

Penney, born in 1875, started out as a retail sales clerk. He soon became a partner in a small western chain, the Golden Rule Mercantile Co. He bought out the two older partners in 1907 and, making the Golden Rule—he should do to others as he would have others do to him—his credo, began to branch out across the nation. In 1913, when there were 34 stores, the chain changed its name and was incorporated as the J.C. Penney Company Inc. Penney relocated his headquarters from Salt Lake City to New York in 1914. Seven years later, weakened by overworking, he moved his residence to White Plains for his health. It was a fortunate move. Penney regained his health and lived another 50 years, dying in 1971 at the age of 95.

James Cash Penney

A decade later a new JCPenney opened up in the founder's adopted hometown. An anchor at The Galleria, White Plains' only mall, the store has become a keystone of the city's busy retail shopping scene. The four-story emporium specializes in men's, women's, and children's apparel and home furnishings.

Like the other branches of "America's only national department store," the White Plains establishment has been focusing on these lines since 1983, when the company decided to reposition to meet the fashion needs of its target customers, middle- to upper-middle-income consumers. In the process it spent more than one billion dollars on renovation and modernization, doubling the space devoted to apparel while reducing or eliminating other lines. The changes are evident in White Plains, where a contemporary and fashionable environment prevails, characterized by an exciting shopping atmosphere and outstanding customer service.

An anchor at The Galleria in White Plains, this four-story JCPenney store specializes in men's, women's, and children's apparel and home furnishings.

Along with commitment to customers, JCPenney stresses commitment to the community. Many local nonprofit groups benefit from its support, including the March of Dimes Walkathon, Heart Fund, Red Cross Blood Drive, and United Way. For a number of years the company has been giving out Golden Rule awards to dedicated volunteers nationwide, and in 1990 it brought the tradition to Westchester County. The five top county volunteers, chosen by the Volunteer Service Bureau of United Way, were presented with JCPenney Golden Rule Award sculptures.

Opening day of the Golden Rule store, Kemmerer, Wyoming, April 1902.

Both kinds of commitment—to customers and to the community—derive from James Cash Penney, who lived his life and shaped his company according to the Golden Rule

HOLIDAY INN CROWNE PLAZA®

With a prime location in the heart of downtown White Plains, New York, the Holiday Inn Crowne Plaza® is geared to serving the disparate needs of business travelers, tourists, and the community itself. The hotel, a striking white stone tower 12 stories high, is just seven miles from Westchester County Airport and less than three miles from Platinum Mile, home of many *Fortune* 500 companies. Courtesy van service is provided within a seven-mile radius. A free enclosed garage is available, but a car is not needed to reach downtown businesses, world-class shopping, or fine restaurants. All are within walking distance.

TOP: ***Guests take refreshment in the elegant lobby of the Holiday Inn Crowne Plaza®.***

BOTTOM: ***The staff prepares for a meeting in one of the 11 conference rooms.***

Especially for business, the Crowne Plaza® has its own satellite communications network, enabling worldwide video conferencing. An on-site audiovisual company can handle everything from renting equipment to staging industrial shows. Eleven rooms accommodate meetings of 10 to 700 people and banquets for up to 525 guests.

The Holiday Inn Crowne Plaza® is a landmark in downtown White Plains.

The Crowne Plaza®, which opened in December 1985, offers amenities of a luxuriously furnished lobby, an indoor swimming pool, whirlpool, sauna, and exercise room. Fenimore's Lounge, an intimate, casual spot, presents live entertainment.

The Post Road Cafe, a bright and cheerful restaurant specializing in American cuisine, offers a varied menu at breakfast, lunch, and dinner. Its highly acclaimed Sunday brunch offers two seatings accommodating 300 people. In addition to the ambience, the menu includes waffles with various toppings, eggs Benedict, and a variety of made-to-order omelets. Other foods include pastas, seafood and salad bars, an Oriental station, a carving table, and a tremendous selection of cheeses, fruits, and desserts.

The 400 well-appointed rooms and suites feature professional work areas. On the executive level, guests are treated to a complimentary continental breakfast, and dinner hors d'oeuvres, and turndown service of a cordial and chocolates, along with other special services.

Very much a part of its community, the Crowne Plaza® hosts many charitable, civic, and political functions. The Crowne Plaza® is involved with such charities as the March of Dimes, Rotary, and United Way. It also hosts the Lions, Kiwanis, and Rotary weekly meeting lunches.

The staff at the Crowne Plaza® places a premium on serving guests well. Excellent service starts on arrival; guests are met by an attentive bellhop and welcomed by an efficient front-desk staff. It extends throughout the guest's stay until express check-out, which eliminates last-minute delays. In addition to price value, the Holiday Inn Crowne Plaza® prides its service as one of its best features, and the key to its ability to deliver a combination of true hospitality and professionalism.

RYE TOWN HILTON

Westchester was still "the country" and the corporate presence there was still new when the Rye Town Hilton opened its doors in 1973. Built as the first combination corporate/weekend getaway hotel, it offered 315 elegantly appointed guest rooms and an unspoiled woodland setting. With meeting and function rooms, ballroom, dining, and recreational facilities, the hotel quickly found its place in the community.

Within just a few years occupancy rates began to strain the hotel's capacity. In response, the Rye Town Hilton launched a $6-million expansion. Anticipated in the original plans, the additions, completed in 1978, did not change the hotel's outward style. The integrity of its design was maintained although the number of guest rooms was increased by more than one-third, to 438, and ballroom space was more than doubled, with construction of the Westchester Ballroom, seating 1,400 people. At the same time, restaurant, conference, sports, and parking facilities were also augmented.

Today the Rye Town Hilton retains its links to both area businesses and residents. It serves corporate traveler and local holiday seeker alike; its conference rooms and ballrooms are heavily booked for business meetings and charitable and social functions.

Nestled amid 45 wooded acres and surrounded by manicured lawns, the hotel presents a pleasing aspect to arriving guests. Its winding, estate-like drive leads up to a brass door. Guests walk through a ceramic-tiled entryway to a spacious lobby where chairs are arranged around a fireplace. Even the registration desk, of green Italian marble, carries out the theme of elegance, suited to both a major business hotel and a fine country resort.

Guest rooms live up to the same standard. Constantly refurbished to preclude any signs of wear, they are fitted with desks and chairs, dressers, comfortable beds with headboards, table and floor lamps, AM/FM radio, and color television offering in-room movies—all the accoutrements to encourage guests to feel at home.

Room service is friendly and timely; wake-up calls are cheerful and accurate. Nearly all rooms have views; many also have such special amenities as two telephone lines, computer hookups, electric coffee makers, and refrigerators.

Proclaiming that "Business is a pleasure at the Rye Town Hilton," the hotel goes to some lengths to

Penfield's Restaurant, the Rye Town Hilton's four-star dining experience.

prove its point. It offers an expedited meeting-arrangement system, permitting meeting planners to dial a toll-free number, explain their needs, and receive answers about rates and availability of conference facilities within 24 hours. The hotel also assigns a personal conference planner to each organization to ensure a smooth and efficient meeting.

With 35 meeting rooms, for a total of 33,000 square feet, the Rye Town Hilton is prepared to accommodate groups of six to 1,400 people. Each room is soundproof, well-lighted, climate-controlled, and some are equipped with a built-in audiovisual system. Many conference rooms also have screens and blackboards.

For social functions, the hotel offers extensive catering services. With poolside barbecue pits, terrace buffets, and formal ballroom dining, the Rye Town Hilton's professional catering staff is ready to meet any need. A personal catering manager is at the disposal of each banquet planner.

Dining is a special experience for every guest. The four-star Penfield's Restaurant, named for an eighteenth-century Westchester tavern owner, specializes in continental cuisine. Serving dinner every evening except Sunday, Penfield's sets its tables with crisp linens, fine china and silver, and bowls of flowers. Picture windows overlook the hotel's gardens.

In summer, Penfield's terrace is open for lunch on weekdays, and for breakfast and lunch on weekends. Meals are simple—hamburgers and hot dogs, salads, and sandwiches—but enhanced by the lovely surroundings.

For casual dining, the Tulip Tree is open every day from 6:30 a.m. to 11:30 p.m. In addition to light meals, available all day, the Tulip Tree is known for its breakfast, brunch, and summer evening buffets and salad bars. Sunday brunches are notably sumptuous, made up of salads, pates, cheeses, meats, smoked fish, omelets, and Viennese and other specialty desserts.

Surrounded by manicured lawns, the Rye Town Hilton's main entrance welcomes guests to its fine accommodations and impeccable service.

The Rye Town Hilton's cocktail lounge, The Den, features intimate alcoves, book-lined walls, and soft lighting. Open daily from noon to the small hours of the morning, The Den plays recorded music.

On-premises recreational facilities include heated indoor, outdoor, and children's pools; whirlpools and saunas; exercise room with weights, stationary bicycles, and a treadmill; lighted tennis courts; and shuffleboard. Guests also find it a refreshing break just to stroll through the expansive grounds, where annual plantings include 11,000 tulip bulbs.

Concerned with the community as well as its own guests, the Rye Town Hilton supports a multitude of civic and charitable organizations. They include the Private Industry Council, Westchester County Chamber of Commerce, Junior Achievement, YMCA of Northern Westchester, Westchester Council for the Arts, National Council for Christians and Jews, March of Dimes, Westchester Lighthouse for the Blind, United Way, Leukemia Society, 52 Association, Adopt-a-School, and several hospital associations.

In the years since the Rye Town Hilton's opening, Westchester has changed, becoming more developed in the course of welcoming new businesses and residents. But the hotel's serene setting remains unchanged, along with its goals of providing the finest accommodations and impeccable service to every guest.

THE GALLERIA

It seems that all of Westchester shops at The Galleria, White Plains, a multilevel center featuring more than 150 fine shops, services, and restaurants. Established in 1980, the 880,000-square-foot retail complex has evolved over the years in response to customers' changing needs. Today's tenant mix inclines toward national chains and strong retailers known for quality merchandise. Anchored by Abraham & Strauss and JCPenney, "the mall for all seasons" has enjoyed the spotlight as the premier mall in Westchester County.

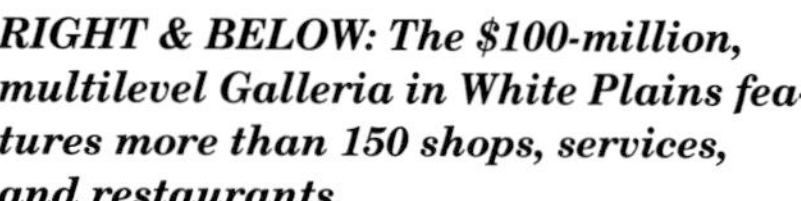

RIGHT & BELOW: The $100-million, multilevel Galleria in White Plains features more than 150 shops, services, and restaurants.

The $100-million Galleria, the city's only mall, was conceived as part of an ambitious urban-renewal project that provided the impetus for rapid redevelopment of the entire area. Its construction, spearheaded by Cadillac Fairview Shopping Centers (U.S.) Limited, sent a signal that the revitalization of downtown White Plains had become feasible. Millions of square feet of office space, hundreds of hotel rooms, and more than 1,000 housing units have since been built within a five-block radius of the shopping center.

Since opening day The Galleria has drawn crowds from an expanding geographical area. With the upgrading of the tenant mix initiated in 1985, sales per square foot rose sharply, placing The Galleria among the top one percent of all U.S. shopping centers.

The center's two department stores, A&S and JCPenney, and more than 150 other retailers sell clothing and accessories, jewelry, electronics, home furnishings, books, and other specialty items. And such services as banking, dentistry, optometry, and hair styling are available, as well as a two-screen cinema.

Located on the Garden Level, the International Food Court features more than 20 restaurants with three-level seating under a skylit atrium. From breakfast and lunch to evening meals, the selections from fast-food and sit-down restaurants offer pizza, hot dogs, hamburgers, sushi, yogurt, tacos, and other specialties.

A variety of special events are designed to keep those who frequent The Galleria entertained and informed. The annual Spring Home & Garden Show features dozens of exhibitors, including contractors, decorators, architects, and patio designers. Other events are just for children, such as Santa's Arrival Breakfast, located at the Food Court. Children of all ages are entertained with clowns, songs, games, and prizes. The Galleria also sponsors such popular local events as the annual 10K Road Race and raffles off prizes donated by its merchants during the post-race ceremony.

Having become an integral part of Westchester County, The Galleria will continue to offer quality selections and convenience to its customers.

STOUFFER WESTCHESTER HOTEL

Set amid 30 acres of woods with a magnificent turn-of-the-century mansion, the Stouffer Westchester Hotel has more than satisfied guests to recommend it. Accolades also come from the travel experts at Mobil Corp. and the American Automobile Association, both of whom have honored the Stouffer Westchester with their highest ratings and made it the only four-star hotel in the county.

Part of the reason is the unique Red Oaks mansion, built in 1906 by noted American architect John Merven Carrere for his own use. Designed in the Normandy style and made of stone from its own grounds, Red Oaks today is divided into six spacious hospitality suites named for the nation's earliest presidents—Washington, Adams, Jefferson, Madison, Monroe, and Jackson. The carefully preserved mansion is used extensively for business and social gatherings. Its patio, the Red Oak Terrace, which seats 200 people for a banquet or 150 people with a dance floor, is among the most sought-after rooms in Westchester for wedding receptions.

In 1976, when the property was acquired by Stouffer, a subsidiary of Nestlé Enterprises, Inc., a new hotel was designed to complement Red Oaks. Opened in December 1977, the Stouffer Westchester's main building offers 364 luxuriously furnished guest rooms, two fine restaurants, an intimate cocktail lounge, a full range of recreational facilities, and 18 well-equipped meeting rooms.

Guest rooms, fitted out with custom mahogany furnishings, come with such amenities as complimentary morning coffee and newspaper, movies, and 24-hour room service.

For all-day dining, The Woodlands features fine continental fare. The wood-paneled Oyster Bar offers a daily dinner menu of fresh seafood. The bar, distinctive with dark wood walls and green sofas and settees, has a library ambience.

A health club, whirlpool, and sauna are available for year-round use. Tennis and paddle tennis courts, a glass-enclosed pool with a nearby game area, and illuminated wooded trails for jogging or walking all offer guests plenty of opportunity to relax.

Built in 1906, Stouffer Westchester Hotel maintains its turn-of-the-century character and appeal.

For meetings and conventions, the Stouffer Westchester is prepared to accommodate any size group, up to 700 people. The hotel's meeting express service can provide same-day confirmation of all details by telephone or facsimile. A professional staff of meeting planners and caterers is on call to help with accommodations, food, facilities, and special equipment. The concierge provides secretarial assistance, car, and other services, while the hotel's complimentary limousine is available for transportation to White Plains Airport, meetings, and shopping within a five-mile radius.

Constantly renovated to keep up its ratings, which it has held almost since opening, the Stouffer Westchester Hotel offers a combination of facilities and services that are ideal for business and pleasure.

The Stouffer Westchester Hotel's main builing offers 364 beautiful guest rooms, two fine restaurants, a full range of recreational facilities, and 18 luxurious meeting rooms.

THE GREAT ATLANTIC & PACIFIC TEA CO.

With annual sales exceeding $11 billion and more than 92,000 employees, the Great Atlantic & Pacific Tea Co., in Montvale, New Jersey, ranks as North America's fourth-largest supermarket chain and one of its strongest. The company operates more than 1,200 stores in 25 eastern, southern, and midwestern states, as well as the Canadian province of Ontario, under the A&P, Dominion, Farmer Jack, Food Emporium, Kohl's, Super Fresh, and Waldbaum's trade names.

Since 1982 A&P has been involved in a total revitalization effort. This has produced financial stability, created a sense of renewed confidence within the entire organization, and led to the development of a new image and new store formats. Today A&P is a market-driven company that has rededicated itself to business excellence and industry leadership.

Now in the midst of a $295-million capital expenditures program, A&P plans to add 43 stores and upgrade 162 existing stores. The stores fall into four basic categories. The first category, upgraded supermarkets, features just what the typical shopper looks for—good quality and value, convenience, the right assortment of merchandise, and good service. Many of these stores also offer such special features as fresh seafood shops and in-store bakeries.

In a strikingly different food shopping environment, A&P's Futurestores appeal to more upscale suburban food shoppers. These stores are equipped with the latest in high technology, such as high-speed computers to track items. Stocked with a wide selection of gourmet foods, Futurestores contain many high-quality perishable departments, including delicatessens, seafood shops, produce markets, and fresh cheese and pasta sections.

LEFT & BELOW: Futurestores focus on gourmet foods and high-quality perishables in an innovative supermarket format.

Early in this century A&P stores were part of the landscape of cities and towns across America.

Sav-A-Centers, A&P's economy stores, appeal to a broad range of shoppers. In addition to reasonable prices, these stores offer variety and good service. Their merchandise includes traditional, specialty, and gourmet items; departments extend to such high-quality perishables as butcher shops, take-out delis, and salad bars.

The fourth kind of store, the Food Emporium, caters to the affluent city shoppper who insists on top quality, extra convenience, and high levels of personal service. Designed to satisfy the most demanding customers, Food Emporiums feature full-service boutiques, including life-styles sections.

All A&P stores reflect current trends. The prevailing consumer interest in diet, health, and nutrition has led to a store design and traffic plan that devotes the lead-off spot to fresh produce. Today's extensive produce selection takes in 350 items, compared with the 100 items that were once the standard. The company also starts trends of its own. In 1988 it opened a two-level Food Emporium in New York City, with an escalator to ferry shoppers between the basement boutique and the street level.

Although the words "new" and "modern" characterize the A&P

A&P has designed its gourmet Food Emporiums to represent the ultimate food-shopping experience.

today, the organization goes back a long way to 1859. As an old, established American institution, it places heavy emphasis on good corporate citizenship. The A&P's main charitable activities are associated with food, specifically the support of efforts to aid the hungry nationwide.

In a 1988 ceremony at the White House, James Wood, chairman and chief executive officer on behalf of A&P, received a Presidential Award from President Ronald Reagan for private-sector initiatives in recognition of its chain-wide efforts in aid of food banks and many other feed-the-hungry programs. Its distribution to food banks that year, in food and money, exceeded one million dollars. In addition, A&P lent its truck fleet for the transportation of government surplus food to local food banks. It also worked directly with vendors and local fund-raisers in a variety of collection activities, ranging from setting up collection bins inside the stores to serving as designated redemption centers for national coupon programs.

A&P continues to increase its food-donation activity, providing emergency assistance in addition to its regular programs. In 1989 the company responded quickly to the Armenian earthquake. It put powdered milk and other dry groceries on board the first plane to fly emergency food provisions into the quake area.

In addition to its food contribution, the firm participates in fund-raising efforts for numerous civic, social, and disease research organizations. Among them are United Way, UNICEF, United Service Organization, Scouting, Multiple Sclerosis, March of Dimes, and St. Jude's Hospital for Children. Many A&P employees join in the fund raising on their own initiative. Members of the company's Bicycle Club have ridden in the American Diabetes Association's 25-mile fund-raiser and the 100-mile event for Multiple Sclerosis.

Beyond such formal activities, the company believes its closeness to the people it serves extends to individual expressions of good will and concern. Employees deliver groceries to elderly shut-ins, managers donate food and supplies to local civic and social events, executives take time to teach Junior Achievement courses at schools, and stores are often the focal points of efforts to aid local families in need of emergency aid. Convinced that supermarkets and their employees are an integral part of the communities they serve, the Great Atlantic & Pacific Tea Co. is committed to supporting a variety of activities designed to improve the lives of all its neighbors.

As chairman, president, and chief executive officer, James Wood puts it, "We're not just another grocery chain. We're a national institution."

RIGHT & BELOW: Geared to economy-conscious shoppers, Sav-A-Centers measure up to 55,000 square feet in area.

J.A. SEXAUER

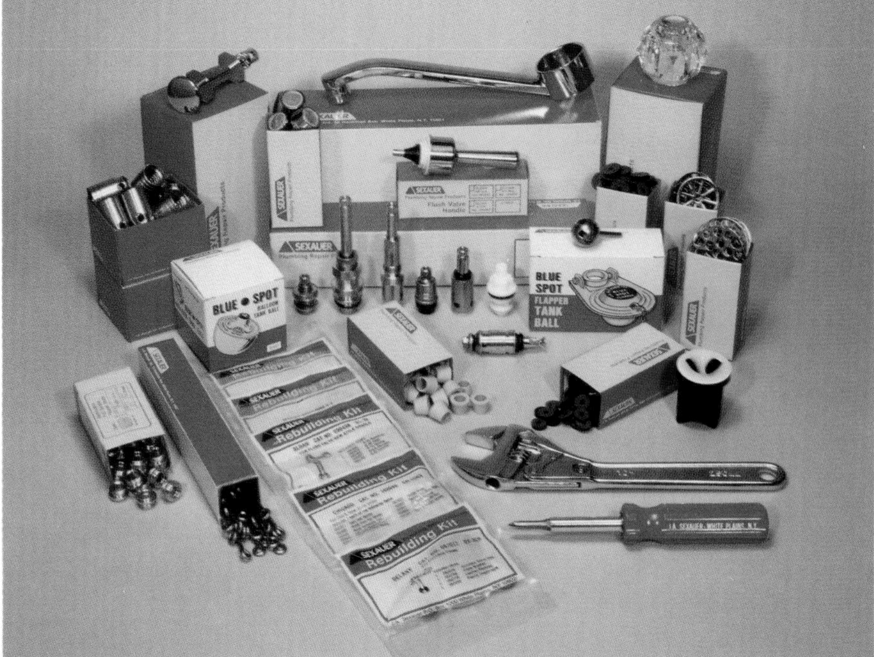

J.A. Sexauer's distinctive red and yellow packaging is recognized as a symbol of quality.

The nation's leading supplier of plumbing repair products, J.A. Sexauer, Scarsdale, was founded in New York City in 1921. The founder was a salesman who, after an argument with his boss, quit and set up a competing operation across the street.

The business prospered from the start, expanding and relocating to Westchester County in the early 1960s. For 20 years Sexauer was quartered in White Plains, before moving to Scarsdale in 1982. When it set up a distribution center in Louisville, Kentucky, in 1973, the company considered relocating but decided Westchester's advantages, especially the superior work force, were too good to give up.

The founder remained at the helm until his death in 1970, at which time his brother, James, took over the presidency. Gil Silva, then a 10-year employee, was appointed president in 1975, and the following year the company was sold to the Dyson-Kissner-Moran Corp., a private investment company. In the next decade the firm more than tripled its sales, and growth continues at a healthy pace.

The company, which sells to commercial and institutional accounts such as hospitals, school systems, military bases, and office buildings, now has more than 160 salespeople nationwide, as well as in Canada and the Caribbean. There are 100 employees at the firm's headquarters. But Sexauer still has the aura of a family company, where employees stay, often for more than 20 years.

Sexauer, which has never had a down year or a layoff, traditionally considered itself recession-proof. The recession in the early 1980s undermined that confidence. Until then, wholesalers of plumbing supplies had stayed out of the complicated repair parts business but, with housing starts down, they went into this niche and stayed in. While troublesome in the short run, it turned out to be a benefit. It challenged the firm to introduce new product lines, better marketing methods, and new locations.

Sexauer picked up the challenge, establishing a branch, Sexauer Ltd., in Oakville, Ontario, Canada, and taking on a new line of electrical maintenance products. The firm also set up a direct-mail operation and diversified into national accounts, strengthening its business across the board.

Widely known and respected in its industry, J.A. Sexauer has also made its mark in civic and charitable affairs. Gil Silva is a member of the Westchester County Chamber of Commerce and of the advisory board of Pace University. Both the company and its employees back United Way and the March of Dimes Walkathon.

Certain that its quality products, top-notch service, and highly professional staff have made it what it is today, J.A. Sexauer intends to keep the emphasis on those characteristics while continuing to explore new products and new markets in the future.

J.A. Sexauer's modern headquarters building.

Photo by Rich Zila

Photo by Rich Zila

12

FINANCE

Westchester County's solid financial base has provided a dynamic environment for the economic growth of both individuals and businesses in the community.

CIGNA INDIVIDUAL FINANCIAL SERVICES CO.

"Serve first, serve better" is the philosophy that drives CIGNA Individual Financial Services Co.'s business relationships. This means putting clients' needs and objectives first. "Our purpose is to develop long-term relationships with a select clientele by providing the finest and most comprehensive financial planning services and products," says regional vice president Richard A. Krim, CLU, ChFC. "We know that the right to do business with a client can be earned only through superior performance and continued support."

When Krim started the Westchester operation in White Plains in 1969, he was the sole employee. Within five years CIGNA had outgrown its original space and relocated to larger offices in Tarrytown. In 1989, with a professional staff expanded to 50 people, the firm moved once more, to spacious new quarters in Elmsford. Reflecting its growth and achievements, the Westchester agency is one of the company's leaders and is a four-time winner of CIGNA's Outstanding Agency Award.

The basis for this success is the range and depth of services delivered to customers in Westchester, southern Connecticut, and the entire metropolitan New York City area.

CIGNA Individual Financial Services Company is truly unique in what it does. It offers a comprehensive custom planning service tailored to each client's special situation and offers investments and insurance products to implement its recommendations. This comprehensive planning includes tax planning, personal investment planning, fringe benefit analysis, business continuity planning, and estate planning.

CIGNA Individual Financial Services Company's primary market is the closely held business and the successful executives and professionals who do not have time to oversee their personal financial affairs. Yet proper financial planning can save them thousands of tax dollars and enable them to meet their business and personal goals.

Standing (left to right): C. William Tanzi, J.D., and John A. Gaines, Esq., CFP. Seated (left to right): Richard A. Krim, CLU, ChFC, regional vice president, and Michael Bucceri, CPA.

Richard A. Krim, CLU, ChFC, regional vice president of CIGNA Individual Financial Services Company, Inc.

At that level, the task takes many skilled professionals who CIGNA has in abundance—attorneys, accountants, chartered life underwriters, and chartered financial counselors, as well as NASD registered representatives. They work closely with each client's own lawyer and accountant, putting 30 to 40 hours into the preparation of a customized report for a client, for which a fee is charged. Once the client is satisfied with the financial plan, the firm has the ability to implement its recommendations with various products if the client so chooses. A yearly review to keep the plan up to date is part of the ongoing service.

CIGNA's philosophy of service extends to the community as well. Among the organizations the firm supports is United Way. For several years Krim has played a leading role in the fund-raising efforts of its business division. In addition, the staff is active in many industry and community associations such as the Estate Planning Council of Westchester and the International Association of Financial Planners.

In the years ahead CIGNA Individual Finances Services Co. anticipates continued growth and service to a broadening constituency.

CHEMICAL BANK

Since opening its first county branch in Eastchester more than 25 years ago, Chemical Bank has been serving Westchester companies and consumers. But its local roots go much deeper, back to 1824, when Chemical Bank was founded as a chemical manufacturer, with a factory on the Hudson.

Headquartered in New York, Chemical today has branches in Eastchester, Pelham, Jefferson Valley, Hartsdale, Elmsford, Thornwood, Yonkers, New Rochelle, Mount Vernon, and White Plains. Nearly 200 people staff those branches, and many of them are active in local schools, government, and charities. The bank encourages volunteerism through campaigns for the March of Dimes and frequent blood drives; employees become salespeople for these causes to enlist the support of coworkers and customers.

The purpose of this commitment—both bricks and mortar and high-caliber people—is to ensure that Westchester has the best in banking services. In addition to complete services for consumers, including private banking and investments, Chemical's specialty is meeting business banking needs. It is the leading bank for growing businesses in the tri-state area, guaranteeing that its officers know the banking needs of those customers and how to tailor bank services to meet those needs.

Many growing companies in the tri-state area choose to bank with Chemical. The bank's Westchester customers are found in office parks such as this one, in retail centers, and in manufacturing districts.

Chemical Bank's system of branches offers a combination of personalized service and technological sophistication. Banking by phone, consolidated business statements, and computerized "windows to the bank" for better cash management are among the services available.

To help companies save time, improve cash flow, and get better control of their finances, Chemical offers a host of financial services. Whenever possible these services are modular. That permits the bank to create special packages that are precisely suited to current needs, yet also capable of growth. Among its financial products are cash management services, enabling customers to use their personal computers to transfer money and monitor accounts at all their banks. MicroLink and ChemLink are standards in banking nationwide.

International services, such as letters of credit and export/import financing, are also available. Chemical is number one in foreign exchange services, according to *Euromoney* magazine.

Chemical also offers lockbox services to speed remittances, turning checks into cash sooner than otherwise possible; account reconciliation services, relieving the headaches of reconciling accounts; controlled disbursement services, allowing a zero balance in disbursement accounts, freeing idle cash; and business checking, savings, and money market accounts to keep cash working.

Chemical Bank is committed to holding its paramount position with growing companies. By providing innovative credit and financial services, the bank believes it earns the right to serve the vibrant business community of Westchester County.

NATIONAL WESTMINSTER BANK USA

In looking at how National Westminster Bank USA has built a sizable presence in Westchester County, one need look no further back than the year 1970.

For in 1970 NatWest USA's predecessor bank, National Bank of North America, purchased First National Bank of Yonkers and became the first bank to have offices in Westchester, New York City, and Long Island. That 11-branch Westchester network doubled a decade later, when the bank purchased 16 branches, 10 in the county, from Bankers Trust Company, significantly expanding NatWest USA's presence in northern Westchester.

"Our top priority is giving high-quality service to consumers," says William J. Laraia, executive vice president/community banking group. "We have taken many steps in the past few years to further improve customer service, and we'll continue to focus on making banking more convenient for customers."

Combine a solid branch representation with an expanding network of automated teller machines (ATMs) and the introduction of VoiceBeam, an innovative touch-tone telephone service, and "you give the customer banking by convenience. That means access to funds around the clock, seven days per week," says Harry Frank, regional manager responsible for NatWest's branches in Westchester and the Bronx. "Offering quality service means providing customers with information when they need it."

VoiceBeam, a unique service introduced by the bank in 1989, gives customers personal account information—including balances, deposits or credits posted, and checks paid—via telephone, day or night. It is also available to small businesses, another very important market to NatWest.

"In the metropolitan area, about 80 percent of all companies are less than $15 million in sales. When you help somebody start out, it is gratifying to see them grow, and generally you get rewarded as they get bigger and stronger," says Arthur Thompson, senior vice president of NatWest's small business activities—firms with less than $10 million in annual sales.

In targeting middle-market customers (less than $250 million in annual sales), NatWest USA offers a broad selection of services, including cash management, trust, trade finance, and commercial real estate. Typical of its innovative approach is Trade Beam, a system that allows customers to initiate letters of credit on their own business computer terminals and transmit them directly to the bank's computers.

Senior vice president Matt Colgan, who oversees the bank's commercial lending activities in Westchester and Connecticut, points out that NatWest's streamlined loan-approval process makes life simpler for mid-size companies. "We have a higher degree of autonomy than many of our competitors in terms of how much

National Westminster Bank USA has conveniently located 24-hour automated teller machines, called Teller Beams, throughout Westchester. The bank is a member of the New York Cash Exchange (NYCE) and the CIRRUS network, which together allow its customers access to funds at more than 30,000 locations nationwide.

Through its "Arts in the Community" program, NatWest USA sponsors more than 100 arts-related programs each year, including this concert at Caramoor Center for Music and the Arts in Katonah.

money we can allocate to a transaction. If someone needs an answer fast, we can often get one the same day. Our customers certainly appreciate that," he says.

NatWest has more than 200 ATMs in New York and New Jersey, including several in key Westchester locations. The bank, a founding member of the New York Cash Exchange (NYCE) network of automated teller machines, is also part of the CIRRUS ATM network, giving its customers access to their accounts at more than 24,000 machines nationwide.

The bank is proud that its ATM network regularly registers more than 99 percent availability for any given month, ranking among the industry's leaders. ATM availability is one example of the bank's effort to be a leader in quality services. All of its 4,600 employees have participated in quality training programs, as the bank strives to give customers the best possible service.

NatWest's published statement of values, mission, and commitment to quality stresses dedication to the communities it serves. Not only is the institution active in community service and a leader in support of United Way, but its officers take leadership roles in many cultural, service, and civic organizations.

In Westchester and throughout the New York area, NatWest USA supports a broad range of cultural events through its Arts in the Community program, including outdoor concerts, music for children and the elderly, performances by local theater groups, exhibitions, radio broadcasts, and telecasts on PBS.

National Westminster Bank USA's exceptional support of the arts has earned it a presidential citation as part of the White House program on private-sector initiatives.

With Westchester headquarters for retail and commercial operations in White Plains, National Westminster Bank USA's activities in the county are part of an expanding regional operation. On February 1, 1988, First Jersey National Corporation merged with NatWest under National Westminster Bancorp, a newly formed holding company based in New York. With that merger, NatWest USA combined its strengths with First Jersey, later renamed National Westminster Bank NJ, the fourth-largest bank in New Jersey. Following the merger, NatWest Bancorp expanded even further into the Garden State with the acquisition of Ultra Bancorporation, parent of First National Bank of Central Jersey.

THE BANK OF NEW YORK

The Bank of New York, founded in 1784 by Alexander Hamilton, the nation's first Secretary of the Treasury, was the first bank in New York State and is the oldest in the country still operating under its original name. Despite its age, this is no old-fashioned, stodgy institution. Sound, reliable banking practices, together with innovation and resourcefulness, have provided uninterrupted dividend payments throughout its history, while the bank has recorded many important firsts along the way.

In 1789 the fledgling U.S. government obtained its first loan from The Bank of New York, in the amount of $200,000, evidenced by a series of 10 warrants, each for $20,000—an enormous sum in those days. The bank still owns and displays Warrant Number One, the first bond ever issued by the U.S. government, in its Wall Street headquarters.

In 1830 the bank established the first bank trust department; in 1920 it was the first to begin investing in stocks on behalf of its customers; and it was the first bank in the country to reopen after President Franklin D. Roosevelt declared a bank holiday in 1933. The Bank of New York also was the first bank to own a computer.

A new chapter in the bank's history was written in December 1988, with the acquisition of the Irving Bank Corporation, the largest commercial bank merger in history, which created the 10th-largest bank holding company in the country. In Westchester County, The Bank of New York totals 75 branches and 33 around-the-clock automated teller machines. It is the largest banking presence in its market.

In 1989, underscoring The Bank of New York's commitment to its market, a major restructuring of the branch banking network was undertaken. The objective was to bring the decision-making process as close as possible to where the clients are. The Westchester/Putnam Division was created, with a division president and senior management team located in White Plains.

"With respect to commercial lending, for example, virtually every decision is made right here in Westchester," comments division president Christopher J. Taylor. "What that means to the Westchester businessperson is responsiveness and sensitivity. Responsiveness means that our customers can expect quick answers by our teams of lending officers without the red tape usually connected with loans that must be shuffled off to a bank's central headquarters. By sensitivity we mean that our clients have the benefit of dealing with specialists who understand the nature of their business, their special needs, and the market in which they operate. My mandate to our lenders and other specialists is to find a way to do the deal."

Experienced officers, situated

From its headquarters in the White Plains Centroplex, The Bank of New York's Westchester Division team of specialists is within minutes of any businessperson in the county.

Rolling hills backed by trees and sky frame The Bank of New York's Consumer Credit facility in Harrison.

Overlooking Westchester Avenue and I-287, The Bank of New York's Corporate Park office serves business clients and their employees along the "Platinum Mile."

throughout the area, offer the widest range of banking services. Trust offices are located in Scarsdale and White Plains, while dedicated experts in municipal and local government finance, cash management services, real estate and construction lending, and international trade transactions stand ready to work with clients from their home base in White Plains.

One of 14 branches situated in White Plains, the Plaza office is convenient for many office workers and apartment dwellers.

"If you're going to maintain the lead position in Westchester, you have to be attuned to all of the different markets here," says Taylor. "People tend to think of this area as a single market, when in fact it consists of a number of very different ones, ranging from centers of business to industrial areas, urban and suburban—middle class, upscale, and poorer neighborhoods. Our job is to see to it that we're providing the products and the service to meet the needs of this wide range of clients. To make sure we get the job done, we've positioned officers throughout Westchester, with specific responsibility for sales and service."

An example of The Bank of New York's sensitivity to its customers is a survey taken at least once each year. Using an outside researcher, representatives intercept customers at every branch, asking them to complete surveys asking for their opinions on staff efficiency, courtesy, job knowledge, and a number of other factors. Thousands of surveys are collected and analyzed. The results tell the bank's management what it needs to know about the quality of service delivered, and where special attention may be suggested.

A strong believer in community involvement, The Bank of New York, Westchester/Putnam Division, provides substantial financial assistance to hundreds of community organizations each year in the areas of health and welfare, urban affairs, civic planning, education and culture, and the arts. This assistance is made in the form of grants, contributions, and sponsorship of special events. Employees of the bank are encouraged to give time and talent to community projects. A recent count revealed that in Westchester County, employee memberships in community organizations numbered almost 300 in 248 different organizations.

In a very real sense The Bank of New York is both the oldest and newest bank in the state—newest in terms of its increased resources now available to customers, state-of-the-art technology installed in each branch, and, most important, its determination to set new standards of service to the community.

"This division offers the best of two banking worlds," says Taylor. "Local people and decision making combined with big-bank resources translates to a new and higher level of service delivery."

THE CHASE MANHATTAN BANK

LEFT: Paul Wise (second from left) and Lynn Bagliebter (third from left), vice president and relationship manager representing corporate banking for Chase Manhattan Bank, meet with representatives of H.O. Penn Machinery, Inc., a large corporate client. Pictured from H.O. Penn are Tom Cleveland, president (far left), and Mike Mulroe, treasurer (far right).

BELOW: Chase's sophisticated ATMs perform a variety of services, including cashing checks and accepting deposits without envelopes or tickets.

A global financial institution, Chase Manhattan Bank is also a local one. Its 29 Westchester branches are attuned to their neighborhoods and are amply supplied with the resources to serve them. Built on a tradition of innovation and excellence, Chase continually researches the needs of its customers and develops products and services to meet the needs of the individuals, businesses, not-for-profit institutions, and municipalities it serves.

The Chase tradition of support for the economic development of and involvement in the communities it serves is nearly two centuries old. The Chase Manhattan Bank traces its roots to 1799 when Aaron Burr founded the Bank of the Manhattan Company. The new bank soon proved its ingenuity with several novel concepts in its first few years, including check endorsements and credit analysis.

Entering the twentieth century, the bank embarked on an expansion campaign through mergers and the opening of branch offices. In mid-century it found a perfect fit in a merger engineered by the much larger Chase National Bank. Chase, established in 1877, was a leading bank to corporate America, but not as strong in the consumer market. The Bank of the Manhattan Company's chain of branches offered an excellent retail distribution network. The merger, on March 31, 1955, gave the Chase Manhattan Bank a solid foundation for growing in both consumer and business markets.

The new Chase Manhattan Bank expanded both in markets and geographically over the years, and reached out to an international constituency by opening locations overseas as well. In the 1960s, as U.S. corporations expanded abroad, Chase Manhattan followed to serve their investment and trade needs. Over the next two decades, as sophisticated electronic linkages among key markets changed the nature of overseas business, banking became a global exercise, with Chase a major participant. Today Chase has a presence in more than 50 countries, making it one of only two U.S. financial institutions covering the globe. And, it is the second-largest banking corporation in the United States.

In Westchester, Chase is proud of its position as the county's oldest community bank, tracing its roots through affiliations back to 1833. In 1984 Chase acquired Lincoln

First Bank, which included the National Bank of Westchester, resulting in a partnership of resources for its Westchester customers. By combining the vast means of a global financial institution with the personalized services of a local community bank, Chase has successfully produced an innovative, committed bank for Westchester consumers, businesses, not-for-profit institutions, and municipalities.

In fact, Chase offers "Better Banking" for its customers, a package of superior products and services that offers enhanced benefits based on the customer's combined balance. These include a full range of checking, savings, and investment alternatives, as well as installment loans, credit cards, lines of credit, mortgages, and home equity credit. Mutual funds and insurance products are also available through Chase branches, as are IRA's, Certificates of Deposit, and automatic teller machine (ATM) cards.

Chase is the second-largest U.S. bank issuer of credit cards, which it markets nationwide by mail, telephone, and related electronic capabilities. Its Advantage Credit, an unsecured revolving credit product, is the second-largest product of its kind in the United States.

The bank's ATM cards are usable nationwide through Chase's membership in NYCE and PLUS and owe their high level of approval to a unique approach to technology. For Chase, producing friendly, easy-to-use technology is a means to improve banking convenience. Its ATMs are designed to minimize the risk of mistakes and make corrections simple. The bank also has well-trained personnel on hand to assist customers. The result is a high acceptance of the technology and improved convenience for the customer.

Other Chase services are also geared to customer convenience. Such tedious, time-consuming chores as getting account information and stopping payment on checks now take only moments for Chase customers. No need for a trip to the bank—a telephone call to the customer service center, open long hours, does it all.

Branches, too, are changing as Chase finds ways to improve the speed and efficiency of its service. Many branches, such as Eastchester, have been remodeled. In addition to a greeter at the door, they have signs to give directions to each department and full automation to speed up each transaction. At the touch of a fingertip, state-of-the-art electronic teller machines cash checks, accept deposits without tickets or envelopes, offer a videotex capability, and deliver printouts—they are fast, convenient, and popular.

For businesses Chase offers a multitude of sophisticated products and services, facilitated by its commitment to technology and multidimensional resources. Products, tailored to the different needs of small, medium, and large businesses include commercial loans, leasing, international trade finance, cash management, and corporate finance, which includes restructuring, leveraged buyouts, and recapitalization.

Chase's global network enables it to help Westchester businesses effectively meet the demands of the international marketplace. Through knowledgeable trade experts based in Westchester, Chase provides classical trade services, such as letters of credit, documentary collections, foreign exchange and international payments, as well as innovative trade techniques.

Technology plays a major role. Chase delivers cash management products through terminals located in its corporate customers' offices, allowing treasurers to monitor their cash positions, create reports, and transfer funds. In money transfer, Chase is the world leader.

What is special about all the products and services Chase provides to business is the way it is delivered. It is local and personal. Chase bankers are on the spot. Many work out of dedicated units, such as the hospital and health care group and the municipal

BELOW: Funding from Chase and other corporate sponsors enabled the YWCA Lila Wallace Center on North Street in White Plains to provide a playground for its newly opened day-care center. This is just one of Chase's commitments to the Westchester community.

finance group. They visit their Westchester customers to acquire firsthand knowledge of their needs, and then they tap the bank's worldwide capability to satisfy them.

For all its size and reach, Chase retains a hometown flavor. It cares about Westchester, as evidenced by its long history of involvement in local civic and charitable affairs. With bank encouragement, staff members volunteer at such diverse organizations as United Way, March of Dimes, Guiding Eyes for the Blind, Grace Episcopal Church, the 52 Association, and Back-to-School Clothes for Kids, which benefits children living in welfare hotels and shelters.

The bank also funds smaller, lesser-known groups through neighborhood grants. These go to combat drug addiction, child abuse, and teenage suicide; help hospitals, churches, and nursing homes provide health and human services; and support programs for senior citizens, the mentally ill, and the handicapped. In 1989 Chase awarded $82,000 to 96 Westchester area organizations.

Regina Greagor, assistant manager at the People's office in White Plains, assists a customer in preparing a loan request. Among Chase's highly specialized services is this Express Loan Center, where a customer can receive personalized loan services tailored to the individual's needs.

Food drives in the branches help the Westchester Coalition of Soup Kitchens and Food Pantries. Contributions also go to recreational activities, from Little League baseball to boccie, and cultural activities, from craft fairs to local symphony orchestras. In addition, Chase makes donations to schools, libraries, scholarship funds, art councils, and music societies.

Most important, Chase recognizes that the bank cannot expect to prosper and grow unless the communities it serves also prosper and grow. By lending money to companies large and small, as well as to individuals, the bank promotes economic development and job creation. It helps entrepreneurs get started and helps established businesses expand. It encourages minority enterprise through the Westchester Coalition, and it works with both business and government to create a favorable climate for economic growth.

Throughout, Chase Manhattan Bank holds unswervingly to three objectives: to be a leading, broad-based financial institution serving corporations and individuals worldwide; to ensure that quality in people, products, and technology is the hallmark of its service; and to be a responsible corporate citizen in all dealings with customers, employees, and the communities where it does business.

Customer Liz Fetoni and Eastchester's branch manager, Dolly O'Neill, stand before the remodeled Eastchester branch's specialized customer service desk, which offers printed bank statements as well as the most current information through an electronic graphics board.

MUNICIPAL BOND INVESTORS ASSURANCE CORPORATION

Municipal Bond Investors Assurance Corporation is the premier name in the municipal bond insurance field. No other financial guarantor combines the Armonk-based company's history, underwriting performance, and record of service.

The core of MBIA Corporation's business is guaranteeing municipal bonds. Issued by cities, states, and government agencies, these bonds finance construction and rehabilitation of schools, hospitals, bridges, roads, water systems, and other essential public works.

MBIA insurance benefits three principal parties: the issuers of bonds, individual and institutional investors in insured bonds, and investment banking firms that sell the bonds on behalf of the municipal government or authority. For the issuer, MBIA insurance automatically raises the credit rating assigned by Moody's and Standard & Poor's to "AAA," the highest possible, resulting in lower interest costs. For municipal bond investors, insurance eliminates the risk that a default will disrupt the timely payment of principal and interest. For investment bankers, MBIA insurance enhances the bond's marketability.

Today municipal bond insurance covers one-fourth of all new issue, tax-exempt bonds, and the business has significant growth potential as the nation works to rebuild its aging infrastructure. In addition to insuring new-issue municipal bonds, MBIA also guarantees bonds traded in the secondary market and those held in unit investment trusts and mutual funds.

In its history MBIA has established a number of milestones. The insurer was the first to receive "AAA" ratings from both leading rating agencies and the first to insure bonds in every state. Another important event occurred in 1987, when MBIA Corporation's holding company, MBIA Inc., sold common stock in an initial public offering. MBIA Inc. is listed on the New York Stock Exchange under the symbol MBI. For the past eight years MBIA has been the municipal bond insurance industry leader as measured by the par amount of new bond issues insured.

Municipal Bond Investors Assurance Corporation demonstrated its long-term commitment to Westchester County in 1989, when it moved from White Plains, where it began operations, to a new facility set in a 15-acre park. There is sufficient room for MBIA's 220 employees, and more for the future—an important consideration since the company began with four employees at its formation in 1973. Some 80 municipal bond analysts on MBIA's staff comprise the largest and most experienced group in the industry.

Underscoring the firm's commitment to the county and its citizens is its sponsorship of the MBIA Invitational, an annual golf and tennis tournament that benefits the Westchester Association for Retarded Citizens and Westchester-Putnam Special Olympics. Employees also participate in civic organizations, and the firm supports a variety of deserving educational and health-related institutions and artistic and cultural endeavors.

In 1989 Municipal Bond Investors Assurance Corporation (MBIA) demonstrated its long-term commitment to Westchester County by purchasing this new facility, which will accommodate all future growth and expansion.

DOLLAR DRY DOCK FINANCIAL CENTERS

Being much more than a bank is what distinguishes Dollar Dry Dock Financial Centers from others in the crowded New York metropolitan area financial services market.

Dollar Dry Dock offers consumers a plethora of services in its 23 financial centers throughout the area in environments patterned after high-fashion department stores, rather than conventional thrift institutions. Gone are the old-fashioned tellers' cages and counters. They have been replaced with visually stimulating offices: color codes for product offerings, freestanding kiosks, telephone hot lines for quick answers to financial questions, and electronic bulletin boards that display the latest financial quotes. It is an application of merchandising techniques used by successful retailers of all kinds.

This strategy grew out of the competitive ferment created by bank deregulation in the early 1980s and was launched following the 1983 merger that created Dollar Dry Dock. Its forerunners were two of the most venerable financial institutions in the area, Dollar Savings Bank, founded in 1890, and Dry Dock Savings Bank, founded in 1848. Together they form a financial institution with $5 billion in assets.

One of the first actions of the newly created institution was to move its headquarters from New York City to White Plains. Today it is the largest financial institution headquartered in Westchester County.

Chairman Robert H. Steele, viewing the crowded marketplace soon after the merger, had a vision: "Just because your bank is a small thrift it doesn't have to behave like one." To survive and succeed in the changing financial services business, he believed that his institution had to provide customers with all their financial needs under one roof.

"Our public should perceive Dollar Dry Dock as a system of financial centers that are capable of creating broad-based financial relationships with customers seeking service, convenience, information, and a range of contemporary products in addition to competitive rates," Steele decrees. He observed that the average individual seeks the assistance of 20 to 25 different providers of financial services in the course of a single year. His aim is to have Dollar Dry Dock customers reduce the number of financial providers they use to 10 and include Dollar Dry Dock among their first five providers.

The key to meeting that goal is the offering of a wide array of products and services: a full line of deposit and credit products with emphasis on relationship accounts; a full line of insurance products, such as savings-bank life insurance, commercial life insurance, tax-deferred annuities, and universal life and credit life insurance; a complete line of brokerage services offering stocks, U.S. government bonds, corporate and municipal bonds, unit trusts, real estate partnerships,

money market funds, and equity and fixed-income mutual funds; and other services such as travel planning, foreign currency exchange, and real estate brokerage.

To translate Steele's concept into visual reality, a design firm was hired to begin in the White Plains office. But instead of choosing a firm that specialized in banks, Dollar Dry Dock chose a retail-oriented designer. The idea was to get away from the familiar, staid bank look and make Dollar Dry Dock Financial Centers look more like department stores, with highly distinctive areas for each product category. One by one, Dollar Dry Dock's other financial centers—in White Plains, Bronxville, Katonah, New York City, and Nassau County—were refurbished with the organization's new look.

To oversee the merchandising of Dollar Dry Dock, a former buyer and merchandising director of Bloomingdale's was hired. The point was to change the way customers were viewed, from a task, as banks have traditionally seen them, to an opportunity, as department stores usually regard them. The new view means Dollar Dry Dock strives to adopt its customers' perspective and concentrates on making financial services more accessible to them and making them aware of all the services available. As part of that accessibility, all Dollar Dry Dock centers are open from 8 a.m. to 6 p.m. daily.

This new approach has won widespread recognition and acclaim. The American Bankers Association recently cited Dollar Dry Dock as one of the most innovative retail banking institutions in the United States. Other financial institutions apparently agree. It regularly receives requests from around the nation to share its marketing know-how.

Community involvement is an integral part of Dollar Dry Dock's business operations. Starting with socially responsible investing in low-income neighborhoods, in which it is a leader, the organization actively encourages its staff to get involved. In recent years Dollar Dry Dock has carried out more than 300 community-based programs and received 150 civic awards. Its people sit on boards and steering committees, work in neighborhood associations, and participate in legislative and charitable meetings and events.

In 1989 and 1990 it sponsored the Dollar Dry Dock Sports Challenge, in which 25 teams participated in a variety of events and raised $50,000 for the Cystic Fibrosis Foundation.

These programs give Dollar Dry Dock Financial Centers a link to the community, enabling it to make a meaningful contribution to the lives of its depositors and the future of their communities. It is one more way for Dollar Dry Dock to show it is much more than a bank.

MUTUAL OF NEW YORK (MONY)

MONY offers the use of a modern on-site fitness center as part of its plan to insure the well-being and happiness of its employees.

Established in 1843, Mutual Of New York (MONY) is a company with a history of firsts. MONY was the first insurance company to issue policies to the general public on the mutual principle, the first to insure the life of a woman, and the first to insure a member of the armed forces.

Today, MONY has grown, through innovations in every phase of product development and customer service, into a mulitbillion-dollar enterprise. MONY offers life and disability insurance, annuities, and pension and investment management services to individuals and businesses throughout the United States and serves U.S. military personnel abroad.

MONY's Westchester Operations Center in Purchase, New York, is the location of the company's pension operations. From this site MONY offers a group of products and services that include corporate-defined contribution, tax-deferred annuity, and managed funds programs as well as guaranteed investment contracts. The key goal of pension operations is to deliver superior quality investment and administrative services for clients' retirement programs.

MONY is also responsive to the needs of its employees and the communities in which it conducts business. Committed to its employees, MONY's Westchester Operations Center has an on-site fitness center, dry-cleaning service, convenience store, subsidized cafeteria, automated banking machine, and credit union. Moreover, employees are offered salary and benefit programs designed to reward performance and meet their diverse needs.

Committed to the community, MONY is known as a "neighbor who cares." Since moving to Westchester in 1985, Mutual Of New York has continuously provided financial support and employee volunteers to many local organizations that address community needs. MONY looks forward to its continued professional and social involvement in Westchester County.

Mutual Of New York (MONY) has been in Westchester since 1984.

Photo by Victoria Lamas

Photo by Balthazar Korab

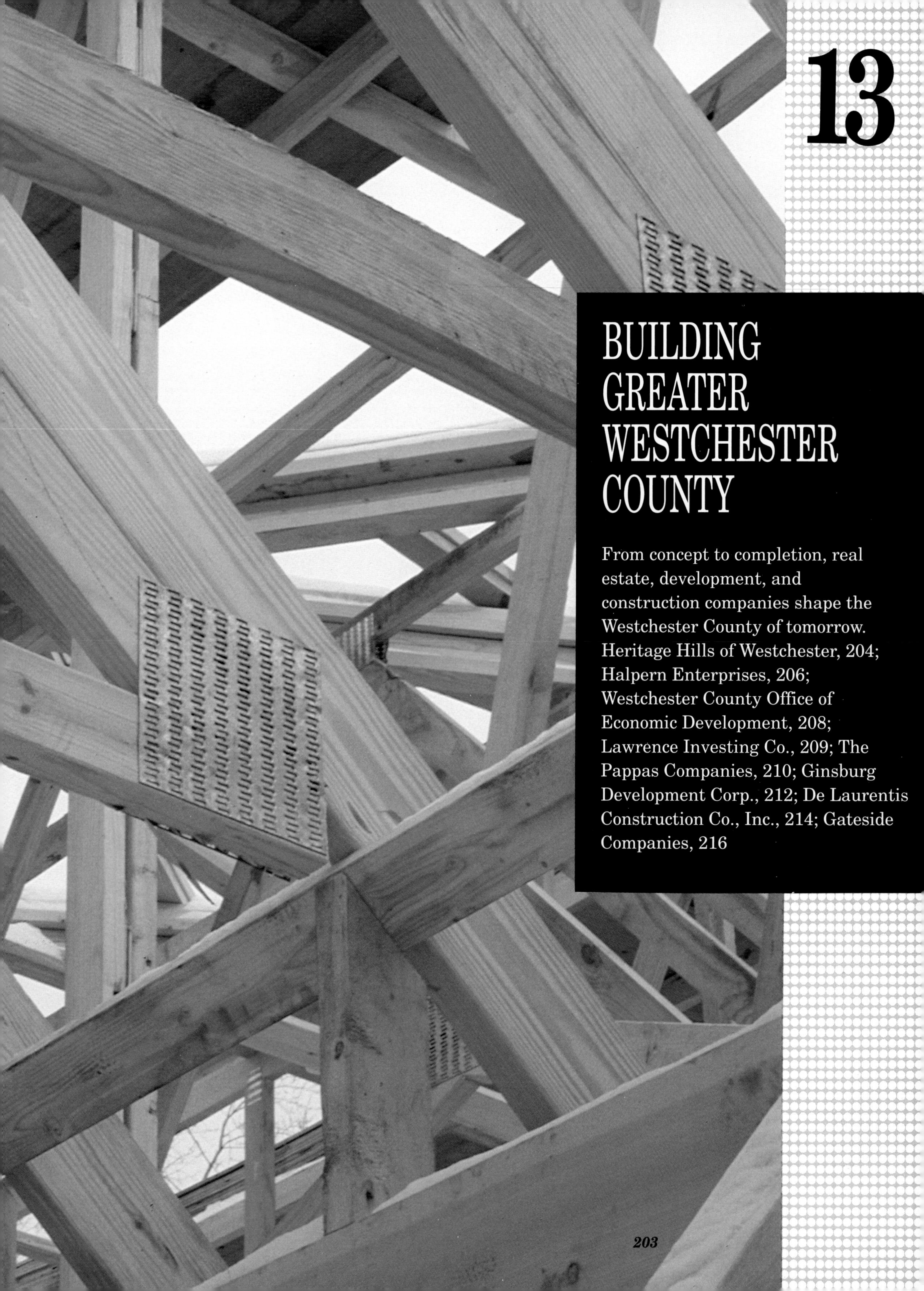

13

BUILDING GREATER WESTCHESTER COUNTY

From concept to completion, real estate, development, and construction companies shape the Westchester County of tomorrow.

HERITAGE HILLS OF WESTCHESTER

The largest condominium community in Westchester County, Heritage Hills of Westchester in Somers has won many national building awards since its inception in the 1970s.

Much of the credit belongs to Henry J. Paparazzo, one of the premier developers in the Northeast and founder and chairman of Heritage Development Group (HDG) in Southbury, Connecticut, builder of Heritage Hills and six other residential communities in the region. "Preserving nature's resources and protecting the natural environment has been our primary objective throughout our years of building Heritage Hills," Paparazzo says, "and it will continue to be our objective through the years to completion." Heritage Hills, planned to encompass 3,100 condominium units, is scheduled for completion in the late 1990s.

The community offers cluster housing set in private courtyards amid the rolling countryside, along with an abundance of social, cultural, and recreational activities. In its early years the novelty of this concept and the project's striking design made Heritage Hills a tourist attraction.

Patios abutting golf fairways and decks overlooking scenic hills are among the distinctive features home owners can choose from at Heritage Hills.

In creating the community, HDG drew upon its experience with its first large project, the 2,700-unit Heritage Village in Southbury, Connecticut. The development won the prestigious Award for Excellence from the Urban Land Institute in 1982. Like its forerunner, Heritage Hills offers 24-hour security patrol, private water and sewage-treatment systems, private roadways and maintenance, and neighborhood recreational facilities with swimming pools and tennis courts. In addition, Heritage Hills runs a free shuttle bus service into Somers and to and from the nearby Metro North commuter railroad station for the 60-minute trip into Manhattan.

But it is design and land use that underlie Heritage Hills' early and continuing success. Within 18 months of its opening, the community received three coveted awards. They include the National Association of Home Builders' Decade 1970 Award for Project Design (1975), the American Institute of Architects/*House and Home* magazine's Homes for Better Living Award (1976), and the Western Wood Products Association's Design Award (1976).

There are 27 holes of golf at Heritage Hills. The private courses are open from spring to fall and offer some of the most spectacular views in northern Westchester County.

These awards recognize HDG's painstaking efforts to preserve and maximize the natural attributes of the land in siting each of the proposed homes. Everything from the views out of each window to how each home will be seen from the homes around it has been planned in detail. Every condominium unit has been designed to harmonize with its immediate surroundings as well as to make the most of residents' views of the countryside.

The exterior design concept of Heritage Hills' homes has re-

The Heritage Hills Country Club features 27 holes of golf, plush locker rooms, a fully equipped pro shop, a casual grill room, and an elegant dining room comprising the open-to-the-public Heritage House Restaurant.

mained unchanged from the start. Emphasizing the relationship between each unit and its environment, HDG uses such natural materials as stained cedar siding and traditional New England stone walls.

Inside there have been many changes from the original designs as the builders adapted room styles and floor plans to match home buyers' changing tastes and life-styles. Today Heritage Hills offers nine different one-, two-, or three-bedroom designs, available in one- or two-level homes.

The community's 3,500 residents enjoy a full complement of resort-style amenities. Three swimming pools, four tennis courts, paddle tennis courts, hiking trails, fully equipped fitness center, and the country club's elegant public restaurant with outdoor dining terrace are among the components of the year-round vacation atmosphere.

Living up to Henry Paparazzo's promise to provide a self-sustaining community, HDG has constructed a small shopping center at the main entrance, on Route 202. Commercial enterprises include a restaurant overlooking a pond, a bank, a beauty salon, and several shops. Installed for the convenience of the community's potential 5,000 residents, the Heritage 202 Center also serves town residents and employees of such local companies as IBM and Pepsico.

Much of the leisure life at Heritage Hills revolves around the Activities Center, a gathering place for the community's interested and involved residents. General Manager Douglas C. Delano calls them "the heart of Heritage," observing that they are well-educated, accomplished professionals in such fields as arts, education, medicine, law, engineering, and diplomacy. Among them, they have organized more than 150 social, recreational, and cultural clubs and groups. The Theatre Guild, Women's Club, Gourmet Club, Bowling League, Hikers Club, Chamber Music Society, Continuing Education Group, Literary Club, Garden Club, and Culinary Club represent a sample of the ongoing activities.

Broadway shows, outdoor concerts, art shows, ice cream socials, St. Patrick's Day dances, Fourth of July picnics, culinary dining, twilight golf outings, and New Year's Eve galas are among the multitude of additional get-togethers residents enjoy throughout the year.

Volunteer activities also play a significant role in the community. Residents and HDG contribute both time and money to a variety of local nonprofit groups. For several years the Heritage Hills swim team ranked as the nation's top fund-raising group for the American Heart Association's Swim for Heart program.

"Heritage Hills of Westchester has been a prominent presence in the region since 1975," Paparazzo says, "and we are looking forward to continued participation in the county's prosperity."

Tennis, swimming, paddle tennis, plays, concerts, art shows, and fine arts classes are among the recreational, cultural, and social events at the main activity center of Heritage Hills.

HALPERN ENTERPRISES

Founded more than 50 years ago, Halpern Enterprises is one of Westchester County's largest and oldest real estate development and management companies, with four generations of the Halpern family having been involved in the organization.

Halpern Enterprises is a full-service real estate organization engaged in commercial and residential construction, development, and management in Westchester County. As developer/owner/builder, Halpern Enterprises has the in-house expertise for handling construction management, basic design, and interior layout for office and mixed-use developments.

Over the years the company has developed several million square feet of various types of commercial space, including the Tarrytown Corporate Center, a multiuse office park containing more than 1.2 million square feet of office space, and the 444-room Westchester Marriott Hotel.

Located on Route 119 in Greenburgh, the Tarrytown Corporate Center is composed of seven modern office buildings. Major tenants at the center include IBM, Citibank, Chrysler, Ford Motor Credit, Fireman's Fund, Continental Insurance, Northrop, U.S. Philips, and Xerox. Approximately 93 percent of the office space at the Tarrytown Corporate Center is occupied. Built in 1972, the center was the first office development undertaken in the Route 119 corridor, an area that has become the focus of a major commercial construction boom.

Located on Route 119 in Greenburgh, New York, the Tarrytown Corporate Center, a multiuse office park, is composed of seven modern office buildings with 1.2 million square feet of office space and the 444-room Westchester Marriott Hotel.

Halpern Enterprises recently invested several million dollars in capital improvements to the Tarrytown Corporate Center, including new lobbies, elevators, and cafeterias as well as an improved internal road network. Also planned for the center is a child-care facility. Future plans for the Tarrytown Corporate Center call for construction of a two-building, 340,000-square-foot complex at 600 White Plains Road. The new complex is to be built on the 16-acre site of the former Westchester Premier Theater.

Led by the senior management team of Harry A. Halpern, chairman of the board; Warren Lesser, president and chief operating officer; and Jon L. Halpern, vice president/development, Halpern Enterprises is pursuing new areas of growth in White Plains and North Tarrytown.

In downtown White Plains, Halpern has acquired the former headquarters building of IRM Insurance at 15 North Broadway. The 27,000-square-foot, three-story brick building is located on a one-acre site opposite Tibbits Park between Main Street and Hamilton Avenue. Also in White Plains, Halpern owns and manages two six-story buildings at 235 and 245 Main Street, containing 175,000 square feet of office space. Major tenants at 235 Main Street include Bank of New York and the State of New York. At 245 Main Street major tenants include AT&T and Peoples Westchester Savings Bank.

The senior management team of Halpern Enterprises includes (from left) Warren Lesser, president and chief operating officer; Jon L. Halpern, vice president/development; and Harry A. Halpern, chairman of the board. Four generations of the Halpern family have been involved in the organization since its founding more than 50 years ago.

In one of the most innovative developments to be proposed in White Plains in many years, Halpern Enterprises plans to build a major mixed-use office complex on a 2.78-acre site spanning the block between Main Street and Hamilton Avenue. The 221 Main Street/301 Hamilton Avenue complex will include approximately 560,000 square feet of rentable office space, ground-level retail stores, a pedestrian concourse, a restaurant, glass atrium lobbies, a child-care facility, a large public plaza, and a 1,024-car enclosed parking garage. With its soaring rooftop gable, the 14-story building at 221 Main will be the focal point of business activity in what is considered the center of downtown White Plains. Located at the foot of Mamaroneck Avenue, 221 Main will also serve as an anchor for that key retail corridor.

In the company's most ambitious residential project to date, Halpern Enterprises has unveiled plans for a major redevelopment of the downtown area of the Village of North Tarrytown. The plan, which would take place in five phases over eight to 10 years, would involve construction of new housing, large-scale public improvements, and creation of a waterfront park and pedestrian esplanade.

While commercial development is the mainstay of the firm's business, Halpern Enterprises is also a leader in the development of affordable housing in Westchester County and throughout the greater New York metropolitan area. The company's residential projects include both private and publicly financed low- and moderate-income housing, middle-income housing, and luxury housing.

ABOVE: An architect's rendering of the office complex to be built by Halpern Enterprises at the corner of Main Street and Hamilton Avenue in downtown White Plains. The two-building complex will include approximately 500,000 square feet of rentable office space, ground-level retail stores, a pedestrian concourse, a restaurant, glass atrium lobbies, a child-care facility, a large public plaza, and a 1,024-car enclosed parking garage.

LEFT: With its distinctive architecture, 660 White Plains Road is the flagship building of the Tarrytown Corporate Center. The 265,000-square-foot building features a full cafeteria and an advanced fiber-optics communications network.

Many of the company's publicly aided residential developments have been codeveloped with agencies such as the New York State Urban Development Corporation, the New York State Division of Housing and Community Renewal, and, more recently, the U.S. Department of Housing and Urban Development and the New York State Housing Finance Agency.

The firm's commitment to provide affordable housing extends to its residential management operations. Through its H&S Management subsidiary, Halpern has extensive experience managing more than 2,000 privately built and owned residential apartments in New York City and Westchester. Halpern Enterprises currently manages more than 1,500 apartments built under federal subsidy programs for low- and moderate-income families, including housing for the elderly and handicapped.

"We are entering the 1990s with a solid foundation for future growth," says Jon Halpern. "Our flagship property, the Tarrytown Corporate Center, has established itself as a proven leader in the Westchester office market. And in White Plains and North Tarrytown, we are moving forward with innovative office and residential projects that will further strengthen our position in the Westchester market."

WESTCHESTER COUNTY OFFICE OF ECONOMIC DEVELOPMENT

The Westchester County Office of Economic Development (OED) views itself as a one-stop service for businesses. As part of the Westchester County Executive's Office of Commerce, OED's primary mission is preserving and creating jobs and increasing the county's corporate base.

Along with helping existing companies to remain competitive, grow, and expand, OED promotes the advantages of a Westchester address to companies interested in relocation. These promotion activities reach nationwide as well as overseas.

Specific help for businesses includes the provision of information on and assistance with financing, job training, energy, and foreign trade. OED acts as a clearinghouse, answering diverse questions and coordinating solutions to business problems on a case-by-case basis, tailoring programs to the particular needs of individual companies.

Working closely with both municipalities and companies, the agency assists in compiling the most effective incentive programs, using county, state, and federal financial assistance, and then helps with the formal applications needed. In Westchester, a comprehensive package of government programs is available for the establishment of new businesses and the expansion of existing ones, but often companies need OED's guidance to reap the full benefit of these programs.

Among its additional services, OED aids site-selection consultants and corporate real estate officers in evaluating such key location factors as costs, labor supply, highway access, water supplies, sewer systems, zoning regulations, and mass transportation. In conjunction with local realtors, OED maintains a data base on available space in the county. The office offers special guidance for small and minority businesses, serving as a conduit for financial and technical assistance.

OED also acts as staff to the Westchester County Industrial Development Agency (IDA), a public benefit corporation organized under state law with county sponsorship. The IDA helps manufacturers and not-for-profit corporations arrange long-term financing at competitively lower interest rates.

In addition to working with individual companies, OED is county government's liaison with business groups, including the County Chamber of Commerce, Inc., the Westchester County Association, and the Private Industry Council, as well as other local business organizations and trade associations. OED also plans seminars, trade shows, and other special events.

Complementing its efforts to foster business, the Westchester County Office of Economic Development promotes tourism to Westchester's historical, recreational, and cultural facilities and events. It prepares and distributes a county travel guide, calendar of events, architectural tour guide, and restaurant guide.

OED helped to assure that Westchester Center, developed by The Morris Companies and designed by Rotwein & Blake Associates, will open in the spring of 1992.

LAWRENCE INVESTING CO.

One of the oldest continuously operating family businesses in Westchester, Lawrence Investing Co., White Plains, celebrated its centennial in 1988. In its first 50 years the organization, founded by William Van Duzer Lawrence, built much of modern-day Bronxville. Later it created some of Westchester's most prominent residential neighborhoods, including Lawrence Park West, Yonkers; Manursing Island, Rye; Lawrence Farms, Chappaqua; and Bedford Village Farms, Bedford.

Several wholly owned subsidiaries are active in the county and beyond. Lawrence Management Co., the operating arm, takes care of all administrative functions in addition to managing cooperative apartments and rental units. Continental Building Co., a development company acquired in the 1950s, handles major land holdings throughout New York State.

The real estate brokerage subsidiary, Houlihan/Lawrence Inc., is Westchester's largest independent real estate firm and the only one to offer complete county coverage. Established in 1888 and expanded in 1984 through a merger with A.T. Houlihan, Inc., the realty firm has 16 offices staffed by more than 400 knowledgeable sales associates. Houlihan/Lawrence salespeople are among the most experienced in the industry. Their comprehensive training program has received national media attention. A large number of the firm's sales associates hold broker/associate licenses, and the majority have achieved the C.R.S. (Certified Residential Specialists) or G.R.I. (Graduate Realtor's Institute) designations.

The residential division is just one of three. The others include relocation, commercial, and land divisions. Houlihan/Lawrence is also the exclusive Westchester affiliate for Sotheby's International Realty. The realty firm handles all Sotheby's real estate referrals, and the two jointly market large estates in the United States and overseas.

In the tradition of their founder, the Lawrence companies emphasize community service. William Lawrence established both Lawrence Hospital and Sarah Lawrence College, named for his wife. His descendants still sit on the boards of both Bronxville institutions. To mark the Lawrence centennial, a series of fund-raising events was held. In addition to the hospital and college, beneficiaries included Historic Hudson Valley, the Bronxville Public Library, Child Care Council of Westchester, and Legal Aid Society of Westchester.

While each Houlihan/Lawrence office chooses its own community activities, the corporation supports such causes as Adopt-a-School, Westchester County Symphony, Caramoor, Heart Association, Audubon Society, and Westchester County Lighthouse.

"We intend to continue to be involved and responsive," says Lawrence Investing Co.'s chairman, George H.C. Lawrence. He envisions "a major role for a concerned family company during the next 100 years."

George H.C. Lawrence, chairman of Lawrence Investing.

Lawrence Investing Co.'s corporate offices in White Plains, New York.

THE PAPPAS COMPANIES

For well over 20 years the Pappas Companies have been the largest developer in the central business district of White Plains. The first to build high-rise office construction in the area, it has demonstrated its commitment to the environment by putting fine art works in all its buildings and laying out plazas for the general public as well as tenants to enjoy. The family-run organization also believes in personal contact. Tenant relations are always handled by a Pappas.

The Pappas story begins in 1908, when Greek merchant Constantine Pappadopolous brought his family to Somerville, Massachusetts. The name became Pappas in the process of immigration. Starting with one food store, he owned a chain of 30 stores by the time he died in 1936. His three sons sold the chain, moved to Boston, and shifted to the wholesale side of the business, importing and distributing food and beverages.

The business prospered. By the 1960s it had expanded to include a fleet of oil tankers and real estate interests in New York and Massachusetts, among other ventures. Today, with the third generation of the family in charge, the Pappas Companies, headquartered in Boston, is still engaged in international shipping as well as real estate. James A. and T. Peter Pappas head the development company, and their sister, Diana, serves as vice president in charge of building operations and leasing.

The company began acquiring land for development in White Plains in 1963 and within a few years began to build. In 1968 Pappas completed its first two major projects in the city—Sears, on Main Street, and the South Tower of White Plains Plaza. Two years later the North Tower, 445 Hamilton Avenue, opened.

Continuing to demonstrate faith in the central city's future while helping to ensure it, Pappas built Hamilton Plaza across the street. The 15-story structure, opened in 1974, contains retail and banking facilities and 385,000 square feet of office space as well as a 700-car enclosed garage.

In 1979 Pappas made another major land acquisition in the Main Street urban-renewal area and put up an elegant office complex called Centroplex to epitomize downtown revitalization. The sleek anodized aluminum structure, opened in 1981, is situated on a 2.5-acre site, with open spaces and tree-lined pedestrian walkways compatible with their surroundings. A 16-story, 420,000-square-foot building, Centroplex features outdoor sculptures by the internationally known American artists Jim Dine and Jim Tyler. Two more Dine sculptures adorn the lobby, along with works by Claes Oldenburg and Larry Rivers.

A few years later Pappas struck a deal with the city to finance construction of the new White Plains Transportation Center's train station, clock tower, and parking garage while acquiring adjacent urban-renewal land. On part of that land the company built Gateway I, a 560,000-square-foot retail and office tower. Opened in 1984, AT&T occupies 70 percent of the space.

Designed to make a statement about urban work styles, the 18-story Gateway is made of gray glass with black anodized aluminum trim, set on solid granite. It rises on a full city block, with half the site devoted to landscaped plazas. A state-of-the-art building, Gateway has four-season climate control as well as natural ventilation; it is protected by sophisticated smoke detectors, sprinkler systems, and emergency standby power. The focal point of Gateway's Hamilton Avenue Plaza is a Barry Flanagan sculpture; the lobby contains no

A tree-lined pedestrian plaza surrounds Centroplex, an office complex noted for both efficiency and elegance.

The 15-story Hamilton Plaza, which opened in 1974, was Pappas' third major project in White Plains.

less than five works by Jean Dubuffet. All the artists represented in Pappas buildings are exhibited in major museums worldwide. Gateway I and Centroplex were joint ventures with JMB Realty of Chicago, one of the largest real estate firms in the United States.

A companion building across the street from Gateway I, the 800,000-square-foot Gateway II, has been designed to incorporate a variety of special features. They include covered skywalks to both Gateway I and the train station, as well as a bus station in the lower-level garage.

On the remaining acre of the land, management at Pappas chose to forgo a third Gateway building in favor of a public park. The civic-minded company has built parks as well as plazas before, notably Gateway Garden, which decorates the entryway to White Plains. Visible from both train station and Tarrytown Road approaches, the garden was donated to the city by Pappas through the White Plains Beautification Foundation.

ABOVE: **Two Big Black Hearts,** ***a 12-foot-tall bronze work, was commissioned from Jim Dine by the Pappas family. Exhibited at the Hirshhorn Museum and Sculpture Garden in Washington, D.C., the sculpture stands in front of Centroplex.***

RIGHT: The 1971 work by Jean Dubuffet, **Erection Arborescente,** ***is a painted klegecell panel exhibited in the lobby of Pappas' Gateway I.***

LEFT: Part of a mixed-used development in downtown White Plains, Gateway I is adjacent to the new White Plains Transportation Center.

Many other local nonprofit organizations also enjoy the company's support. Among them are the Boys Club, Music in the Parks, Pace and Mercy colleges, and St. Agnes Hospital.

As the largest single contributor to the city's revitalization effort, the firm has made a significant impact. Each of its projects has earned a reputation for responsible planning, architectural excellence, and economic success. Pappas has always drawn upon the talents of the best practitioners of contemporary

architecture and engineering, and demanded that every phase of construction exceed industry standards.

A developer and owner of 5 million square feet of commercial and industrial real estate in the Northeast, the Pappas Companies particularly values it role in Westchester. "The future of the White Plains central business district is vibrant and strong," T. Peter Pappas says. The Pappas Companies plans to strengthen and expand White Plains operations.

GINSBURG DEVELOPMENT CORP.

An architect-led company, Ginsburg Development Corp., Hawthorne, operates on a philosophy of pragmatic idealism. Founders Martin and Samuel Ginsburg believe their responsibilities go beyond the short-term economic gains and include moral obligations to the community, surrounding neighborhood, and the ecology of the site itself. Reflecting this sensitivity, GDC projects adhere to high standards of architectural design. A long list of prestigious awards bears this out.

The Ginsburg brothers, architects since graduating at the top of their class from Rensselaer Polytechnic Institute in 1958, began by working for others but soon launched their own enterprise. Their earliest business ventures included a third brother, Jerome, who subsequently left the business. "It started out as a sideline," Martin Ginsburg says of their partnership, formed in 1963 to build a single house with total initial capital of just $8,400.

GDC built, owns, and operates the River Hill Tower overlooking the Hudson River in Yonkers.

On the success of that project, the sideline turned into a full-time business. "In the early days we were not averse to helping out with digging trenches," Samuel Ginsburg says. "We were not gentlemen builders. But on weekends we put the suits on and were out there selling."

During more than 25 years in business, brothers Samuel (left) and Martin Ginsburg, both architects, have made Ginsburg Development Corp. a diversified real estate company with acquisition, design, planning, development, construction, sales, leasing, and management capabilities.

The first big project, Stone Ridge, whose name describes the difficult site, was a 25-lot subdivision for single-family housing. "Because difficult sites were the only ones we could afford, we cut our teeth on some serious rock piles," Martin Ginsburg says. Taking on projects other builders declined enabled the Ginsburgs to gain the expertise that has proved the basis of their success. "Even today, whenever the brokers have a mountain that no one can build on, they immediately think of us," Martin Ginsburg says.

Primarily residential developers, the Ginsburgs did not switch to commercial projects, as many others did, when prices rose in the late 1960s and early 1970s. Instead, the Ginsburgs turned to multifamily housing. Among the earliest condominium developers, the Ginsburgs also constructed low- and moderate-income apartments and senior citizens' housing. In the late 1970s they went into rehabilitation and recycling deteriorated apartment buildings.

A decade later the company began expanding out of state and now owns residential properties in Pennsylvania, Tennessee, and Florida as well as New York. But GDC remains most active in Westchester residential development as witnessed by its current developments of Boulder Ridge, Clarewood, and Pondside—totaling almost 500 residences.

Boulder Ridge in Scarsdale

Clarewood Village is a low-density condominium community of 85 town homes on a 46-acre parcel.

sports one of the area's most complete recreational facilities, with its four tennis courts, pools, and clubhouse with entertainment area, eating facilities, and exercise center. Well before completion Boulder Ridge attracted national attention with two of its models, and the community in its entirety has won awards in major competitions.

Clarewood, in Hastings-on-Hudson, is a more recent development and combines 85 luxury town homes with 40 moderately priced condominiums. The heavily wooded, hilly setting surrounded by 46 landscaped acres distinguishes the community. Featuring a complete recreational center, Clarewood also offers such amenities as master suites on the living level, cathedral ceilings, whirlpool tubs, and private rear yards. Clarewood was recently given the regional American Institute of Architects' Award for outstanding design.

GDC's Boulder Ridge condominium community (LEFT) has won national recognition for combining quality design with environmentally sensitive planning. The home owners enjoy an on-site country club (ABOVE) with outstanding facilities, including an 80-by-40-foot swimming pool, four tennis courts with the services of a tennis pro, and a fully equipped exercise room.

In late 1989 GDC broke ground for Pondside, in Greenburgh, a 190-unit town-home and garden-style condominium community situated on 17.5 acres, including two ponds in a parklike setting. While holding prices to moderate levels, the Ginsburgs cut no corners on the site planning and quality construction for which they are noted.

Their interests extend to a variety of community projects. Martin Ginsburg is a past president of the Builders' Institute. He and his brother, Samuel, have long been active in housing initiatives. They were instrumental in creating the Yonkers Neighborhood Preservation program, a model adopted by other cities, whereby declining properties were renovated through the combined efforts of the developer, city, and financial institutions. GDC contributes to local charities through the Sol and Rose Ginsburg Foundation, named in honor of Martin and Samuel's parents.

As a full-service company employing 260 people, Ginsburg Development Corp. has capabilities ranging from analyzing initial development potential and feasibility to developing architectural designs and providing complete marketing and property management services. The company's plans include commercial as well as residential development. In the future as in the past, the Ginsburg brothers are pledged to make every project they undertake enhance their reputation as conservationist developers with a deep concern for Westchester's people, communities, and environment.

DE LAURENTIS CONSTRUCTION CO., INC.

Cofounders Joseph (left) and Edmond De Laurentis at the National Environmental Award ceremony at the White House.

Recognized as one of the nation's top five site developers, De Laurentis Construction Co., Inc., in Mamaroneck, is a well-established family company dedicated to creating a better environment.

An endorsement came from former First Lady Nancy Reagan, when she presented an award for outstanding achievement to cofounders Edmond and Joseph De Laurentis for their work at Corporate Park on Gannett Drive in White Plains. The prestigious White House presentation of the award from the American Nurserymen's Association was but one of many received by the company over the years. For four consecutive years—1986, 1987, 1988, and 1989—*Landscape Management* magazine selected De Laurentis Construction as one of the top five landscapers in the United States. In addition, the company has citations from most Westchester municipalities for its work on public parks and tennis courts.

Founded in 1963 by brothers Edmond and Joseph De Laurentis, the firm has grown from a two-man lawn-care operation to a corporation with $17 million per year in revenues.

One of the company's first customers was the noted Japanese landscape architect Kaneji Domoto, who was impressed with the brothers' skill and ability to get a job done on time. A long-term relationship developed among the three men, inspiring Edmond De Laurentis to study landscape architecture himself. Edmond holds a landscape architectural license from the State of New Jersey. The relationship also influenced the firm's development of its unique style—a westernized-Japanese effect, combining aesthetics with efficiency.

"I like landscaping design, and I particularly like stone sculpture," says Edmond De Laurentis. "We use the rocks we blast out in preparing a site to create outdoor sculpture gardens. To make it today you must diversify. We became the first landscaping firm to take on the entire job from beginning to end. Investing heavily in excavation and construction equipment, my brother, Joe, earned a blasting license, and we went into site development, which is the term that describes the whole operation from blasting to earth relocation, drainage, masonry, paving, landscape design, and planting—the total package. From the beginning to the end, every detail is our concern."

As the firm grew, family members joined in and cultivated their own specialties. With Edmond as the company's president and landscape architect, vice president Joseph concentrated on contracting and horticulture, while Edmond's wife, Mary, took over administration of the growing company. Edmond and Mary's sons, Joseph III and Lawrence, function as on-site job supervisors and can step into senior positions at a moment's notice. A third son, Edmond Jr.,

The De Laurentis' park and residential garden landscapes stress natural preservation and beautification.

worked with the company until he went on his own to form De Laurentis Development Company, which is now building condominiums in White Plains. Today De Laurentis Construction has a staff of 50 full-time employees. In peak season the firm has an additional 100 people.

Over the years the company has worked closely with many prominent developers. Lowell Schulman, the master builder of the Platinum Mile office parks, was the first developer to allow the brothers a free hand in designing his parks. Not surprisingly, the Gannett Drive project was awarded a National Environmental Award, presented at the White House in 1986. Recently, Louis Cappelli of Saturn Construction commissioned Edmond to design the landscaping at The Summit at Valhalla. There, the waterfall and Shibui Pond was also awarded a National Environmental Citation for its preservation, beautification, and collaboration with nature.

The De Laurentis designs for the Platinum Mile Office Park (ABOVE) and The Summit at Valhalla (LEFT) each earned National Environmental citations.

As the De Laurentis reputation grew, other developers in the tri-state area of New York, New Jersey, and Connecticut enlisted the company's talents on major projects. Today steady clients include HRH Construction, Property Resources, Sigma Land Corp., and Rosenshein Associates. In New York City, De Laurentis is also involved in a major landscape at Roosevelt Island.

For all its contributions to the beauty of Westchester, De Laurentis Construction's commitment to the county goes beyond business. Family members are active in many local service organizations. They have been honored by the Westchester chapter of the National Conference of Christians and Jews for distinguished civic and community service. Edmond De Laurentis has been presented with the Family Award from the American Committee for Italian Migration, and he and his wife have received the Humanitarian Award from the Westchester chapter of Boys' Town of Italy. De Laurentis Construction Co., Inc., has also been lauded by the Westchester Lighthouse for the Blind.

Underlying the quality of De Laurentis Construction Co., Inc.'s, dedication of the family to the county is the De Laurentis' goal: "For the present, a better quality of life; for the future, a legacy of creative design to symbolize the highest standards toward which we aspire."

GATESIDE COMPANIES

A large portfolio of commercial, industrial, residential, retail, and marina/waterfront properties distinguishes the Gateside Companies in Rye. Multifaceted Gateside is involved in development, management, investment, and joint ventures. "We are very good at finding locations where there are underdeveloped properties," says Norman M. Feinberg, president and chief executive officer, "and at developing values in properties."

Founded in 1962 by Feinberg and two partners, Gateside began modestly by purchasing two walk-up apartment houses in Brooklyn. The company had no employees besides the principals then, but it soon acquired Manhattan property and spread out farther.

In the early 1970s Feinberg undertook his first Westchester venture—the gutting and rebuilding of an office building in White Plains. The 80,000-square-foot project, at 7-11 Broadway, won the coveted Mayor's Award for Excellence for helping to make White Plains a more beautiful city.

Since then Gateside, which now has 125 employees nationwide, has acquired an impressive portfolio of more than one million square feet of class A office space, 2,500 residential units, 550,000 square feet of shopping center and retail space, 1.5 milion square feet of industrial property and several world-class marinas.

The International Corporate Center at Rye is one of Gateside's impressive development projects.

Major office projects include the International Corporate Center at Rye and the Taconic Corporate Park in Yorktown Heights. The 17-acre Rye property was an obsolete industrial facility owned by the old Continental Baking Co. when Gateside bought it on December 31, 1986. After gutting the three buildings and stripping them down to their steel skeletons, Gateside developed a 174,000-square-foot complex interconnected by glass-enclosed passageways and marked by a unique package of amenities. The Taconic project, a 210,000-square-foot, three-building complex on 25 acres, includes both redevelopment and new construction.

Many Gateside tenants are *Fortune* 500 and other blue-chip companies. Boeing Corp., Chrysler Corp., Kaiser Permanente, Metropolitan Life Insurance Co., Nordbanken of Sweden, Dan River Corp., Rohr Industries, and Scott Paper Corp. are among its tenants, in Westchester and elsewhere.

Involved in the betterment of the community in a variety of ways, Norman Feinberg serves as a director and vice president of the Association for Mentally Ill Children, which runs the Clearview School in Scarborough. He has also served as an arbitrator for the American Arbitration Association and was a member of the Young Presidents and is currently a member of the Chief Executives organization. An avid art collector and a trustee of the Brooklyn Museum, Feinberg uses art extensively throughout his projects—a Gateside trademark.

Characterizing Westchester as "extraordinarily beautiful and a good community," Feinberg says Gateside Companies "will remain and continue to invest in the area."

PATRONS

The following companies and organizations have made a valuable commitment to the quality of this publication. Windsor Publications and The County Chamber of Commerce, Inc., gratefully acknowledge their participation in *Westchester County: The Golden Apple of New York.*

Aerotech World Trade Corp.*
Ain Plastics, Inc.*
Arrowwood*
AT&T*
The Bank of New York*
The Chase Manhattan Bank*
Chemical Bank*
CIBA-GEIGY Corporation*
CIGNA Individual Financial Services Co.*
College of New Rochelle*
De Laurentis Construction Co., Inc.*
Dollar Dry Dock Financial Centers*
Empire Blue Cross and Blue Shield*
The Galleria*
Gannett Westchester Rockland Newspapers*
Gateside Companies*
Ginsburg Development Corp.*
The Great Atlantic & Pacific Tea Co.*
Halpern Enterprises*
Heritage Hills of Westchester*
Holiday Inn Crowne Plaza ® *
Jackson, Lewis, Schnitzler & Krupman*
J.F. Jelenko & Co.*
Lawrence Investing Co.*
Metro-North Commuter Railroad*
Municipal Bond Investors Assurance Corporation*
Mutual Of New York (MONY)*
National Westminster Bank USA*
New York Medical College*
New York Power Authority*
Northern Telecom Inc.*
Pace University*
The Pappas Companies*
JCPenney*
Rye Town Hilton*
Safe Flight Instrument Corporation*
St. John's Riverside Hospital*
Saint Joseph's Medical Center*
J.A. Sexauer*
Southern Westchester Board of Cooperative Educational Services*
Stouffer Westchester Hotel*
Texaco Inc.*
Transamerica Leasing*
Union Carbide Corporation*
United Hospital Medical Center*
Universal Voltronics Corporation*
Westchester County Office of Economic Development*
WFAS AM & FM*
WHUD-FM/WLNA-AM*
WZFM*
Yonkers General Hospital*

*Participants in Part Two, "Westchester County's Enterprises." The stories of these companies and organizations appear in chapters 7 through 13, beginning on page 123.

BIBLIOGRAPHY

CHAPTER I

Metropolitan Transportation Authority Commuter Relations Office data.

New York Facts—A Comprehensive Look at New York Today—County by County. Dallas: Clements Research, Inc., 1986.

1989 Westchester Golden Apple Guide to Business and Livability. White Plains: The County Chamber of Commerce, Inc.

1986 Survey of Vocational Opportunities in Westchester. White Plains: The County Chamber of Commerce, Inc.

Survey of Higher Education in Westchester County. *Westchester Commerce* July/August 1989.

Walker, Barbara. *Westchester County, N.Y. Profile.* U.S. Impressions, Inc., 1989.

Westchester County Airport data from the Office of the Airport Manager.

Westchester County Atlas. New York: Columbia Marketing Corporation, 1984.

Westchester County Department of Transportation Annual Report for 1988.

Westchester Planning Department data.

CHAPTER II

Baird, Charles W. *Chronicles of a Border Town 1660-1870.* New York, 1970.

Bolton, Robert. *The History of Several Towns in Westchester.* New York, 1881.

Davidson, Marshall B. *New York—A Pictorial History.* New York: Charles Scribner's Sons, 1977.

Duncombe, Frances R. *Katonah—The History of a New York Village & Its People.* Historical Committee, Katonah Village Society, 1961 and 1978.

Eastchester Historical Society. *Tricentennial Journal, Town of Eastchester.* 1964.

Eichner, Frances, and Helen Ferris Tibbets, eds. *When Our Town Was Young—Stories of North Salem's Yesterday.* Board of Education, North Salem, New York, 1945.

Lamb, Wallace. *Lamb's Sectional Histories of New York State.* Phoenix, Ariz.: Frank E. Richards, 1941.

Lewisboro History Book Committee. *A History of the Town of Lewisboro.* Lewisboro, New York, 1981.

Oechsner, Carl. *Ossining, New York—An Informal Bicentennial History.* Croton on Hudson, New York: North River Press, Inc., 1975.

Scharf, Thomas. *History of Westchester County.* Philadelphia: L. E. Preston & Company, 1886.

Shonnard, Frederic, and W.W. Spooner. *History of Westchester County, New York—From the Earliest Settlement to the Year 1900.* New York: The New York Historical Company, 1900. Reprinted, Harrison, New York: Harbor Hill Books, 1974.

Westchester Lighting Company and the Yonkers Electric Light and Power Company. *The Story of Industry in Westchester County—A Unique Radio Series.* Mount Vernon, New York, 1948.

CHAPTER III

Commercial Reporter. Stamford, Conn.: County Publishing Corp., April 1990.

Crain's New York—1989 Edition Top Business Lists Vol. IV, No. 52. Crain's Communication, Inc., 1988.

Davidson, Marshall B. *New York—A Pictorial History.* New York: Charles Scribner's Sons, 1977.

Gordon, Dorothy Gay. *The Social and Cultural Development of Mount Vernon, New York.* Mount Vernon: Mount Vernon Public Library, 1951.

Hufeland, Otto. *Early Mount Vernon.* Mount Vernon: Mount Vernon Pubic Library, 1940.

Keen, James D., and Doris B. Keen, eds. *Landmarks Lost and Found: An Introduction to the Architecture and History of Yonkers.* Yonkers Planning Bureau and Yonkers Environmental Impact Advisory Commission, 1986.

Kitchen, Ruth. *New Rochelle—Portrait of a City.* New York: Abbeville Press, 1981.

Lederer, Richard M., Jr. "Post Roads, Turnpike Roads and Milestones—Part I." *Westchester Historical Society Journal* 63:2, Spring 1987.

_____. "Post Roads, Turnpikes and Milestones—Part II." *Westchester Historical Society Journal* 64:1, Winter 1989.

Miller, Louise Stevens. *Story of the Stevens House 1851-1882.* Mount Vernon: Mount Vernon Public Library, 1951.

New York State Department of Labor, Division of Research and Statistics. *Annual Labor Report, Westchester County, 1989.*

Scharf, Thomas. *History of Westchester County.* Philadelphia: L.E. Preston & Company, 1886.

Shonnard, Frederic, and W.W. Spooner. *History of Westchester County, New York—From the Earliest Settlement to the Year 1900.* New York: The New York Historical Company, 1900. Reprinted, Harrison, New York: Harbor Hill Books, 1974.

Weigold, Marilyn E., Ph.D., ed. *Westchester County: The Past Hundred Years 1883-1983.* Valhalla, New York: The Westchester County Historical Society, 1983.

Westchester News 1:17 (January 24, 1854). From the T. Edward Oakley Collection, Mount Vernon Series #4, Mount Vernon Manuscripts.

Westchester Lighting Company and the Yonkers Electric Light and Power Company. *The Story of Industry in Westchester County—A Unique Radio Series.* Mount Vernon, New York, 1948.

Westchester County Department of Planning. *Westchester at a Glance.* July 1988.

_____. *Westchester County and Municipalities Population Estimates for January 1988.* July 1988.

CHAPTER IV

Barron's Profiles of American Colleges—16th Edition, New York: Barron's Educational Series, Inc., 1988.

"Education's Future in Business." *Westchester Commerce* 4:7 (July/August 1989) Chase Communications Group, Ltd., Mount Vernon, New York.

The Educational Register 1987/88—47th Annual Edition. Boston: Vincent Curtis.

Handbook of Private Schools—63rd Edition. Boston: Porter Sargeant Publishers, 1982.

Northern Westchester Hospital Center 1988 Annual Report. Mount Kisco, New York.

Peterson's Directory of Private Schools. Princeton, New Jersey: Peterson's, 1989.

Sterns, Michael, ed. *The New York Times Guide to Where to Live In and Around New York.* New York: Times Books, 1985.

The 1988-89 Facts & Figures Survey of School Districts. Scarsdale: Westchester/Putnam School Board Association, 1988.

United States Department of Education. "Excellence in Education." News statement, May 1989.

Wirth-Vogt, Toni. *Westchester 1989—Golden Apple Guide to Business & Livability.* White Plains: The County Chamber of Commerce, Inc., 1989.

Westchester County Department of Planning. Statistics on the county's educational institutions from Information Center/The State Education Department, 1989.

Westchester County Office of Economic Development. *Health Care Fact Sheet.* Prepared from data submitted by the Hudson Valley Health Systems Agency, Tuxedo, New York, 1989.

CHAPTER V

The Council for the Arts in Westchester

Cultural Events Listings—December—Gannett Westchester Rockland Newspapers

Cultural Events Listings—December—*The New York Times* Westchester Weekly Edition

North Castle History 5:1. The North Castle Historical Society, Armonk, New York,

1978.
Westchester County Department of Parks, Recreation and Conservation
Westfair Office 2000 Business Expo Directory. The Gannett Specialty Marketing Department, White Plains, New York.

CHAPTER VI

Berkery, Patrick. *Occupational Needs, Hudson Valley Region 1989-1991.* Albany: Bureau of Statistics, New York State Department of Labor, 1988.
The County Chamber of Commerce, Inc. "Our 75th Year of Making Things Happen for Westchester—1988 Assessment Report."
Prezioso, Sal J., ed. "Visions & Views Into the 21st Century." Westchester 2000, 1989.
Westchester County Department of Parks, Recreation and Conservation, Office of Public Information. "A Pattern of Growth." 1989.
Wirth-Vogt, Toni. *Westchester 1989—Golden Apple Guide to Business & Livability.* White Plains: The County Chamber of Commerce, Inc., 1989.

INDEX

GENERAL INDEX
Italics indicate illustrations.

A

B

C

D